ENCHANTED SAFARIS

ENCHANTED SAFARIS

Roy E. C. Griffiths

The Book Guild Ltd
Sussex, England

The Book Guild Ltd.
25 High Street,
Lewes, Sussex

First published 1995

Set in Times
Typesetting by Acorn Bookwork, Salisbury, Wiltshire

Printed in Great Britain by
Antony Rowe Ltd.
Chippenham, Wiltshire.

A catalogue record for this book is
available from the British Library

ISBN 1 85776 028 X

CONTENTS

PREFACE

I've felt I had a story to tell since 1974; that's when I started this book. It's taken nearly twenty years to complete the job! The delay wasn't caused by lack of interest but mostly because of the sheer pressures of earning a dollar. I have tried to restrict my thoughts, my feelings and the story of my family life to points that would be of interest to all my readers and not only my immediate friends and family. I have tried to cut out as much superfluous verbiage as I can without ruining the spirit of my message. I have been told that prolixity is the amateur writer's greatest enemy, so I have tried not to let my book suffer in this direction.

Because of the nature of my profession I have been able to travel quite extensively and whilst in the process of performing my work, I have encountered many unusual and interesting situations. This book is nothing like a travelogue; my travels were only the nourishment to help create my story. Countries where I was only a tourist I have not mentioned. My story confines itself only to those countries where I stayed long enough to learn about it, its people and at least a splattering of its language. This book is about these people and places as much as it is about myself. I have spent my whole life as a land/hydrographic/engineering surveyor and so much of it supports the theory that throughout history the surveyor was almost always the first man in! Fortunately, the surveyor is not required to be good-looking but, generally speaking, he is required to have a strong body as well as a scientific mind to cope with his job and to enjoy the type of adventure that his profession has to offer him. This book is about my life as a surveyor, not only to include many of my professional experiences but some of my personal endeavours as well. There were people who helped and inspired me to try and achieve higher levels of life and I write about these people, especially those whom I found so colourful and interesting; I feel that they add value to my book as they added value to my life. There were others. Perhaps my readers will enjoy comparing some of my characters with people that they knew.

I've introduced into my story the difficult life-style of working (making maps) in the loneliness and barreness of the Arabian Desert, where your only other fellow human being, apart from your driver, were Arabic speaking Arab Legionnaires. Then I go on with life amongst the beautiful lakes, mountains, prairies and frozen wastes of Canada. Then the dangerous, close to nature, sensuous and exhilarating living in that beautiful country called Kenya. The heavenly atmosphere whilst working and living in the colourful and romantic Tahiti. The exciting and high standard of living and working in modern California. I don't forget the cold and calculating life of the oil and gas engineering world of the North Sea. There is a generous ration of descriptive love, hate, happiness, sadness, life, death, sex, wealth, poverty, swaying palms, blue lagoons, golden sands and white crisp snow. I know that I'm not a celebrity, but had I been, I can't help but wonder if I would have been able to have had such an intimate and rich experience. I hope that readers that enjoy a book on love, travel and adventure, will find prime entertainment in these pages.

I have spent many years on 'safari' in one place or another; mostly under canvas. These are the sort of safaris occasionally portrayed by Hollywood. However, they are rarely performed today, if ever. Much of my story, although certainly not all of it, is about East Africa and I suspect the tale is one of the last to be written by a still living professional safariman. I think this is significant; we are a breed becoming extinct. Now there are hard-top roads and modern hotels all over East Africa but it hasn't always been like that. Things have changed so much in only forty years, and you can feel these changes taking place in the following pages.

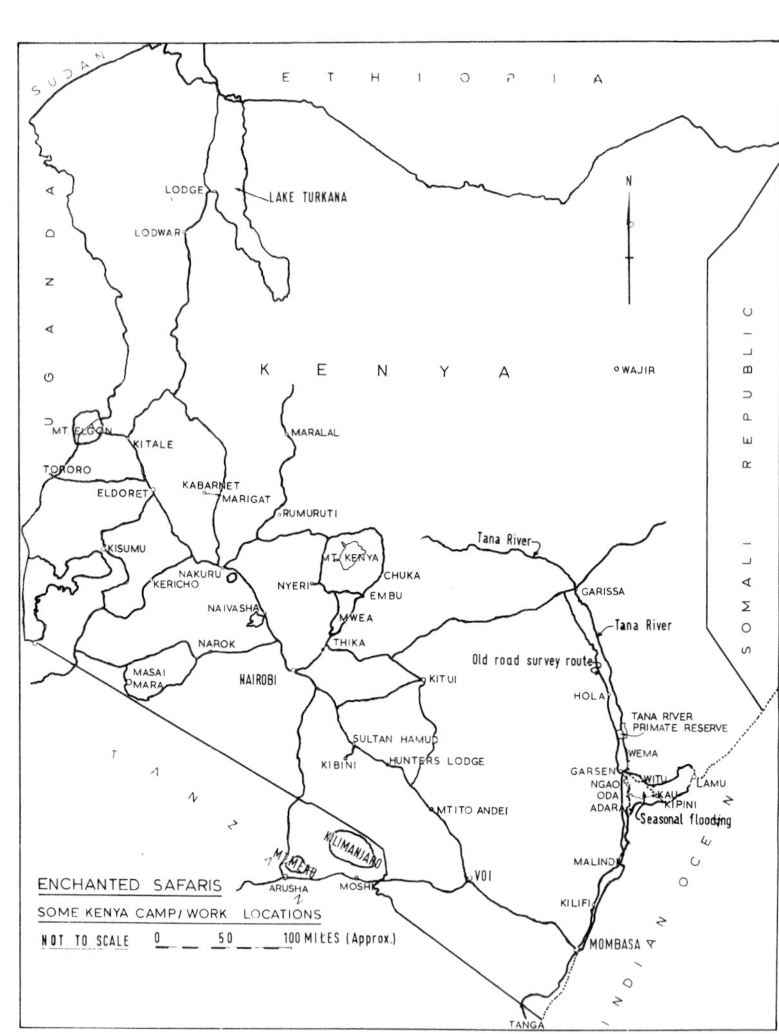

SUDAN
ETHIOPIA
UGANDA
KENYA
SOMALI REPUBLIC
TANZANIA
INDIAN OCEAN
N
LODGE
LAKE TURKANA
LODWAR
WAJIR
MT. ELGON
KITALE
MARALAL
TORORO
ELDORET
KABARNET
MARIGAT
RUMURUTI
KISUMU
MT. KENYA
Tana River
NAKURU
KERICHO
CHUKA
NYERI
EMBU
GARISSA
NAIVASHA
MWEA
Tana River
NAROK
THIKA
Old road survey route
MASAI MARA
NAIROBI
KITUI
HOLA
TANA RIVER PRIMATE RESERVE
SULTAN HAMUD
WEMA
KIBINI
HUNTERS LODGE
GARSEN
WITU
LAMU
NGAO
ODA
KAU
ADARA
KIPINI
MTITO ANDEI
Seasonal flooding
KILIMANJARO
MALINDI
VOI
ARUSHA
MOSHI
KILIFI
MOMBASA
TANGA
ENCHANTED SAFARIS
SOME KENYA CAMP/WORK LOCATIONS
NOT TO SCALE 0 50 100 MILES (Approx.)

1

Jordan – Where It All Started

To write this book I'm sitting in the lounge of my cottage which overlooks the Bay of Erbusaig, near the Kyle of Lochalsh, and it takes in a magnificent view of the Isle of Skye and some smaller adjacent islands. It's a beautiful sight, one which I have come to love dearly. I am not a Scot by birth; in fact, I settled here only in 1988. My home before this was in that lovely county of Wiltshire; in a 300-year-old house. It was while living in Wiltshire that I was set back with a rare illness associated with diabetes, but I am now happy to say that I have that under control. In the initial painful stages of that illness it gave me time to reflect on my life, as they say. Whilst sitting out on my lawn, taking in some early morning summer sunshine and watching my housekeeper cutting some roses for my lounge, I thought to myself that apart from my illness, which I hoped was only temporary, why was it that I was always feeling so discontented? I have been fairly successful in business and I have had, I suppose, more than my share of love. On top of this, I have been able to travel quite extensively and, up until now, have always enjoyed a good healthy life. So, what is it that causes this current discontentment? Well, I have found the time to sit down and think the matter through. Out of the blue, I found the answer. It was because I wasn't living, in this point in time, where I love most of all, where I had worked many times during my working life – the Islands and Highlands of Scotland.

Kenya has also been a love of my life but I will have more to say about that later!

My story begins in the winter of 1949/50 when Blondie and I had walked for many hours and had covered many Jordanian miles. We were not exactly lost but we knew that we had a long way to go before we would reach base camp. It was doubtful if we would see another living soul before our journey's end. There were plenty of 'dead souls' around as was witnessed by the small stone cairns on the hillocks, marking their resting places. I thought God, what a place to finish my life! We said very little to each other for we were so tired. It was January so it was bitterly cold. Both my knees had been bleeding quite a lot from where I had cut them from stumbling over lava rocks. There was blood down the front of my tunic, too, which had come from my cracked septic lips. We had learnt how thirsty one can get, even in this bitter cold. Unfortunately, there was no chance of a drink of any kind and I had foolishly disposed of my urine many hours ago! I knew that some of our men have had to revert to such drastic actions on such occasions as these before. Blondie and I were serving regular soldiers in the Topographic Squadron of a Survey Engineer Regiment of the Royal Engineers.

The previous morning, quite early, Blondie and I left base camp with our driver. At the same time, a second jeep left with a fellow surveyor, Mick Rooney, (believe it or not, that was his name!) and his driver. We were both driving a good bit further north of base camp to identify selected points on some air photographs and then heighting these points by means of a battery of aneroid barometers; a process in making maps. There were few identifiable tracks and no roads in this part of Jordan. There were no maps either for that was our task – to make them. We were driving along without too many obstacles and making good progress when out came the 'war cry' from the other jeep – 'Gazelle!' In response, I looked around and indeed, over to the left of us and about 200 yards away there was quite a herd of them. The chase started. I hasten to add at this stage, this was not indulging in a blood sport. Many of us lived up to three years almost entirely on tinned food, so an occasional fresh meat steak was extremely appreciated. It didn't take long to isolate one of the gazelle, chasing it to the left, then turning sharply to the right and then back again; all at considerable speed. Then the driver slammed on his brakes and Blondie stood up, took aim with his .303 rifle and brought the creature down with a single shot. It was 'cleaned out' and we were on our way again within fifteen minutes. I could shoot at an enemy, on command, but I don't think I could shoot a gazelle!

After this short excursion we had strapped the gazelle to one of the jeep bonnet's and then continued our journey northwards. Driving slowly, we picked our way through patches of lava and wadies when suddenly we came across some small buildings but, strangely, there appeared to be nobody in them. It was still bitterly cold even though the sun had made a brief appearance. We stopped and called out a greeting in Arabic but there was no answer. Cautiously, we went inside one of the buildings and behold, sitting all around the inside of the room were skeletons of men, women and children; all fully clothed in black clothes. Suddenly, the sun disappeared plunging the room in near darkness. The cold wind was finding its way in from everywhere. All this gave the scene a very morbid atmosphere. We were very respectful to the dead and sorrowed with what we saw and in low voices we expressed that we couldn't figure out under what circumstances these people had died. Neither could we understand why these skeletons retained their sitting posture. True, a few of the skeletons had collapsed and some had fallen to one side. There was an odour that we couldn't quite identify as well. I secretly whispered a small prayer and we all left this morbid place and got on our way again.

The time had come to identify our first point on the air photographs and for the other jeep to part company with us to carry on with the other strip of photographs just to the north of ours. Gosh, it was so damn cold and we didn't have an overcoat between us. We studied our photographs and estimated that our first 'point', which was in a wadi, was about thirty yards further west, so we drove on to carry out the identification when . . . splosh! We were up to our axles, front and back, in a wet rut. We could see the other jeep disappearing into the north and, as hard as we tried, we could not attract their attention. There were several of these ruts around left by some recent rain. You don't find many of these small areas where the rain doesn't get soaked up or drained rapidly away. It wasn't from the lack of effort that we subsequently couldn't free ourselves. Stranded in the ruddy desert, I couldn't believe it! Very little food, no safe water and not an overcoat between us. Blondie calculated that we were approximately five miles from the lone railway line that runs north/south, Ma'an to Amman, the Hashemite Railway; the railway that Lawrence of Arabia passed away some of his time on. The train passed twice a week, going south one day and back north the following day. It had already passed today. Blondie also calculated that not far north of where we would strike the railway, Catranā Arab Legion Fort was situated. Right, let's go for it! We decided to leave the driver the few compact emergency rations that we had, the rifle and the gazelle that we had shot that day. We told him our plans to go and get help and then left him with our ears ringing under a barrage of sarcastic remarks.

Now our plans were to leave the driver, head for Catranā Fort, get on their radio to the Arab Legion Fort at Ma'an who, in turn, would contact our OC at the Arab Legion Camp at Ma'an and pass on the information of our whereabouts. Once we had decided what we were going to do to help ourselves, it seemed a good and clear cut plan; in fact, we had already started to congratulate ourselves on our integrity. In spite of three years' training back at the survey school, I knew nothing about working and surviving in the desert. That's why I had been put with Blondie for a few weeks, he being a little more experienced.

True enough, the railway line was only five miles away; walking west-wards we couldn't miss it. The number of mirages we both saw was absolutely incredible and, of course, a stage of never ending 'dancing devils'. There was no sun and we didn't have a compass but there were distant hills we were familiar with. We left a mark at the first railway bridge that we came across, so that we could identify it later if needs be. Then we continued our 'hike' northwards. We walked fifteen miles along that track and found nothing but for the ruins of an old station situated all by itself and looking very lonely and forbidding. It looked like another one of those places that Colonel Lawrence had been having a go at during the Great War. During my work in Jordan I came across several remains of twisted railway tracks, old engine boilers, rusted footplates and other debris left from the Colonel's scuffles! The Topo Squadron were living under pretty austere conditions to get this job done, but I thought what a man Colonel Lawrence must have been to get 'his' job done, under the conditions prevailing in those days. Anyway, we walked another six miles which made the accumulated distance greater than anything Blondie had assumed. So, without any ill feelings or unkind comments we decided that we had gone far enough.

It was nearly dark so we sat down on the bank and rested a while, about an hour actually, waiting for the moon to rise. Hardly a word was spoken during that long cold wait and eventually I found considerable cheer when the moon did show itself. It was unfortunate that the cold wind was picking up even more; however, the clouds were disappearing thus giving us the full benefit of the moon. I tied my bootlaces back up in the process of giving myself a vigorous rub from my head to my toes. Meantime, Blondie had already faced south and was putting one foot in front of the other, so I fell in right behind him. We made the six miles back to the deserted station (which I later learnt was Menzil Station). We were now feeling very tired, cold, hungry and horribly thirsty. We again spoke very little; I assumed that Blondie's mind, like my own, was full of occupying thoughts. Mine were mostly of my parents and Eleanore, the Scottish lass that had cast my love to the wind. The hours passed very slowly as we lay shivering on the bare cold stone floor. No way could we get out of the ice cold draught as sage bushes blew in one entrance to the ruin and then out the other. We were aching with shivering as this persistent icy wind blew all around us. I tried to sleep but I was far too cold, thirsty and hungry. We were once visited by a wildcat, or something, during the night and it sounded just as lonely, cold and hungry as we were!

My diary has the following entry for Friday, 6 January 1950, '. . . at last, it was dawn. My colleague and I held another conference and decided that we would return to the jeep and when there, compose further plans that would be governed, to a certain extent, by the condition we were in when we got there. Oh, for some ham and eggs and a cup of tea! I lifted my aching body from the floor but I must confess, I felt a little better for the rest. On we walked to the bridge from whence we started. We had a long rest before we then started the bash on to the site where we had left the jeep. The thought of chewing a couple of hard compo biscuits seemed appetising, let alone cooking a bit of gazelle steak! Horror struck us . . . the jeep had gone!

Thank heavens, though, in this spot there was plenty of water around in the ruts, so we could at least have a drink. The water tasted absolutely horrible, a brownish green and full of goodness only knows what. However, we drank first and then complained afterwards. Well, there was only one thing we could do now. We assumed that the jeep had been found; that alone was miraculous; then pulled out by some mechanical means and then returned to base camp. So, we followed on. We had already walked nearly forty miles since yesterday and we had had no food and very little to drink – and no sleep. Now we had another twenty-eight mile walk ahead of us! Oh dear, it was very hard to find one's sense of humour. Walking came automatically and painful. Our morale was very low at this point in time. Still, few words were exchanged between us and those that were were of a survey technical nature, although we admitted how hungry we were. My lips showed new deep cracks caused by the strong wind and the lack of fluid. On we bashed. We lost our way two or three times but managed to correct our course when we could identify certain hills or wadies. My memory was working overtime. Apart from the intricate details of my young life, like the two lovely girls that I had kissed at one time or another, I started to think of what I was going to say to my troop sergeant if I ever got out of this. At last we could see the distant hills, behind which our base camp was situated. However, once again we thought that fate was against us as darkness fell. Indeed, it turned very dark and even colder. We were really done in. We both willingly fell to the ground and seemed to fall into a deep sleep. We woke up in about one and a half hours later, when the moon was just beginning to rise, letting us see the hills again. I felt much fresher for the kip but I was very cold and quite damp. Feet were rubbed very sore in places; however, we got up and bashed on. We now moved very slowly with rests becoming much more frequent until we reached the foot of the hills.

We had to admit (although we didn't do that very often) we were completely exhausted again. Our legs refused to cooperate when we tried to advance; they just wouldn't move. We knew that the base camp was only about three miles away but we still decided to rest for a few more hours before trying the last stretch. We hoped that they hadn't moved base camp! A few days ago we remembered that there was talk about doing so.

While I was down on my back, studying the various constellations in the heavens above my head, a sudden chill of excitement went up my spine to the roots of my hair. Was it possible that I heard what I did? Yes indeed, Blondie confirmed that it was the purring of a jeep engine. I don't know how we managed it but we both shot to our feet as if we had sat on red hot ashes! Then we saw the lights of that wonderful vehicle. Blondie went wild as he ran towards the direction of the oncoming lights, waving his arms and shouting out at the top of his voice, 'It's about time you bloody well showed up!'

I tried to run but it was impossible, so I did what I thought was the next best thing – I stood waving my arms, hoping that they would see me in the moonlight. They saw us! You would have thought that it was V.J. Day by the way that they behaved when they finally stopped their jeep. And, oh boy, were we glad to see them. Men can be strange creatures. The part of the troop that happened to be in base camp gave us a terrific welcome. Food! What it is to be young! We left seeing the troop sergeant until next morning.

They are over forty years' old now; nevertheless, I still have Mick Rooney's notes, written in his own hand, giving his account as to how he had found our vehicle, how he had searched for us for two days and how he found us when he did. This was one adventure of many on this tour.

I had three years in the Middle East and, on the whole, I enjoyed it. Much of that time I would go many months when my only accommodation was a sleeping bag along the side of my vehicle. All my meals had to be cooked by my driver and myself. We lived almost entirely on the tin and I lost five of my adult teeth. The water truck got back from Amman or Ma'an about once every week to ten days and usually brought our mail with it. Each of us collected our mail when we got back to base camp, which was at about the same frequency! Much of the time we could not spare the water to have a good wash, however, there was a good powder that killed most things. We mostly washed our hands and plates in the sand. Sand flies and dung beetles were our worst enemy. What an old soldier's story this must sound. When possible, we used to enjoy a visit to Petra, by horseback. There were no signs of tourists or accommodation for the suchlike, in those days.

The jobs I enjoyed most of all during this tour in the Middle East was the six months spent on the N.E. Jordan Triangulation and the six months spent in a field astronomy team in Fayid, Egypt. On the last mentioned job, we had the good facilities offered to us by the then Egyptian Astronomer Royal, Dr Madwar. We were able to do much of our work in the Royal Observatory at Helwan. For this job the Army issued us with civilian clothes and accommodated us in a first class hotel; quite a contrast to life in Jordan! The Army also issued us with an instrument known as a 'broken transit theo,' together with a full chronometer, radio, chronotape, loads of mathematical tables, all very high-tech for those days. I had to spend more time computing than observing. The team consisted of only two officers and two NCOs.

Towards the end of my tour I was promoted to troop sergeant and as strange as it may sound, we were all issued with plain clothes again, to do a job in the north of Iraq via Baghdad. I still wonder if I'm allowed to say what exactly our job was – perhaps the less said the better.

On one of my return trips to Fayid I met an old fellow student friend of mine who eventually turned out to be my brother-in-law. He had been at the Survey School with me in England. Now he too had to do a three year tour in the Middle East. I couldn't think of a worse way to punish oneself than to go home to England on leave half way through your tour – he did – but he had a very good reason, he married a lovely lady. On his return to Fayid, after the wedding, I too had to return to Regimental HQ from Ma'an. This not only created the chance to meet up again, it gave him the chance to show me his wedding photographs! It was then that I saw a lovely girl standing next to the bride and groom.

'Who is this?' I asked him.

'Who?' he asked.

'This lovely girl,' said I, pointing to her in the photograph.

'Oh, her! That's my sister Molly.'

In the weeks that followed, I fell madly in love with her. Over the course of time letters were exchanged between him, his mother and his sister and the outcome was, I was informed, Molly would enjoy having a letter from me, if I would care to write. I thought deep about it and knew that I had yet another year to serve in the Middle East but my feelings got the better of me, so I wrote. They were important events, getting Molly's letters over the following months. They were cheerful, newsy and pleasant but never once did Molly even indicate that she got the message of my sometimes cheeky letters! If I had been successful in conveying my feelings towards her then she was equally as successful in not letting me know that I had done so.

Of course, it is a long time since I worked in the Middle East and I dare say that things have changed in leaps and bounds – and are still changing. I have read about the terrific improvements in parts of Jordan and who is to say that Egypt hasn't changed and come a long way since the days of King Farouk. I am sure that some things will hardly ever change and what comes to mind is the peace and reverence of the early morning call to the faithful to prayer; the magnificence of the Creation of the desert dawn and sunset. I feel man will always be able to pass through the 'fault' in the mountain to enjoy the thrill of coming face to face with the timeless grandeur of the 'Treasure House' of Petra, '. . . the rose red city half as old as time . . ;' the quiet friendliness of the Bedouin residing in his black tent, that being his only address; the pomp and tradition of the excellent Arab Legion Bagpipe Band.

October 1951 saw the end of my tour in the Middle East. Unfortunately, my dear mother was very ill at that time and I couldn't leave her for more than a few hours at a time. However, Molly, whom I was desperate to meet, managed to arrange to come down to Salisbury from her home in London. This she was able to do for several weekends so that we could meet and get to know each other more. I shall never forget when I first met her on Salisbury Station. She was tall, black-haired, wore a green coat and black beret on the back of her head. She looked gorgeous. I met her in October; we got engaged at Christmas and married at Easter 1952. At that time she was one of the

English secretaries of a famous American film producer and, as such, she was able to meet many celebrities. She was well-read, very good-mannered, polite, very feminine, good-tempered, pretty and sexy! I rather 'bush-whacked' her into marrying me and it took her thirty two years to pluck up the courage to tell me to 'buzz off' and then divorce me!

2

The First East African Tour

Once I had made up my mind that I was leaving the Army there were all kinds of help available to me to find a job and get myself settled down to a civilian life again. Some years ago, when I had decided to take up a life of surveying, I realised that I would have to travel quite a lot and that I had to accept this. To me, this was one of the main attractions. However, I was now a married man and I realised that I would have to look at my choice of employment very closely. Not necessarily to give up my type of work but to try and fit it in with an acceptable standard of matrimonial life.

For a number of years I was very keen to try Australia where I knew there were ample opportunities in my kind of work. In answer to an advertisement, I was successful in securing a post in Australia on the Snowy Mountain Scheme. But, oh dear, this came up against a lot of opposition from my in-laws! I feared it might. In hindsight, I could understand that this was quite natural. Indeed, my wife's family were a very close-knit lot. The thought of Molly going so far away was more than her parents could stand. Understandable. It was wise to try and plot another course.

Soon after deciding not to go to Australia I was out of the Army and I had to do something fairly quickly about finding a job because now I had a wife to support. Gratefully, I accepted a post as surveyor with the Open-Cast Coal Executive of the National Coal Board. They posted me to Nottingham and that was a very beautiful part of England; the natives were extremely pleasant too. Anybody coming from that part of the world can be justly proud. This job lasted me out until May 1953.

When I look back I feel that for many years my life was pointing towards Kenya. I had read many stories about it and my instructor colleagues, back at the School of Military Survey, had told me many tales of their service in that magical country. In all, I was very intrigued with the place. And, of course, the founder of the Boy Scout movement was buried there.

In answer to another advertisement in *The Telegraph*, the gentlemen of The Crown Agents called me to No. 4 Millbank. On arrival, they sent me to Harley Street for a medical before announcing that I was successful in winning the post as surveyor with the East African Railways and Harbours Administration. What a great day that was! In spite of the Mau-Mau campaign, even my in-laws agreed to me taking this job! I've never really known if this was because they were hoping that the Mau-Mau would get me or because it was close enough to England and within their resources to come and see Molly at any time, if need be.

We had very little money but my Dad was able to help us a little. We certainly couldn't afford a weapon which everybody purchased in those days, even if only to defend themselves. We never did afford a weapon. After saying our farewells to our friends and families in an old Nissen hut at Heathrow we were off to Kenya. We flew in an old Hermes which was a pretty up to date aircraft in those days and the journey seemed to take for ever. We had to stop in Rome, Khartoum, Entebbe and then, at last, reached Nairobi.

There is one event that always comes to my mind when I reminisce so far back. We were on our way to Kenya and we had never been so happy. In less than one year of married life I had come to find Molly a tower of strength and in me she trusted her protection, happiness and well-being. That's the way it should be. When we got to Rome, Molly wasn't feeling too well and we both put it down to her pregnancy and likely air-sickness. Continuing our journey we arrived at Khartoum at approximately four o'clock in the morning, both feeling uncomfortable and hot. After we had refreshed ourselves poor Molly had to retreat to the ladies and be violently sick. The poor wee soul, when she reappeared she looked so ill and absolutely beat. I consoled her by saying that it wouldn't be long before I would have her comfortably in a nice cool aircraft. This became a fact in about another fifteen minutes.

So, there we were, comfortably seated, the cool air vents directed towards our faces, the stewardesses making a last minute fuss of us and checking our seat-belts. We could now hear the rumbling of the aircraft wheels as we twisted and turned towards the start of the runway. I gripped Molly's hand and she gave me a weak smile in return. Entebbe next stop. Wait a minute, there was a waiter running towards the aircraft and wasn't that Molly's handbag he was waving in the air? The plane stopped and the stewardess took the handbag aboard. I believe it was the captain who asked us to check the contents of the bag! My God, we could see instantly that the travellers' cheques were gone! My stomach wrenched and I could feel water flooding to my mouth. Immediately the plane's radio went into action. They spoke to Khartoum, to Entebbe and Nairobi. What on earth was going to happen to us now? How much more of this could poor Molly take?

Even though we were burdened with anxiety, we couldn't help but be very impressed with the beauty of Entebbe, the greenness of the lush foliage, all dappled with patches of sunshine whilst dancing in the breezes. We could hear the sound of distant drums. The flight from Entebbe to Nairobi was, as predicted, a little 'bumpy'. Behind us, we could hear a returning farmer saying to his accompanying passenger '. . . there it is – that good old Kenya red earth – by Jove, I can even smell it!' Indeed, with the position of the sun relative to the position of the plane, the land stretched out below us looked ablaze, like the glow of burning ashes being fanned by the breeze. So, this was Kenya. I had already fallen in love with her!

We were met by a Mr Brown from the Chief Engineers Staff Section. He sincerely welcomed us to British East Africa as he tidied his shirt and tie – and the position of his revolver! He showed compassion towards our misfortune (HQ had already heard about our troubles.) However, he cheered us up with the news that he had booked us in at the New Stanley Hotel for our first ten days pending posting. This was with the compliments of our employers, EAR & H. The next day they further assisted me by advancing a 'sub'.

Nairobi was larger than we thought it would be and there were so many people of different races. The mass was staggering. But what were all these sand-bags for? The way many of the buildings were faced with these bags rather reminded me of London during the war. At certain vantage points on the corners of some of the roads they had built small huts of corrugated iron and sand-bags and each were surrounded by barbed wire. These must be some form of defence against the Mau-Mau, I thought. Our surprise was intensified when we arrived at the hotel and saw many ladies dressed in their pretty summer frocks and white gloves and wearing pistols strapped around their waists. This was 1953, of course, and the height of the Mau-Mau campaign.

We had a quick shower and changed for dinner. We were both very nervous. I thought that Molly looked very pale but very pretty. We agreed to call in on the famous Long Bar and have a Tusker lager before we went in for dinner. The waiter who served us, a young Kikuyu chap, taught us our first Swahili word, which was JAMBO. I think that no other greeting in any other language has such a cordial and sincere meaning to it. Whilst we were sitting there we were astonished at the large number of navy blue and khaki-uniformed police that were also sitting in there. Like some of the civilian-clothed ladies who were sitting with them, they were all armed. Suddenly, in their midst, there appeared a very heavy set man with an attentive crowd sitting around him. He wore long, very tattered trousers and bush-jacket with a greasy bush-hat perched on the back of his head. He clearly had several front teeth missing and appeared to be in his mid-forties. Across his chest were two bandoliers of bullets and propped up between his hands was a machine-gun. Hanging down his side was a sheathed panga and he also wore a pistol. This was the famous pseudo-Mau-Mau terrorist, Davo Davidson; the man most wanted by Kenyatta's followers. You will hear more about this very colourful man later on.

The next morning I entered the HQ of East African Railways & Harbours which looked as much like Buckingham Palace as anything. There I met the chief engineer. The following ten days were spent on documentation and familiarising myself with my employers' specifications with reference to performance of my profession. I became impressed, quite early, by the way the railways knew their job and I felt their standards were commendable. Molly was still being sick and was suffering with an uncomfortable tummy condition but she still didn't complain. On the first night in the hotel I secretly wept when I thought of what I had let her in for and I could see how she was suffering. And yet, to help us out over a sticky patch, she had dragged herself out to a typing agency, which was just around the corner from the New Stanley Hotel. She thought that in this way she could earn a quick bob or two to give us some immediate cash. So that she could continue her efforts and because she hoped her condition was only temporary, she had taken frequent calls in at the chemist to take 'a draught' to try and settle her! I ask you! One night I found that her mosquito-net had been pulled back and her bed was empty. I found her sitting on the balcony gripping her tummy and suffering a raging temperature. She was in full view of any terrorist who wanted to chalk up another victim. The next day a visiting 'white man' was shot dead on the opposite side of the road. That morning the railway doctor called into the hotel and Molly was admitted into

Nairobi Hospital. Dysentery! When I got back to the hotel, after watching Molly being fed 'crushed charcoal' in hospital, I overheard on someone's radio that at that very moment Her Majesty Queen Elizabeth was being crowned Queen of England.

Twelve days had passed and I had been summoned by the chief engineer. A survey party was returning to Nairobi in a day or two and I was then to join the safari which was going to Sultan Hamud. I froze in horror. On my next visit to the hospital I told Molly.

'You are not going on safari without me,' she said.

She got out of her hospital bed and the two of us walked along to another ward where the doctor was caring for some Mau-Mau victims. We told him of our plight.

'Might be the best thing. Keep taking the medicine, boil all your water and be careful of what you eat. You can go out tomorrow morning, Mrs Griffiths,' he said, to our amazement.

I promised him that I would take great care of her and would drive her back to Nairobi should I least suspect the necessity. Although very thin and looking very weak, she was very, very happy.

A crisp Scottish accent, belonging to the engineer-in-charge of safari, commanded, 'Get the boys to put your tent up here and George's tent up there and mine can go up over there. We will put the office tent next to mine and the boy's tents can go nearer to the station.' We had arrived. This was Sultan Hamud. By evening we had all the tents up and the grass had been cut well back to prevent fires and the invasion of snakes. The vehicles had been re-fuelled, the survey instruments unpacked and inspected and I was downing a really cool Tusker bought from Amir Ali's duka. Molly and I had experienced our first safari bath; a canvas bag about three feet square and six inches deep which was held up by a thin unfolding wooden frame. When one has it set-up, the cook poured in one bucket of hot water and one bucket of cold together with at least four tablespoons of Dettol to kill whatever might be lurking around in the water! You could just about sit up in the thing and we claimed that even though we had stayed in some of the most luxurious hotels in the world, no other bath was ever so appreciated, or enjoyed as much as that safari bath in the back of our only home – a tent! Quite often, a column of safari ants would pass through this part of the tent but we learnt to pay little heed to them; should you kill a 'bull-ant' whilst filling your bath the smell is unique and quite insufferable! The water was heated up in a makeshift kitchen outside and around the back of our tent by John Matibu, our newly employed cook. John was a Wakamber boy and a Christian with a small splattering of English language.

It was wise not to roam too far from the tent in the dark. Even in broad daylight Masai warriors were lurking around the camp and were gaping at Molly in awe.

Although she was very tired, Molly's health had already improved immensely, judging by the new bloom in her cheeks. We got up from our camp chairs, put our Tilley lamp out and then embraced each other as we looked across the moonlit bush and wondered, was this really happening to us! We kissed goodnight and turned into our camp beds, tucked in our mosquito nets and slept like we had never slept before.

Mr Thompson, the engineer in charge of Safari was in his late sixties, a fine engineer and loved his work. I never did know his Christian name. One day, when we were up in the back of the truck returning to camp, after just having done a day's surveying, he confided in me. If you bide your time, sooner or later you can catch most people in this mood. He said that throughout his life, when he had worked on other engineering projects, he often thought of himself as nothing more than a glorified accountant, always worrying about other people's money or where the money was going to come from. But, on survey work, he only spent money and didn't have to worry about where it came from. He was a bachelor himself and had absolutely no time for married couples, especially on his safari (some wife must have given him a real rough time once!) and made his point of view quite clear to Head Office. Nevertheless, he was stuck with us. Strangely, he and Molly became quite good friends and his only complaint that I heard of, was how quickly Molly read through his Book Club books. Mr Thompson was short, very thin, deaf as a doornail and very experienced. He wore steel-rimmed spectacles and a bush-hat with a thick brim of double felt. He always drove his own old khaki-coloured Austin Countryman.

We were at Sultan Hamud for about six weeks all told and our job was to find a railway route to a limestone deposit at Kibini, about twenty miles away from the station. It's now well marked on today's Survey of Kenya map. Shortly after our arrival we met a Swedish driller who had made the test boreholes to prove the deposit. We also met the Danish prospector who had found the deposit for the cement company; he said he had been looking for diamonds! Both men were very charming and they clearly enjoyed Molly's company. I always thought that made up the European complement but, twenty-five years later on, Molly told me there were two more. Apparently, two European Permanent Way Inspectors (who would eventually lay the railway track on the new extension) had stopped at the station siding in their 'caboose'; a special railway carriage fitted out as accommodation for railway operation and field staff. When the engine left them at the siding they walked across to the camp to see if they could find Mr Thompson or anybody else. I was working out along the proposed line and Molly wasn't with me on that day. They invited Molly across to the caboose for coffee and she went. The morning was very bright, sunny and getting quite warm but inside the caboose it was still cool yet. The caboose had a noticeable background aroma of curry and coffee but the place looked spotless and the table had been nicely set by the cook for morning coffee. The topic of conversation one can only guess but she said that as time went along a situation was developing very fast. The inspectors were young, single, sunburnt and handsome. She pulled herself together and quickly analysed the situation and declined their offers, gracefully retreating back to her tent. Such is life in the bush. Africa has strong vibrations which sometimes overactivate a young person's sensual instincts; it happens to everyone.

Molly was looking browner, stronger and was settling down more each day. Inches were slowly increasing around her tummy as our baby grew. More days than not she would go out to work with me. She would plonk herself down in a camp chair by the side of my theodolite and the chap that was holding the sun umbrella over my theodolite would make certain that the area of shade would encompass her as well (sometimes forgetting my theodolite). I would read out my observations to her and she would book them in my field-book. This speeded up the sections work considerably. Of course, I as well as some of the chainmen loved her presence. She also coped with the visiting Masai tribesmen and the flies they brought with them. One day, at about one o'clock in the afternoon, a chainman came running towards us and whispered, 'Bwana, we must go quickly because ahead of us there is a rhino and when it gets wind of us it will kill all of us.'

So, what else would you do but pack up and walk quickly back to the truck and then head back to the camp? True, we did too, only we ran!

'What are you doing back at camp this time of the day?' said Jock. I explained.

'One can tell you are new to Africa. They will pull this one on you as often as they can. They know you will not chance your luck against a rhino, especially when you haven't got a gun.'

I was embarrassed, but there you are, it happened.

Seven o'clock next morning, we were off again. Molly and I were standing on top in the back of the truck and leaning over the cabin roof. It was a five-ton Austin. Sharing the ride with us were about ten African chainmen and bush-cutters. We were all highly amused at the herds of dik-dik and Thomson gazelle who were trying to race with us. A whole herd of impala shot across our tracks and over there, to the right, was yet another herd of motionless wildebeest. The whole scene was dappled with early morning sunshine and the air was fresh and cool. All of a sudden, just as we drove over a slight rise, there stretched out before us was Kilimanjaro. What a magnificent sight! Molly and I clasped hands together as we drank in this breathtaking picture. It was a very emotional experience for at the same time the men were softly singing, in absolute harmony, that old Swahili song, 'We are going to Mombasa.'

That was a moment we shared that could never be taken away from me by anyone.

That morning my survey was going well until about one o'clock and then, blow me if it didn't happen again. 'Rhino, bwana! Rhino, bwana! Rhino bwana!'

Now what do I do? Mr Thompson's lecture flashed through my mind. That was all the thinking I did. You should have seen us scatter. I grabbed Molly's hand and took off back to where we had left the truck which was now about a mile back. Molly's pregnancy, now about six months old, did not appear to bother her or hold her up at all. In fact, at times, she was pulling me along! After we had gone about a quarter of a mile we met the Danish prospector with two African game scouts.

'Good morning, what seems to be the trouble?'

I very reluctantly had to stop and take the precious time to tell him.

'I heard about your trouble that you had yesterday, yes. I've been given permission from the game warden to deal with the situation as best fits yes. If you and a couple of your men can come back forward with us, we will try and put the matter right.'

I was not consoled by the bravery of the Dane but I was impressed by the steel look in the eyes of the two scouts; more so when I saw them taking the brown sticky material off the tips of the arrow heads. These, I thought, obviously must be poisoned tips.

I told Pompillio, a two metre tall Uganda Chainman, to stop here and take care of Mama and help her up this tree if needs be. Molly persuaded me to go with the Dane and convinced me that she could manage. Right, off we went, nervous and excited. Suddenly the Dane said 'Now we will stop here and your men must work their way round forward and make plenty of noise!'

It was like being in the movies. Orders were given to my men and the two scouts got down on one knee and took aim at heavens only knew what! By this time I was really jittery.

'Mr Griffiths, you climb up that tree there and I will go up this one because there is not much else we can do except keep out of the way.'

I now wondered what I was doing there at all but I was willing to take instructions from anybody who had some idea of what to do when a couple of tons of wild meat comes hurtling through the bush at you. I found climbing the tree difficult, it wasn't an easy one, but so what! As I was going up I thought how supple the tree was and when I was nearing what I thought to be a safe altitude from ground level, I could hear a devil of a commotion going on underneath me. However, for the seconds it was all happening, I couldn't see anything because of the difficulties with the climbing and the concentration it demanded of me. I was probably huffing and blowing more than the rhino. It was slowly revealed to me that the tree wasn't coping with my weight at all. The wretched tree was slowly bending over until my bottom was only four feet from the ground. This was a frightening sort of thrill. I let my feet drop to the ground and then I let go of the tree. I looked around and it had turned very quiet. Where was everybody? It must have been only seconds since I started to climb the tree and yet now there wasn't a soul around except me and I presumed the Dane, somewhere up the other tree. I couldn't even hear any sign of the rhino; what could have happened in only such a flash?

Not finding any sign of my wife, or Pompillio, I kept running back towards the truck. Pompillio and several other of the chainmen were inside the trucks cabin with the doors and windows not only closed but locked. There was Molly, hammering on the door of the truck but nobody was taking a blind bit of notice. I almost threw Molly onto the back of the truck and then jumped up there with her. We then just looked at each other in breathless astonishment. It was now as silent as the grave; even the tropical birds were quiet. Slowly, one man appeared from the bush and then another and again another. The Austin gradually became as noisy and as active as a wagon load of monkeys. As it turned out, it was a cow rhino and her baby that was giving us all this trouble. The scouts chose not to shoot. The rhino were subsequently captured and evacuated to another part of the plain. So much for 'old timers' ' theories about natives trying to pull the wool over the eyes of young officers!

We had to get used to life without TV, cinema, theatre, sports, pubs or even decent radio. Never mind, it seemed we still filled our lives to the brim. Another thing, we at least enjoyed talking to each other. We also had the interest to talk to other people and they to us. With the way of life in Africa in those days it seemed that everybody we met conveyed the message that we needed each other. I observed clearly that most people cared about each other and expressed themselves in that light. We had more time for each other, I'm sure, without all these other time absorbing distractions. I doubt if we would have had the time or inclination in England to meet someone like Amir Ali. I have mentioned him before. He was the owner of the shop (duka) in Sultan Hamud. His was an Asian family and their shop sold just about everything; if they didn't have it on stock, then they would get it the next time one of them went to Nairobi. They mainly traded with Masai tribesmen; therefore, perhaps, with all due respect, the standards of hygiene and presentation left a lot to be desired. Most of you who have been to Kenya these past few years, wouldn't know the duka because the new road sort of bypasses the 'downtown' area of Sultan Hamud. You have to go off the main road if you want to visit the shop. If you do visit the place in the future, please convey my warmest regards to them and tell them that I have mentioned them in my book!

Amir had a sister that used to work in the duka too; her name was Khartoum. I used to rather fancy Khartoum. We would go over to the duka every evening for a 'sundowner' before it got dark and the cook had our dinner ready. During this hour we would share many a tale and learnt much about each other's culture and different ways of living. One of the days we were at Sultan Hamud was the Aga Khan's Birthday and they invited us to share in his birthday celebrations with them. They had been preparing a huge curry over these last several days and it was absolutely delicious. Very hot but still delicious. Molly drank several bottles of Fanta Orange and Coca-Cola with hers as well as a jug of water! But, eat it she did – and even had seconds!

Two months had passed and the survey was completed. It wasn't long afterwards when the spur was built, as was the huge cement works at Athi River to where the limestone was conveyed. Now we were on our way to Mombasa. I can't say the word MOMBASA, let alone type it, without my heart thumping and I get to feel terribly homesick. To us, it became Paradise and today I could happily put my bones there to rest. Well, this was our introduction to Mombasa by having to do another small job there which only took a couple of months. We had to survey a route for a railway line running from Kwa Jomvu Station, which is located just off of Mombasa Island, to Kilindini Port (Mombasa Port) via a new causeway at Kipevu. This line was partly for the use of 'boat trains' from up-country. Years later, when on a return visit, many a day I enjoyed waving back to all the pretty sun-burned mums and their happy children as the train passed along this newly constructed route. They were either boarding or had just disembarked from one of the smart steam-ships that served British East Africa from England. Some of these passenger ships went down as far as South Africa.

Mind you, I did get sunburned at Mombasa myself, badly! It was on a rare day off when we went to a very lovely beach on the North Coast, called White Sands. There was a hotel there made up of a few timber, coral blocks and corrugated iron buildings with *mikuti* roofs. One could get a good lunch and ice-cold 'Tusker' there, for less than a pound each. I went into the Indian Ocean for a good swim for two half-hour periods and for the rest of the time I kept a shirt on. I wasn't daft. Molly didn't go in swimming at all because a swimsuit hadn't been designed yet for ladies in her 'condition'. That night I had huge, long, yellow blisters right across my shoulders. Because of the severe discomfort I could have willingly hanged myself if it hadn't been for the understanding and compassion of my Molly. If I did get any sleep over the next few days, then it was sitting up at the dining table with my arms and head on a pillow. I got over it. If you are going to Mombasa, be warned. Incidentally, you should see the Whitesands Hotel today!

Tanganyika. Don't you think that is a lovely sounding name? That's what Tanzania of today was called then. Before and during the Great War the Germans built a railway line from Tanga to Mombo and it served the country well for very many years. However, it was not compatible with modern demands and standards. There was at least one gradient that I was told about where the train only just made it to the top – and that was only after it's third attempt! The engineering drawings were a treasure of engineering culture. However, not only was everything in German but they were all in METRIC. Everything is in metric today, even our surveying equipment. This nevertheless was my first encounter (I knew it was going to happen sooner or later). Tanga has been called 'the Jewel of the Indian Ocean' by Vasco de Gama or some such colourful person and I go along with that. Most of the town was made up of single storey buildings, many of them just made with mud and wattle although some were made of coral blocks and all had either corrugated iron or *mikuti* roofs. There were some exceptions and one of them was the old German Hospital; this was double-storeyed, heavily built and typical of the old German Empire Tropical lines; well, it was the way I thought of it. You expected to find German army officers inside with their spiked helmets and waxed moustaches, white-coated doctors with shaven heads and steel-rimmed glasses talking to nurses in their starched stiff uniforms. Another exception was a small block of offices and shops belonging to an Indian gentleman who owned much of the land adjacent to the railway line. The streets were narrow but orderly and were lined with sweet smelling jasmine trees – how delightful was the perfume of those trees on those family strolls at sun-down! The foliage was in abundance, including palm, banana, euphorbia, kapok, gum, jacaranda and many others. Marvellous. Tanga is where the job started and we had to re-align much of the track all the way to Mombo.

Our first camp was at Muhasa. It was decided to work down to Tanga from there and then up-line for as far as was practical. Muhasa was the sort of centre of the sisal-growing plantations. The 'town' comprised a few dozen houses similar to those described for Tanga and all occupied by either African or Asian folks. Quite near there was a Catholic mission hospital staffed by nuns, some of whom we had the pleasure to meet. One of them insisted on calling me 'the man of the sea'; I think she must have once known somebody else with a beard like mine. Lovely and dedicated ladies all.

Didn't it rain whilst we were there! The tent roof hardly let in a single drop of rain but that didn't stop a torrent of a river passing right through the inside of the tent. We had a large suitcase which Molly kept all her future baby's clothes in and a lot of other things that would be needed when the time came to deliver her child. You had to provide these 'things' yourself when you lived in the bush. Every day Molly would take her baby's clothes out of the case, look at them lovingly and then put them back. They looked so out of place on a safari camp bed! Most of these things we bought in Nairobi or Mombasa but some of them were sent out from England. We were assured that many of these things would not be available in Tanga. The lot got soaked. We were able to salvage and wash a lot of the stuff but a lot was a complete write-off. Molly didn't complain but I had a gut feeling that she was pretty upset. Two days later, while Molly was resting on her camp bed, a damn great python passed right through the tent and parked under her bed. I still shudder when I think about it. She flew off the bed and ran to the other tents shouting for help. Everybody was out but she did see her kitten spitting at it.

Well, because of our predicament and because the baby was due in just a week, the doctor in Tanga decided that Molly should stay at the Tanga Hospital and use it like a hotel until the event. I was able to drive back to Tanga every four days to see if there was any news of the new arrival and to see how Molly was faring. Three weeks went by. Molly was so fed up at having nothing to do and, I suppose, not being with me in this unfamiliar environment that she talked both the doctor and myself into taking her back out to camp! Would you believe that?

Ten more days of bush-bashing went by and the survey was surging ahead. Mr Thompson said to me,'You know Griffiths, this is ridiculous. That girl is going to have her baby right here in this camp, if we don't do something about it! I'm sure that you had better take her back into Tanga now – anyway, I want some petrol and some "posho" for the men.' (And for the moment, I thought he was being so considerate and human!) Anyway, he was too late because Molly and I had already decided to go to Tanga the next day; after all, the baby was now a month overdue.

On arrival in Tanga we went straight to a new friends' house. On the journey in it rained so hard that we lost the track a dozen times. We noticed how the rain brought the snakes out. These kind friends invited us to stay with them 'until the time came'. The Good Lord would provide. Jim Aylward was a PWI on the railway and his dear wife, Amy, was one of the best. That evening Molly and I went to see a movie that I had enjoyed seeing once before. We had often talked about it. *A Cure For Love.* A jolly good film; I had seen it at the RAF cinema in Amman, Jordan. The late Robert Donat was excellent; so was Miss Dora Bryan. As I have said, I had often chatted to Molly about this film so I was very pleased when the opportunity came for her to see it. Afterwards, we drove along the front to cool off a bit where we parked on top of the cliff overlooking the harbour. Close to the shore below us was the vessel *S.S. Uganda*, dressed overall and with her lights aglow. We could hear the music of her small orchestra. The Sisal Growers Association were having their annual dinner on board that evening. It was a romantic atmosphere, a beautiful evening; we were happy, contented with our lot, young and deeply in love.

It was a long time since we had eaten but I was able to buy some locally dry-roasted peanuts from a vendor nearby. These nuts still have their husks on and are salted. To squeeze the nut between your fingers so that the nut pops into your mouth, leaving the husks between your fingers, takes lengthy practice. A good chew on the end result is a treat for your palate but plays havoc with your waistline. We were doing it for about an hour!

We gave our bedroom a second spray of mosquito-killer and turned in at about half-past-eleven. At about one o'clock that morning Molly woke me up to tell me that those peanuts had been giving her dreadful wind. My friends were disturbed by the light and came to administer assistance – if required. Everybody was on edge anyway. 'That's not wind' declared Amy, '. . . you had better get dressed and get Molly to the hospital poste haste, my boy!'

Gay was born at two o'clock that afternoon. Molly had a pretty awful time although her main complaint was the row the pile-driver was making down at the new port then being constructed.

Gay is now an SRN and is married to a doctor. She has often expressed her strong desire to go back and work in 'her country'. This is an observation that Molly and I have made on numerous occasions. Whatever country a child is born in, no matter if the parents move afterwards, that child has deep feelings for its country of birth. I wouldn't like to get into any arguments over this! These feelings often get stronger the older the child gets. They feel that this is their country, their home, no matter what the politicians say and regardless of what their parents' relationship is with that country now. That country can mean as much to them as Wales does to the Welsh, Scotland to the Scots or, even, England to the English!

Whilst Molly was in hospital we moved our camp from Muhasa up line to Korogwe. Here the station reserve was much the same as the last one, as indeed were the living conditions. We still had the same tent, two camp beds, two camp chairs, camp table and food safe. The food safe was a cupboard built of wire mesh and stood on four tins of paraffin to stop the ants getting in at the contents. Together with our canvas bath, wash bowl and water filter, that was it and I was worried! I couldn't afford a paraffin operated fridge and even if I could, I couldn't see it standing up to the travelling from camp to camp. There was a further worry too; Mombo would be a lot further from Tanga and civilisation, such as it was, should an emergency arise.

George, an older colleague, lent me his car, a brand spanking new one, into which I loaded my brand spanking new and precious little daughter, her mummy and a good supply of fresh fruit and vegetables. The nursing sisters were glad to see the back of me, the person they connected with the noisy Land Rover that, having lost its silencer, used to wake them up when they came off of duty and were trying to get their rest. This was at a frequency of once every three or four days and I subsequently understood that they used to mark their calendars up to show the dates I was due in! Mind you, that day they couldn't recognise me because I didn't turn up in a Land Rover and for another reason I had shaved off my 'forty-niner' beard. I had shaved it off because I had a daughter and not a son! That was the deal.

The drive to Korogwe was very hot and humid and the further we got from Tanga the more mixed our feelings were. That night we had to put the legs of Gay's cot into tins of paraffin because already the safari-ants must have smelt milk; they had started to swarm the cot! Molly lost sleep over this. (I guess these pages are mainly for my lady readers because they could appreciate the situation Molly was in and no doubt feel for her.)

'Griffiths, we must send the water-truck out to find water. Our usual source has dried up!'

This was an annoying situation for we were swamped out only a couple of weeks ago. (The luxury of just being able to turn a tap on in the bathroom or kitchen and pure, clean, cold and fresh water coming out!) For the last few days our water supply was very restricted indeed and it was a dark brown in colour. Molly never belly-ached, not even under these conditions; even so, I saw her bathing Gay many times in just a mug of water from the water-filter. After which, she would have to wait at least an hour for another mug of water to filter through to drink. Because of the water, all Gay's napkins were becoming permanently stained brown. I could see clear signs in Molly of post-natal depression and who could blame the poor lass! I had the symptoms as much as she did! On top of all this, there was no end to the attacks of things that crawled which Molly still seemed to handle better than I. I'm ashamed!

The job was going well. I had completed all the field work of the re-alignment/re-grading survey nearly to Mombo and I had not lost an hour's work because of my 'family'. I worked eleven hours a day, six days a week. When I think about it, I can't recall anybody asking me to work so many hours; I just did it because I thought it was expected of me. Several more weeks went by and now the time had come to move to Mombo. Still shortages of supplies and never a lot of water. Then, for days we could see a nasty spot growing on Gay's tummy and then in horror we actually saw a mango-worm crawl out of the 'boil'. That was it!

The time had come to pull myself together and change this situation. How on earth, I thought, could I continue to serve EAR & H but in a more rational manner? As long as my only home was a tent, I couldn't. In the strongest of terms that I could muster, I persuaded Mr Thompson to speak to Head Office in Nairobi, over the railway signal system (which they didn't normally like you doing), and tell them that as far as I was concerned, I no longer wanted to be Dr Livingstone! 'They' tried to call my bluff but it didn't work; I had become desperate. Things have a way of sorting themselves out. The powers that be must have known that we were beginning to find it a wee bit tough living under these conditions with a new-born baby, and must have thought that they had had their ounce of flesh off me, because within a couple of days, I was posted to Mombasa Harbour Construction.

I soon found out that I was able to work just as hard but at the same time I was able to cope a lot better. I thought being posted to Mombasa was a sort of reward for services rendered. Or was I joking? Many years have passed since then and now I have my own survey firms operating in other parts of the world so there is one thing I know; to run an efficient organisation like EAR & H, the chiefs have to be very tough on their staff and sometimes even ruthless.

The port was under complete reconstruction. It was a couple of miles long and there were future plans for making it bigger than that. However, Mombasa is an island with very little land to spare so everything fitted in very tightly. Because of the list of priorities, drawn up by the Commercial Departments, different parts of the port had to be constructed at different times. Nevertheless, ultimately, the whole lot had to fit together. For this reason, instead of each section engineer doing his own setting-out, the resident engineer developed a survey section to look after this aspect. This section was run by an extremely competent surveyor, a Mr Arthur J. Rusk, M.I.C.E., A.R.I.C.S., B.Sc.

(Hons in Maths, Physics and Geography.) I was to assist him because his work was certainly piling up. I was thrilled with the challenge. The new port consisted of a lighterage wharf, ten deep-water berths, a slipway, a causeway (for the 'boat train' I have previously mentioned), a large marshalling yard, a high/low level line (to take the traffic from the dockside to the higher Mombasa Station Area) with all the other sheds, buildings, special rail/crane crossings, electricity, sewer and water facilities. An eye had to be kept further afield to Kipevu, to the north and west, for future developments, such as a refinery. In all, a nice bag of surveying, setting out and hydrographic surveys.

Arthur Rusk was then a man in his middle fifties, of good build and sporting a fine set of grey whiskers. He was a good engineer and a superlative surveyor. Very meticulous and scientific in his work. I understand that he spent most of his life in Africa and spoke Swahili like a native. He was educated in Edinburgh. Like myself, he had also taught surveying as a subject. He wore nylon socks and kept parrots. He enjoyed the respect of his employers as well as those who worked with him. He spoke like a cultured gentleman. I think, as we go through life's journey, we become partly made up of each of the people we meet, particularly of those we work with. Rusk was one of those people that made a great impression on my life. It was valuable experience to co-author with him several technical articles, at least two of which were actually published. He had a great sense of humour and was good for a laugh at least once a day. He used to keep a doormat hung up behind the office door and occasionally, when returning to our office from the resident engineer's office, he would be wearing an angry expression on his face because, obviously, something had upset him. He would then close the door, take down the doormat and stamp on it. Then he would hang the mat back up, sit down with a smile on his face, pass his cigarette case over to me and say, 'Now old chap, do have a cigarette and tell me how your lovely wife and little girl are coming along.'

Great stuff! We never talked about that doormat. I often recall the many times he said to me, 'Oh well! Do remember this; all situations, yes, all situations, are only temporary, even cancer!'

I understood what he meant and I have often found comfort in those words. I learnt much from Arther John Rusk which I hoped made me a better surveyor and perhaps a better person.

When we arrived at Mombasa we stayed at the Manor Hotel for the first ten days, as was the custom. During this time Molly went out house hunting. There were no railway houses available at that time but she found a private house for rent at Tudor Creek. The resident engineer was prepared to pay the rent and gave us his blessings and even some furniture, so into the house we moved. Gay seemed delighted with everything.

On reflection the next two years were probably the best two years of my life. The work was interesting; the climate was heavenly tropical; food was good and cheap and in abundance; social life was very happy and entertainment was good and varied and at a price we could afford. Our working colleagues were all pleasant, without exception, and we only worked from eight o'clock in the morning until noon and then from two o'clock until four o'clock. Saturday afternoons and Sundays were off. Of course there would be times when I had to work odd hours; to catch the tides. So, no wonder Joy was born before these two years were up.

Our doctor, Dr Watson, had asked us weeks previously, when exactly were we due to go home on leave. He appeared shocked when he realised how quickly time had flown and that we now had only three weeks to go. On this particular day it was the usual hot sunny morning for this time of year and it was going to remain hot until about two o'clock in the afternoon; that's when the breeze comes off of the Indian Ocean, a welcome relief! There was no one in the doctor's surgery so we were soon sitting in front of the doctor.

‘I want Molly in the maternity ward by lunchtime because I’m going to carry out a surgical induction. We don’t want things to go on like they did in Tanganyika for the poor girl,’ said Dr Watson. He thought her time was just about right.

Joy was born at six o’clock that afternoon; just in time for her sundowner! Now we had two girls, Gay and Joy. At the time of writing, Joy is out in Khartoum (or is it Hungary?) organising some teaching. Some years ago she took a degree in Modern Languages at Bath University and since then she has worked in Russia, Austria, Malawi, Sri Lanka, Solomon Islands and Germany. Talk about like father like daughter!

Our first tour of duty was over and the Number One Up was due to leave Mombasa Station at four o’clock that afternoon. The careful packing of many almost worthless possessions was executed by Molly. The farewell parties were over and the account with Inland Revenue was settled. All there was left to do was to catch the Number One Up to Nairobi and then our onward flight to London.

We were very touched by the number of people that were at the station to see us off. The number was made up of several Races. There were Pat and Ken Macdonald, Joan and Dick Howard, Doug Valpy, Juma (my head chainman), Mohammed (the cox’n of my survey launch, *Morag*), a young Harbhajan Singh, who at that time I hardly knew, the station master (Mr McDermott) and a number of folk from Molly’s office in the DTS’s Dept. There were a good few more other people whose names I cannot recall as I sit here writing, but I can never forget our old faithful servant, Musa.

I’ve got to be careful that I don’t get criticised for over discussing my friends in this book; I would be told that they are of very little interest to my readers, but I’ve got to tell you about some of them because I feel they contribute towards the fabric of this chapter; they add the spices and the flavours. The richest part of the story of Mombasa is its people.

Ken and Pat were a couple of real Kenya Red Earth people; born in the heart of Kikuyu Country. That is the land which white, black and brown people can be proud of. The land of the greatest of them all – Mzee Jomo Kenyatta. Ken was the son of an American who farmed in Kenya and Pat was the daughter of a game warden (he lost an arm doing his job!). Ken, a good-looking blighter, so the girls tell me, had been a warrant officer in the African Rifles during the war and was now an inspector of works on the railways. He spent a lot of time keeping my motor-bike on the road as well as sinking a good few sundowners with me. Often, little Gay, Molly and myself would be standing at Pat's kitchen with our mouths wide open, waiting for a serving of Pat's fabulous home-made potato soup; yes, that's right really, potato soup – it was scrumptious!

Mohammed was a tall slim man, a coastal tribesman if I remember rightly. He had a perpetual grin on his face and handled the boat so perfectly he was as good as having another Surveyor on board. I can remember that one day, I was standing on the bow of the *Morag* and old Rusk was standing on the stern. Suddenly, for some reason or another, poor old Rusk fell overboard (it happens to all of us!) into the shark-infested water of the Kilindini Deeps. He yelled out to Mohammed, '*Leti Kamba* Mohammed! *Leti kamba*!' which meant throw the rope Mohammed, in this sense. Mohammed hastily let go of the helm, pulled his throttle back, picked up the coil of rope and threw it at Rusk – both ends as well! I didn't understand the Swahili poor old Rusk used on that event!

What can I tell you about dear Doug Valpy? He was born in Kenya of New Zealand parents, who were farmers up at Kitali. Doug won his Civil Engineering degree at Natal University, South Africa. I first met him at Sultan Hamud Station when the train from Nairobi (the Number Two Down) stopped at ten o'clock at night. Actually, I took over from Doug in Mr Thompson's party. Mr Thompson and George wanted to exchange notes from the previous job that they had all worked on together. My two colleagues spoke so highly of Doug that I felt some extraordinary jealousy towards the poor chap. My feelings didn't improve when I saw him get down from the train for ten minutes. A fine figure of a man with a cleft chin and good looks to boot. He wore a broad smile and carried an air of quiet confidence. Molly said he was the ideal star for a film ad for some cigar or pipe tobacco company. Ha! The next time I met him was in Tanga, when he was Assistant District Engineer. After speaking to him for only a few minutes the urge to want to box his ears ceased and I thought that perhaps I could grow to tolerate him. The third time we met was when we became neighbours at Mombasa. We became almost like blood brothers. We had to work together often, we went sailing together and ate often at each other's houses. Gay loved him. Living was a laugh a minute – and that was a fact.

We were upset when Maria, our ayah (our children's nanny) didn't turn up to say good-bye. Maria had been with us since we had arrived in Mombasa. I suppose she must have been in her late twenties, not fat and not thin and with a cheerful disposition. (Sounds like a character reference! Forgive me.) We didn't know her tribe or even if she was married, although we did know her 'man' by sight and we knew where she lived. She cared for Gay as if she were one of her own. Molly was very pleased with her and satisfied with her standard of work. Maria went everywhere with us. She had Saturday afternoons and Sundays off but she was always willing to let Molly and I get out by ourselves for one evening a week. We were always back by ten or ten-thirty and then I would always run her for the two miles home on the back of my motorbike. The silly kitten would always start laughing as soon as Molly helped her onto the back seat and screams of laughter would be the situation all the way home. (Again, this part of my story is mainly written for my lady readers!) The daily routine, when she left the house at the end of the day's work was to shout out, all the way down the road, '*Kwaheri* Gay' and Gay would answer, '*Kwaheri* Maria' and so the repetition would go on and on: '*Kwaheri* Gay,' '*Kwaheri* Maria,' '*Kwaheri* Gay,' '*Kwaheri* Maria,' until Maria was out of earshot. I'll remember until my dying day the time I brought Molly and Joy home from the hospital. My pick-up stopped outside the kitchen door of the house where Musa and Maria, with Gay in her arms, were standing and waiting to welcome Mamsaab back home. Maria and Musa looked jubilant with broad happy smiles on their faces and smelling fresh and clean of Sunlife Yellow Washing Soap. As soon as Molly and Joy got out of the pick-up, Maria plonked Gay into Musa's arms and ran forward to Molly, shouting out in her strong Swahili voice, 'Thank you Mamsaab, thank you Mamsaab,' grabbing the baby as she said so. That was the last we saw of Joy for the next hour! She was showing Joy off to all her ayah workmates, who were sitting around in a circle under the big mango tree. They had all been waiting, with their charges, for our homecoming. Another very happy day.

Musa was our houseboy, as we used to call them in those days; I cannot remember his tribe either. I believe he liked working for us and likewise, we enjoyed having him almost as a member of the family. Our friends liked the chap as well and his cooking wasn't bad! He was always surprising us with his cake baking; I can still remember the long periods of heartburn! He was very proud, well-built and respected by his people. He owned a very good bicycle – which was a symbol of respectability! He had a very pretty little wife who bore him a strong son. He kept our home immaculate and his dhobi was superlative. He was honest. What else good can I say about him? Oh yes, he always removed his fez when he bade his farewells. We loved Kenya people and perhaps sometimes it shows!

They were all there on the platform, even Maureen, Jean and their dad. The Number One Up sounded his whistle to inform us that business was imminent. The station warning bell had rung. Molly was in tears and I was trying to get Gay out of the arms of affectionate friends; the carriage doors had already been closed. The station master gave us a friendly 'fourpenny-one' as I thought how smart he always looked in his uniform and pith-helmet. The monster show-off, a Garret steam engine heaved his first tug as I quickly noticed the shadows of his steam and the dancing palm trees on the sunny platform. I was cautious not to show any emotion on my face; my voice had already gone but I made sure that no one knew. My chest hurt like hell, as did the lump in my throat, and my tender wife was grizzling even more than ever. The Garret was eager to deal with the problem ahead as he blasted off his whistle again. The platform had soon left us and as it did so, I didn't know whether I was looking or waving to any one person in particular. The train started to collect speed.

Then the worst thing happened. Half a mile from the station, at a lonely level-crossing, there was the lone figure of Maria. Barefooted, thus showing her two big toes, and with a galabia draped attractively over her head and shoulders. She had a lovely smile on her face but I could see tears in her eyes and she was calling, '*Kwaheri* Mamsaab. *Kwaheri* Bwana. *Kwaheri* Joy. *Kwaheri* Gay . . . *Kwaheri* Gay . . . *Kwaheri* Gay . . . *Kwaheri* Gay.' Until the train shuddered round the next curve when we could see her no more.

On the flight back to England Joy was nursed a good deal of the way by Dame Flora Robson!

3

Canada and the St Lawrence Seaway

To try and reduce the length of this book I decided to try and retain much of my story about East Africa but considerably condense my tales of other parts of the world where I have had the good fortune to live and work. But still, there is nothing that I would love more than to expand the details of my adventures in a later subsequent book. I only hope that you are enjoying travelling along these roads with me. Now, here are some yarns about Canada.

It was May 1956 and we were in England, just starting our six months' leave. In two weeks' time, we would be setting sail for Canada. In the mean time, Molly's parents offered to look after the children whilst we took off for a few days break to my beloved Scotland. For this trip I had purchased a BSA 350cc motor-bike. (I can hear you saying 'Oh dear!') That morning, prior to visiting the motor-bike shop, I'd bought Molly an attractive pair of shoes that had caught my eye for several days, I thought they high-lighted her pretty ankles and put the finishing touches to a pair of very lovely long legs. We took delivery of the BSA and gingerly returned home for lunch. Molly had absolute confidence in me. Creating a case of chronic indigestion, we again shot out to give our steed another try. It hadn't rained in London for months but, at this moment, it decided to drizzle. The surface of the road became lethal. We were going down Putney Hill towards the shopping centre, when a young mum, pushing a pram, decided to cross the road without giving as much as a glance in any direction. If a motor-bike could have jack-knifed, it did it then. Silly woman. Molly and I went sprawling in one direction and the shiny new motor-bike went in another! The mum carried on across the road muttering something about crazy, stupid motor-cyclists! In Kenya we had rhinos and here we had mums! Only the other day, we saw a TV safety film pressing the line, 'Think bike! Think bike!' Poor Molly's shoes were ruined and I lost skin off of my ankle which took a year to grow back again. The bike . . . not a scratch! Such were British made motor-bikes in those days!

The next day was the Trooping of the Colour. 'Why don't you two nip up to the city on your bike and witness the real thing? See the Queen. I'll look after the girls,' said Mother, We went off like a shot. Naturally, there were thousands of spectators and to leave the BSA anywhere seemed impossible. Impulsively, I went up to a uniformed gentleman, who was guarding a famous building and said, 'I'm from Crown Agents and we have just come back from East Africa. Please may I leave my machine in your archway?' I expected to see the flash of a pair of handcuffs or at least feel the draught of a policeman's truncheon. Instead, in a matter of minutes, we had the privileged close-up of Her Majesty as she rode past on her horse, It was a dream come true.

A couple of days later we alighted from the train at Kilmarnock and I can still remember the faces, in great detail, of the two railwaymen who watched me struggle to manoeuvre my heavy BSA out of the goods wagon. I said more than thank you to those two, I can assure you! It was very early in the morning when we rode to Ayr for breakfast. It was bitterly cold and it rained every day whilst we were in Scotland, but never mind, we enjoyed ourselves. We took in many of the sights tourists were expected to take in as well as re-visiting some of the places where I got my early training on the Ordnance Survey, pre-military days. Molly loved it and declared she did.

Back in Putney, we had now been home six weeks when through the letter-box came our immigration papers in response to our interviews and medicals. We could now confirm our passages to Canada. The sea voyage was sensational, even though Molly and I had to sleep in separate cabins. However, people were most considerate and compassionate and understanding and tactful, so we didn't miss much! We didn't have the girls with us either!

While we were in England, Ron, Molly's brother and my good friend, had decided to take the jump and was successful in getting a job with an air survey company in Montreal. We were able to pool some of our resources and ideas and mutually agreed upon a plan which all of us would benefit from. Molly and I would go first, leaving our children with Lillian and Molly's parents. Ron would leave a couple of weeks later, after he had satisfied the Canadian Immigration and then Lillian would leave by air, soon after Ron had found somewhere to live. She would bring our two girls and my niece. We, of course, were going a lot further than Montreal.

The St Lawrence River was breathtaking and the further you got up-stream the better it got. The first siting of Quebec was quite a thrill; millions before us had the same experience. Because both Molly and myself were still officers of EAR & H we had complementary tickets to go right across Canada and back on both railway systems. We boarded the CPR train at Montreal and started the journey westwards, stopping to look at Ottawa, Winnipeg, Regina, Medicine Hat and ending in Calgary; we felt that we had gone far enough. Anyway, we fell in love with Calgary. We got there whilst the Calgary Stampede was in session! You haven't seen anything until you have seen a chuck-wagon belting along being pulled by six horses with a further four outriders, all in real life. I can see, hear and smell them still. The Calgary people were outstandingly kind and courteous, a fact that was demonstrated over and over again throughout each day by bus drivers, store clerks, mailmen, employers and the girls in the offices. Talking about girls, the most popular song out at that time was 'Standing on the corner watching all the girls go by.' This I used to hum as I stood outside Hudson Bay Company waiting for my bus connection. The ladies of Calgary were intoxicating in their pretty dresses, some with their summer coats on and most with white gloves. Their skin brown and their hair bouncy with a sheen that can only be donated to them by sunshine and that good prairie air. I soon learnt that when I wanted to cross the road I had to walk to the end of the block to do so. Strangely, I never felt comfortable when car drivers, without exception, would stop and allow me to cross the road. Such courtesy was a way of life in this civilised city. I could willingly go on and on about these fine people.

The wad of dollars in my back pocket was getting thinner and thinner. It was clear that I should find work as soon as I could. After a week of trying very hard I finally got a job. This is again where I had the advantage of a strong encouraging wife. She gave me such strength. When I got the job, we were so happy – what it is to be young!

We over-indulged in delicious soft ice cream dipped in chocolate and covered with chopped roasted peanuts. We simply adored the huge hamburgers with relish and French fries. We ate peaches by the pound and T-Bone steaks . . . a single portion of which was nearly as big as Mother's weekend joint. We shall always enjoy the memory of the service we got from the drug stores and restaurants. The smile that was offered with a warm greeting from the pretty waitress, together with a napkin and a glass of ice-cold water before she even took your order; even though she knew your request may only be for a cup of coffee! That was another thing too, you only paid for the first cup of coffee; the refills, if required, were on the house. At first, I couldn't believe it. But why did those glamorous waitresses always wear those horrible hefty white shoes with those thick soles and why did they always have to make such a racket and clatter when they collected and washed up the china and cutlery? The juke-boxes were always answering demands; nine out of ten times it was either for Elvis Presley or the Everley Brothers. We always put a dime in for Pat Boone! I had a job as an engineer with a firm of civil engineers – that would fill a volume alone!

In the meantime Lillian had arrived in Montreal with the children and a few days afterwards Molly also arrived in Montreal on her 'free ticket'! If I remember rightly the journey used to take about three days each way! Molly didn't stay there very long before she, with the two girls, were on their way back to me. What a happy day when I went down to Calgary Station to meet them. The massive train came in very slowly with its large bell clanging. One carriage after the other slid past me, each one slower than the one before. As I peered through each window looking for them, I found myself becoming slightly breathless with the excitement of seeing them again. The train stopped. By far, most of it had gone past me. Where on earth were they?

'Daddy!' Gay cried as she came running down from the rear of the train to meet me, As she got closer to me, she threw her arms open and without stopping she leapt up into my arms. She nearly broke my neck with her strong little hug. I have never had such a cuddle from anybody, before or since, like the cuddle she gave me on that day. Soon, I had Molly and Joy in my embrace. My, how Joy had grown in such a short time! From her mother's arms she just looked down her nose at me with the hint of a smile on her face. What pretty little girls they were. Molly and I looked into each other's eyes; only our eyes talked as she kissed me with her moist tender lips; her mouth always had a lovely fragrance about it. We quickly came down to earth when Gay said to a lady that was standing by us, 'Look, here is my Daddy, I have found him!' The lady, who had been accompanying them, just burst into tears! There was a Royal Canadian Mounted Policeman standing near by us; he smiled at us and even his eyes looked moist. Another great day, Lord.

A few weeks after the girls had joined us I made the usual middle-of-the-week phone call from Red Deer to Molly to see how the girls were doing. Molly said, with a very nervous voice, 'There is a letter from Nairobi. It said that you have been upgraded from a Grade III Surveyor to a Grade II Surveyor and did you still want the post? If so, when did you intend returning to London prior to flying back to Nairobi?' Hardly the right way of saying it but this opened up all the old wounds, if you can understand. The following weekend, when I got home, we were in a right turmoil over this letter from EAR & H. I thought, because we had been in Canada for only a few months and because we virtually had no friends (although plenty of acquaintances), we were very vulnerable being confronted with such a decision to make. Our free ticket back to Montreal was good for another week. To pay our fares back to Montreal would cost nearly as much as our fares from Montreal to London! We didn't have that kind of money. Canada, the buses, large cars, the houses, the supermarkets, Canadian dollars, the way of life, all these things were pulling us one way. The strong love of Africa was pulling us the other. We made another one of our lists of advantages and disadvantages for living in Canada or East Africa; both lists were long. On that Friday, while Molly was making our sixth cup of coffee at midnight, we suddenly completely disregarded the lists and decided that I would give a week's notice to my employers; less if possible; and start back on that very long journey, to our home – Africa.

The train journey back to Montreal was enjoyed by one and all, as the saying goes.

During the time we were gallivanting around Calgary, Ron, Molly's brother, had secured a job back in Montreal and had found a comfortable home, an apartment in St Lawrence. Ron was at Montreal Station to meet us and how lovely it was to see him again. He couldn't believe that we wanted to go back to Africa. 'Surely you don't want to go back to "that place", with its malaria, its diarrhoea, and look at the horrible skin infection you brought home and passed it on to poor old Dad!' Then he started to narrate about Canada and the advantages for us and the children in living here, all of which we had thought out for ourselves! I must confess, however, hearing it from somebody else was pretty convincing. In only two weeks I had got a job and we were comfortably established in our new apartment in Montreal West!

That winter was my first experience at trying to work in temperatures at forty degrees below zero, or worse yet! The girls were always kept warmly dressed against the weather and the cold didn't seem to bother them too much! The following spring I saw an advertisement in the local newspaper for a hydrographic surveyor for the St Lawrence Seaway Authority, but they stipulated that the applicant must have a federal or provincial licence. That let me out. A few days later Ron asked me if I had seen it. He said that he had noticed the advertisement periodically over these last few weeks and it seemed as if they couldn't fill the post. What could I lose if I tried? The pay was attractive, the conditions looked favourable, it meant that I could get home every night, so I went for an interview. And, what a project was the St Lawrence Seaway! Another great day when I started with them a week later. Because I didn't have a licence I couldn't legally call myself a surveyor in the Government service but they overcome this by giving me the title of Technical Officer. My job was to answer to the resident engineer for all hydrographic survey work from Cote St Catherine to the Barharmois Lock. The men working with me were a great bunch of fellows; most of them were French Canadians but I witnessed no antagonism between us in the whole two years we were together. We had the best equipment available at that time and some fine watercraft. The office was right alongside the Lachine Lock and was very pleasant.

Our heroes were Boom Boom Jeffreon, 'the Rocket' and his brother 'the Pocket Rocket'. Our team was the Montreal Canadians, of course. Everything was big and glamorous. Good food was in abundance as were big cars and other material things. It all seemed to be in everybody's reach. Most people seemed to be working and earning. Friday night at the huge Dorval Shopping Centre was the family night out for my family. Boxes of peaches filled the car with their mouth-watering aroma and five pound bags of Washington Delicious apples with their rich juices just straining to leak down your shirt when you took the first bite. French Canadian apple pie, maple syrup, large cartons of health-giving orange juice, pineapple juice and tomato juice. Large beef steaks and chef's salads; all of these things most people seemed to be able to afford. But the winters . . . in my profession that was something else!

In the winter of 1958/59 Molly presented me with another daughter, Wendy. She was another great charmer in my life. She left a gaping cavity in my life for no other crime than growing up. She completed her training at St Bartholomews Hospital, with her older sister, qualifying, not as an SRN but as a radiographer.

The Seaway construction was coming to a close and everybody knew it, although there was still another year's work before completion. I had to think about the future. I had already developed warm feelings about the USA, cultivated by our frequent visits to that country. Molly and I sat down and composed another one of those lists containing all the pros and cons of working and living in the States, compared to Canada. You'll find this hard to believe but on 5 December we tore up that list as the last boat for England was leaving Montreal – with us on it!

We loved Canada, there was no doubt about that. I still miss Canada and the people, for we made a lot of friends. They are easy people to make friends with. The country is beautiful and rich. Mind you, the winters are very cold and it costs a lot of money to keep warm. However, if anybody wanted to move to Canada and they could satisfy the necessary pre-requisites, then I say go for it, I thoroughly recommend it.

4

The Second Tour of East Africa

We all know how miserable January and February can be; it's enough to make you eat your young. In 1959 these months were no exception. It rained and rained and rained. We didn't have much money to buy a house (who did?) so the type of accommodation that was available to us was nothing less than soul-destroying. However, as luck would have it, we were able to find a comfortable home in Pontwalby, near Neath and my work. In spite of the shocking colds and coughs that we all had, the children were happy and Molly, as usual, was a tower of strength; this last point being so important at times like these.

But if there was a time when everything in the garden wasn't rosy, then it was at this time. The standard of living was totally different from that of Canada and we had great difficulty in making ends meet on what I was earning from the NCB. Life was very much one of liver and faggots! We needed but couldn't afford anything that resembled a car; we had a thing made back in 1936 and it was nothing but trouble. I recall one day, when we were passing a speed sign which read '30 MPH', Molly turned her head away from me and mumbled, 'They must be joking!' We could hardly afford coal to keep ourselves warm and at night we put newspapers between our blankets for insulation against the cold. I worked as hard as I did everywhere else but the results, in terms of standard of living, indicated that there must be something wrong somewhere. At that time I couldn't see things changing. However, I remembered what old Rusk had told me: '. . . all situations are only temporary. . .' and I consoled myself that the situation that I had found myself in was only transitory – there were greener pastures ahead.

One day in April 1959 I returned to the Crown Agents Offices after just having had my medical in Harley Street. The interviewing officer then said to me, 'OK Mr Griffiths, when can you leave for Nairobi?' Yet, another one of those great days. I walked through Westminster to the Underground absolutely intoxicated with happiness. I was on my way back to my beloved Kenya. I was sure I would scream if I couldn't talk to somebody soon! However, I had to contain myself all the way back to my Welsh valley home. Molly could read my joy and responded with screams and chuckles and arm waving and tears of joy and happiness. Such was the way of life and we enjoyed every moment of it – especially moments like this one.

Although we were happy to be going abroad again, I must admit there were moments of sorrow to be saying good-bye to Wales. Bless me if the sun didn't shine for the whole of the last three days we were there! We loved the people of our valley; they were strong stuff, kind and human. They too were always ready for a good laugh. We will go back there one day and I'm sure we will find a 'Welcome in the Hillside', just as the song tells us.

Molly's aunt said, 'Just look at those girls. Anybody would think that they were catching a bus to go shopping instead of a plane to Africa. They just take it in their stride.' We were all at London Airport waiting for the announcement of the departure of the flight to Nairobi. Reason? To take up an appointment with the Hydraulics Department of the Ministry of works, Kenya Government. It wasn't very long before we were at Nairobi Airport, being met by the Department's staff surveyor, Mr Stan Longdon. I spent the first two weeks or so in Nairobi with Stan, learning how things should be done, getting fixed up with housing and preparing for safari. Stan hailed from Northumberland which one could easily detect by that rich accent. We enjoyed the company of Stan and his lovely wife, Nora, on many occasions out at his coffee farm at Kiambu.

As one would expect, I had to spend much of my time on safari. These safaris usually lasted three to six weeks. This was horrible for Molly as she was going through a stage of her life of not knowing what to expect next. In the meantime, she had got an excellent ayah and had found a job in Nairobi. This not only helped to pay for the new car but also kept her busy and gave her a chance to meet and talk to other interesting people.

When I went on my first safari, up to North Kinankop, on a water distribution project, I had nobody to tell how much I missed Molly and the girls. It seemed to me that no matter what I wanted to do in life, there was always a price to pay. I had come to terms with this philosophy, although I couldn't always find comfort from it when I felt I was paying too much. Molly went along with this philosophy too, but with the same reservations. For sure, I felt that if my wife and children were happy and comfortable and everything was being done to care for them, then I shouldn't belly-ache. If I didn't like the conditions of my job, then change it. The only trouble was, I couldn't imagine spending my life in any other way than being a 'peg-thumper'.

Maybe others agree with this philosophy but are not prepared to pay the price as Molly and myself did. Every night, Gay, my oldest daughter, would be in tears and would pour out to her mummy how much she missed her daddy! One night Mummy consoled her by telling her that perhaps Daddy could do something about it the next time he came home from safari. When I did get home, all was revealed. Whilst I was in the office, bringing my drawings up to date, I explained the situation to Stan. He said, 'Well, for heaven's sake, if you think that you could manage, then take her with you.' This, again, was another one of those great days. It was a very reluctant mummy that gave a faint-hearted sign of approval, but Gay was over the moon and had her packing done in fifteen minutes. I wasn't due to go out on another safari for at least another ten days!

My next safari was up to Maralel, which is getting a bit up north and is at about 7,000 feet above sea level. It's only about one degree North of the Equator. On the eve of that safari, I said prayers with the family and when it was Gay's turn to be tucked in and to kiss me good-night, she looked up to me with those lovely big brown eyes and said 'Good night, Daddy. You won't forget to wake me up will you?'

Wasn't that lovely? She was seven.

That was one of the many safaris during which Gay was my right-hand man. I can honestly say that on all those trips, some of them lasting six weeks, she chatted in a cheerful mood about her sisters and her Mummy. There was never any sign of sorrow. She kept herself very busy day by day. Tidying up behind me in the tent gave her quite a lot to do. Fortunately, I had brought an extra supply of notepaper and coloured pencils because she had got through one box of coloured pencils, drawing up her own 'maps'. During the day she would stay with me whilst I was surveying in the bush and whilst I was doing this, she would be carrying out an investigation of everything that crept and crawled in the bush; believe me, there were plenty of things to inspect! She would go about her business in a very scientific manner, but I can assure you that all my African chainmen were keeping a weather-eye on her to make sure that no harm would come to her. They would often have to intervene because of a rather menacing snake or angry scorpion. Sometimes she would pester my African driver, Charles, until tiredness would overcome her when she would have a doze on the seat of my Bedford Safari Truck; awfully uncomfortable, I thought, but she never made any complaint.

On Sundays I would like to spend the day in camp if I could. Doing the calculations in my field-books, a rough trace to make sure that I had got everything that I was there to get and such things as this. I would have fresh clean clothes on and I would thoroughly enjoy the frequent pots of tea which my cook would produce in the canopy of my tent. On these days Gay would do her 'important drawings' for her mummy and sisters; these she would give to her Uncle Stan the next time he visited us. Then she would go round to the back of the tent and tell the cook that he wasn't doing this or that correctly. More times than not, Kasuba, my head chainman, would come and collect her and take her for a walk; this is when they would collect flying-ants (for eating!), snakes and goodness knows what. I'm not saying she ate the ants but I'm not sure she didn't. She became an authority on the skill of catching snakes and killing them before they could perform their deadly skill on you. She never had difficulty in doing what comes naturally; she would just head for the nearest bush, no fuss or bother. Things were often more difficult in the midst of civilisation! Sometimes, I would be concerned when I looked across towards the men's tents, just a few hundred feet away, and see her crouched down on her haunches, with her dress pulled forward and tucked between her knees, eating the food that they had prepared in the manner that they too adopt when eating! That is to pick up the food in the scoop of your hand and place it in your mouth. Would she quickly grow up in a culture that perhaps was not too adaptable to the way of life of her own people? Maybe, these *were* 'her own people'!

They were great days when Uncle Stan visited us, about every couple of weeks or so. He would bring us a letter from home, some nice fresh fruit and vegetables, some meaty pork chops and always a little something special for Gay. He would have a meal and perhaps stay with us the night or move on to another safari somewhere. Each of these visits would give Gay and I something to talk about for days. That day would be the only day that she would forget to make sure that we both took our anti-malarial tablets. It was lovely having her with me. She was very personal to me and somebody I could say, 'I love you' to and cuddle now and again. In turn, I would enjoy the little fusses this little seven-year-old would make of me in a life that was quite tough and certainly one where you wouldn't expect to find such tenderness. God really blessed me when He put this charge in my hands.

A fever would spread throughout the safari when we all knew the time was near for going back to Nairobi – and home. When we broke camp I would pay off the casual labourers and the permanent staff would travel back on top of the Austin lorry except for the head chainman who would travel back with us in the Bedford Safari Truck or Land Rover. In those days there were few tarmac roads so our journeys usually took at least two days and we nearly always bore down on Nairobi in the evening. What a warm and exciting sight Nairobi always looked! It is becoming very modern and yet it retains its prettiness. It is the one city that feels more like my home than any other city in the world.

The Mau Mau days were over but not forgotten. The main topic of conversation in any office, in any bar, was the anticipated date for Kenya's independence. These were very anxious days for many people; for some it was the end of life as they knew it; one that they had created. Already, farms were being sold by the dozens and the European owners were pulling out. Some people were saying it would be ten years before independence would materialise and some were saying only two! For the black Africans it was an exciting time too; I doubt if they would ever experience such a period again in their whole lives. Changes were happening; in fact, we were witnessing them day by day as the Independence Day came closer. Fortunately, I didn't own a house in Kenya, I didn't own anything and I certainly didn't look upon my job there as my lifetime career. So, I tried not to get too emotionally involved in the independence situation; I just tried to enjoy the privilege of working in such a lovely country. But I did feel a secret satisfaction in knowing that my work, in a small way, was helping them to build their very proud and lovely country.

After I had been back in Kenya a year I went on safari to the slopes of Mount Kenya. My job was to cut and survey a route down the slopes for a controlled channel of water to supply a mission and the village of Chuka. During my time there the boss paid me one of his usual visits. Over a Tusker, he informed me that I was to be stationed, for a while, at the Mwea Tiberi Irrigation Scheme. This was on the south side of Mount Kenya, not far west of Embu. He said he would try and get hold of a couple of aluminium Rondavals and, with a bit of effort on my part, I could soon join them together by building a sort of living-room between them out of local materials which wouldn't cost anything. What this meant was that I could have Molly and the girls out with me – full time. Another one of those great days!

In a few weeks' time, the Chuka job was completed and by an awful lot of scrounging, by friends as well as by myself, we had a pioneer type shack built and filled with local made rustic type furniture. I had bought this furniture from African local craftsmen at Kiambu. When I got the family out there they were all pleasantly surprised. Thank goodness! It consisted mainly of two rondavals; one for our bedroom and one for the girls; and these were joined together by a fairly large room. I managed to procure a few bags of cement so we had concreted floors throughout. There was a wall all around the room waist high and made of hammer-dressed stone. Three of the sides were made up to the corrugated roof (swiped from some old disused army huts), with woven wicker fencing panels (the sort that you see being used at horse trials!), the front being left open. Mind you, I did have a long papyrus curtain made which could be rolled up and down to close out the night or protect us from the rain. The curtains and rush matting were made by local lads, as were several other items which were useful in making up a home. Around the back of the complex we were able to build a hut which substituted for a kitchen. The water was piped a few hundred feet from what was a disused camp. The hydro system worked very well actually because the water was 'solar heated' in the pipe running over the ground. It was often too hot for a shower (at the back of the kitchen) so we often had to wait for the cool of the evening.

Of course, Gay's schooling could have been a problem, but thanks to the Rift Valley Correspondence School this situation was very well taken care of. Molly became mother and teacher. Poor Molly; however, she did both jobs superlatively. The system worked very well and the experts back in Nairobi thought Gay had progressed well.

Saturday mornings was the time we took off for Nairobi, to purchase supplies, to visit friends, to collect items from the office and to deposit all the data that I had collected over the past week. Lots of cups of lovely Kenya coffee too. The day was highlighted in the evening by a visit to the drive-in-cinema. As a family, there was nothing that we enjoyed so much, before or since, as those Saturday evenings at the drive-in. We always saw the most up-to-date films; all the good stuff and never the rubbish! This last comment leaves me open to contention. The road from Nairobi Centre is a bit up and downish, often blocking the view ahead, so, we entered a contest; who could see the drive-in first? I'm sure my family would never believe this and I'm not going to tell them either, but try as hard as I could, I'm blowed if I could ever see the drive-in first!

The next little story may seem childish at first, but please read on. Why am I telling you this story? I think it's because there are some hidden messages. It's because few people in this day and age are affected in such a way as chance found myself. For a long time I hadn't been distracted from my children by TV and the like as I was in my Western world; we hadn't even had neighbours. Whether we liked it or not, we had to make do with our own company for that is all we had; I'm not complaining about that. We seemed to take more notice of what each other was doing. One seemed to fob each other off much less and developed the habit of paying attention to each other when one had something to say. One retained interest at all levels of intellect and tried to show this interest. The following is a moment shared with my children. One night, when we were driving back from the drive-in, I accidently ran over a young gazelle and all the occupants of my car demanded I stopped, got out and see what I could do. On inspection, I found it was a mother. She was dead. Trying to hide my sorrow, I pretended to take a further look around in the dark and then reported to the car that the gazelle must have been stunned and subsequently had got up and ran away. The trouble was, she had left her little baby behind, I don't know if it thought that I was its mother for it showed no fear of me as it hung around my feet. There were unanimous shouts of 'Put it in the car Daddy and we will look after it!' I could see by the lights of the car that Molly also had that tender, loving and caring look on her face, so what could I do? We fed and cared for that little soul for several days, but alas, on the third or fourth morning I looked for it, to see how it was getting along. It was dead. I tenderly lifted the little creature and took it out to the back and hid it until I could bury it later in the day. I convinced the girls that the mother must have come to the house in the night and taken her baby away. We all thought that the mother showed signs of ingratitude; nevertheless, we were all happy that mother and baby were back together again. Actually, in our book of rules – they were . . .

I was always surveying within a couple of miles of 'home', working on an area that was very soon to be under irrigation; hundreds of acres of it. Before that gorgeous sun was at its upper culmination Molly would often come out to the fields in the car and bring with her a lovely fresh flask of coffee. She would do the same again at about three in the afternoon, after wiping the perspiration from my face and neck; this used to go down well, I can tell you. It was always lovely to see her too! Some days it would be just too hot to survey in the middle of the day, about the middle four hours. Under these circumstances I would carry on for as long as I could and then stop. Then I would carry on doing whatever it was I was doing in the cool of the evening. It always got dark around seven o'clock, give or take a few minutes, every day of the year. The evening session was always pleasant because I would take the girls out with me. They enjoyed this and so did my chainmen and this is the way the girls learnt Swahili and my men picked up their English. The girls kept pretty busy carrying the pegs and ranging-rods.

This brings me back to the very colourful gentleman I mentioned earlier; Davo Davidson. Beyond all doubt this man was a one off. The family loved him. No wonder, when during the Mau Mau campaign, every time we saw him he was surrounded by friendly people. Not for one minute am I putting him up on a pedestal, but very rarely do you see such a person like Davo Davidson drawing people around him with such apparent magnetism. Now we had him all to ourselves and we were sure that we were in for many an interesting evening listening to his tales. He was now living by himself in a hut in the disused prison camp behind us. This camp sounds an awful place but it wasn't really. The whole place was covered with colourful bushes, shrubs and flowers. Davo had his beard shaved off and looked clean and smart now. Soon after shaking the huge hand of this man, I noticed he was looking and smiling at my children. Quite frankly, this knocked me back because in no way could I see this big rough man, this ex-pseudo-terrorist having any interest in little girls. I was wrong. In a very short while this legend of a man won the hearts of my little nippers. They all became dear friends. Every other evening, if not more frequently, Davo would come over to our shack and have a beer and a natter. One evening, he was telling us about the time he was in Al Capone's gang; in fact, for some reason that has gone out of my head, he had to get out quickly because they were going to 'rub him out' or 'bump him off'. Can you believe that? He had no end of newspaper cuttings to back up his stories. One afternoon, when I had finished work, I got back to my wee house and there was Davo teaching Molly how to throw a big snake knife! I heard him say, 'No woman, don't throw it like that, throw it harder. Throw it so hard that even if the blade doesn't stick into him, the handle will knock him out!' He had a farm in the Kinangop country which wasn't doing very well for reasons unbeknown to us. Every time he came over he used to ask us to put 'that' record on. 'That' record was called 'Here comes the Show Boat' and was a jolly record playing all the old river songs, the ones that everybody knows, regardless of age. The last thing I heard about Davo was that he was making a living in South Africa somewhere, running some sort of self-defence school.

I repeat myself – I find it hard to write about Kenya without writing about people – to me they play a significant part in the story of Kenya. There were three other Europeans in that disused camp. One was an ex-Battle of Britain pilot who was now performing the duties of a surveyor, an excellent fellow with a sharp Yorkshire wit. The second was his wife, who was the secretary to a senior cabinet minister and a lovely lady. These were another two people you were richer for knowing. The third person was an Italian by the name of Maccaroni; unfortunately, I would keep calling him Spaghetti, no malice you understand, just a repeating mistake. He used to come and collect me and take me out to the nearby lakes to shoot duck. The outstanding feature of those little excursions – at least to me – was the overwhelming picture we would encounter of hundreds of crested cranes. What beautiful birds they are, no wonder they are the national bird of Uganda! The noise demonstrating their objections wasn't exactly deafening, but those were the terms of reference. Maccaroni had a charming manner, especially with the ladies; no matter whether they were six or sixty! I think that one of the main characters of the Italian male image is the way they have of showing a sincere adoration of the female; any and all females are to be adored and ceremoniously performed to. Whenever he met Molly or Gay or Wendy or any other female, it was always the same act; 'Bella Bella . . .' as he greeted them with his arms outstretched and his flashing smile showing beautiful white teeth. Us other blokes never knew where we stood with our women, because of them.

Do I detect that note of jealousy again? Now I'll stop being silly and admit I enjoyed the very special attention he was able to pour on my ladies and it tickled me pink to watch the girls go all coy and sweet, if you know what I mean. All great fun, so it was.

There was one event that happened in Mwea which turned my stomach over and over again during my stay there. The last day of building my little bush-home I arose very early to drive into Nairobi to collect my family. The sun had not yet shown itself to this lovely land. When I looked about a hundred yards beyond the house I could just make out an African lying on the ground. It was getting lighter by the minute. Just then an African police officer in a Land Rover drove up to the body. He appeared to move the prone body slightly and then jumped back into his vehicle and drove off, leaving a second man in plain clothes behind. After I drank my tea the man in plain clothes also left, leaving the man on the ground alone. I was almost sure of what may have happened over there but, out of morbid curiosity I suppose, I just had to go over and have a look. What a ghastly sight! He was a small built man and was wearing rather delapitated khaki shorts and shirt and he was also wearing a pair of those sandles that they make out of rubber car tyres. He was on his side in a running posture and his throat had been cut from ear to ear a third of the way through the thickness of his neck. He was in a pool of blood which was soaking into the ground but the stain had a black perimeter of ants. Terrible. As it turned out, on my return to camp, a local told me that the murdered man was, in fact, an ex-Mau Mau prisoner and for some reason, beyond the jurisdiction of this book, a fellow inmate had it in for him and this was his first chance to settle the score. Anyway, the girls didn't find out about it and all enjoyed our lives there immensely without the knowledge of that event.

One weekend, while on our weekly trip to Nairobi, the boss said, 'I've got a nice little job down at the coast. Should only take about two or three weeks. Do you want to take the family down there, under canvas and do the job?'

Oh boy! Stan had just about all my stores ready for me, so it didn't take long before we were on our way again. The drive down to Mombasa was very hot indeed and the corrugated roads nearly dislodged all my teeth but all I got from Les Girls was to tell me to stop complaining. We stopped and had lunch at Mtito Andei, a sort of oasis half way down to Mombasa, where everybody stops to refresh. The beer was always cold and the food was very good, but the whole hotel used to have a fousty smell about it. The children were always highly amused at the lizards that used to run up and down the walls. Sometimes these creatures would engage in mortal battle, when before our very eyes, we would see a warrior lose a leg or certainly a tail. After feeding and watering and cleaning up, we continued to Mombasa. The thrill of watching the road turn sandier and sandier as we got nearer the Coast. The tall palm trees would now appear which would play havoc with our expectations of things to come. We had already left Maji Chumvi (Salt Water) behind, a reminder that the coast was imminent and now Kwa Jomvu was in sight. After Kwa Jomvu it was only a matter of minutes before you saw the sea. The first sighting of the sea has always been a thrilling moment for me and I expect that is the case for you, many of my readers. At last, there was the sea and there was Mombasa. She had changed very little since the last time we saw her. Kilindini Road had been presented with a very impressive and decorative pair of elephant tusks which arched across the road. Not far from these there was a new western looking excellent Fish and Chip Shop! We thought the standard of the hotels that we knew and loved so much had gone down a bit, but, along the front (the sea front) there was a brand new hotel called The Oceanic which could probably toe the line with some of the best foreign jobs. Anyway, to get on with the story, we stayed at The Manor for the night and the next morning we drove north, up the coast, for about twenty miles to a place called Bamburi.

When I saw Bamburi many years later, I just couldn't believe my eyes. Progress! Here, we set up our base camp on the beach itself. We chose a picturesque spot on the cool white sand under a clump of coconut trees – after my chainmen had cut down all the loose nuts and fronds! Off with our clothes and on with our swimsuits and down to the task of setting up our temporary home. We got everything off the truck first and then the odds and ends out of the car. Then we sorted out the tent for heaving up. Right, that was the tent up, now for the ground-sheet. At this point there was some hair raising noises from Wendy.

'What's the matter, darling?' said Mummy, 'What on earth have you done?' she said again, as the three-year-old Wendy started to go blue and to vomit something terrible. Molly caught sight of a cordial bottle, the one in which we kept paraffin for the primus stove; the top was off it!

'Roy, Roy, Roy, Wendy has been drinking the paraffin, what on earth shall we do?'

Panic hit me but I thought hard.

'Get her to drink some milk,' I said, as I dragged on my trousers and closed the tent doors and told the cook to take charge; all at the same time. I shoved Molly and the girls into the car and found my way back to the road post haste. I can't remember the drive back to Mombasa. I put my foot down and it stayed down until I got to the hospital. Poor Molly, she was in a pathetic state too, but I tried to console her as best I could. As soon as I opened my mouth to the sister, Wendy was whipped away to the theatre where they gave her tummy a good pump-out. You could smell the paraffin all over the hospital, the Matron complained. Poor little soul. The doctor decided that Wendy should stay in the hospital for one night, just so that they could be sure she was all right. We stayed with her for another hour or so and when the excitement had died down a bit we left to go back and get camp organised. In my unpredicted absence, the cook and my chainmen had done very well; even the beds were all made up and there was a salad ready. Next morning Wendy was back with us and as right as rain. Molly and I felt very guilty about the accident; we tried desperately to look after our nippers and stop them from coming to any harm. This was one time when our system broke down. It should not have happened; but it did.

By the end of the second day in camp all was almost forgotten and we were back to our normal state. The girls just loved to go for a dip when the tide was in or, if the tide was out, we would all go exploring in the shallow lagoons. Paradise. I started my actual survey on the second day I was there after the equipment was unpacked, tested and adjusted where necessary. My task was to find a route for a freshwater main to go from Bamburi to a prison at Mtwara and then survey it. The first week we were there we had brilliant moonlight. There was no doubt about it that this moonlight stirred up feelings in Molly and myself which would fill a book alone! Suffice to say that when the children were safe in their beds and asleep we enjoyed a few moments of being alone together, swimming in the nude in the Indian Ocean under a canopy of bright stars. A few hundred yards down the beach were a couple of African fishermen's homes but apart from these, we had the beach, miles and miles of it, to ourselves. I shall never forget.

The African fishermen were a race of their own. Their women were bright-eyed and in those days they still walked around naked from the waist upwards. At least half of them showed large firm rounded breasts but the other half showed the natural depletion at various stages through age and use. Whatever, it all looked so natural in this setting. These men would go out to their work in tiny dug-outs with just an outrig lashed to one side. They would go out in the Indian Ocean for miles and you would often see them disappearing in the trough of a wave. We would hold our breath when they didn't reappear when we thought they should! I used to inspect their crafts when they were high and dry on the beach and, honestly, nothing was joined securely and nothing was square to anything else! There were cracks and splits all over the place, including below the water-line as well as above. They were literally tied together with bits of string. Two things came to my mind which gave me a chuckle. One was I wondered if some of my friends, with their expensive crafts, would be so lucky with their fishing as these hardy men; and secondly, I wondered what our various ministries in the UK would say if they saw men, going out to work, in such things! But what a happy and jolly lot these people were! You felt that they knew what they were doing, they knew well the risks involved and you knew they would always get back.

This was the last job I did for Stan. I had been with the Ministry for just over a year now but whilst on these weekend trips to Nairobi, I had been having meetings with my old employers, East African Railways and Harbours. The outcome was a small promotion on transfer from the Ministry back to the railways. Pulling off the transfer alone was a good thing but I could hardly believe my ears when the chief engineer said he was posting me to harbour works at Mombasa.

There followed another two good years, although I didn't get it all my own way all the time. There is always a price to pay. One time I had a temporary posting, by myself, to the Soroti/Lira Construction in Uganda. These were the worst type of postings; you didn't know whether you would be away a week or months and months. I was very unhappy about this posting right from the start. It had all the characteristics of an open bridging loan, if you know what I mean. I was sent up there to help get things started; in fact, I and another European were the only two up there for a long while. My job was to start the setting out of the first few miles of the new railway line; the first peg going in the middle of Soroti Railway Station. I didn't see eye to eye with my new colleague from the first moment I cast my eye upon him, even though experience had taught me that this was one of the worst things that could happen under this set of circumstances. I could hardly ever find the chap when help was needed. There was a sort of club at Soroti and he was able to attend there all hours of the day or night and no matter how much 'beverage' he consumed there, it never seemed to have any effect upon him. I will say this for him, he was always on 'parade' first thing in the morning to help get 'me' out! This part of Uganda was a bit tucked away and I found it very uninteresting, to say the least. There was nowhere to go on the one and only day off each week; not even any shops; so I worked on. It was all blooming horrible. Day by day, I never had any idea of when I was going back to Mombasa. Honestly, when I think of the way we used to be treated in those days. I set out about twenty miles of 'centre-line'. Some days I would only be able to get a couple of hundred feet out because of the ruddy great trees and the antiquated method we had of cutting them down. At the end of the sixth week I'm sure that the powers that be knew that this boy had had enough. I was on my way back to Mombasa. I remember arriving at Mombasa Station at eight o'clock in the morning and seeing my little girls running up the platform to meet me. They were in pretty green dresses which their mother had made for them whilst I had been away. Molly looked so radiant and pretty. Straight to the toy shop and then home for coffee.

Another time I didn't get away with it was when I was travelling down Kilindini Road on my Vespa scooter. Some clot came straight out of a service station in a Karman Ghia; he shot across the road to the centre reservation before turning right to go up Kilindini Road. In this mere flash of time I was looking at the driver and could see that he didn't see me coming. I started braking like fury but I couldn't stop in time, so I hit him right in the middle, flying over the top of him and landing on my head on the other side in the gutter. Out cold! As a result of that accident it was many years before I got my senses of taste and smell back again. I didn't even get the cost of a new shirt out of that little lot! But this is life isn't it? It's a matter of picking yourself up, dusting yourself off and starting all over again. No pun intended.

The rest of the two years was on the good side. Molly worked as secretary to the District Traffic Superintendent at Mombasa Station. Our working hours were from eight o'clock in the morning until noon and two o'clock until four o'clock in the afternoon. This divided the day up perfectly; time for love, time for the children, time for work and then time for more love. Day in and day out, month in and month out, you could never get tired of this routine. To watch the port grow was so interesting too.

My head chainman at Mombasa was a good African by the name of Bernard. He was an extremely fine man to have in your team. He was the son of a Tanganyikan chief, a conscientious worker, a good runner and swimmer. Going back to the time of my accident again, whilst I was laying in hospital, apparently in a bad state, Molly rose early to unlock the door to let the cook in. She also opened the door to let our cat out and when she did so, in rolled Bernard on the floor! He quickly and embarrassingly picked himself up.

'What on earth are you doing there, Bernard?' my wife asked him.

'Oh, I'm sorry Mamsahib, I thought that because the bwana was in hospital, I had better sleep out here all night, just to make sure that you and the Totos are safe.' He slept on the doorstep every night whilst I was in the 'dock'. Talk about the Brotherhood Of Man! I have always thought and wondered how black and white men would get on together if they weren't subjected to the hostile jeering and buffeting from such people as some politicians. I think it would do no harm if the relationship between the races was played down a bit. Just let integration grow with education (on both sides) and let things take its natural course. We would all be less aware of the problem if we paid less attention to it. Mind you, perhaps a little jesting or comedy between the races, as seen on TV from time to time, could be healthy and a good thing. It would allow the safety valve to let off a little steam now and again. The whole thing would demonstrate how ludicrous discrimination is, black or white. Well, that's how this Joe sees it.

There was another interesting exercise that we pursued, the sport of badminton. We formed a 'club', for the want of another word, consisting of a membership made up of the people we worked with, about some twelve folks. Harbhajan and I built the court with our own hands in my back garden. The ground was a sort of compacted sand so there wasn't much use in putting white paint all over the place. We overcame this task of marking the court by digging a trench, wherever a line should be, just deep and wide enough to accommodate a line of normal house bricks. All the scuffing in the world wouldn't destroy this line. The club was very successful too, playing on Monday, Wednesday and Friday nights and Sunday mornings. Singles and doubles. This went on for months and months. We even threw in a couple of barbecue evenings as well and always got full attendance to these! Our 'membership' included a Sikh wife and the Muslim wife of a sheikh and they played in their customary clothes, suffering with fits of laughter whilst indulging in sheer enjoyment. This was the modern world coming to terms with itself really; naturally and without interference.

My survey assistant/trainee was a man named Harbhajan Singh Juttla. He turned out to be one of the best friends of my life as the years rolled by. He was ten years younger than myself and had a happy and magnetic personality. Fit as a fiddle and full of cheek. According to my reckoning he was a good Sikh. Harbhajan was a tremendous help to me at work and would quite often come up with some very helpful suggestions. Warm mutual feelings were developed between him, Molly and the girls too. This is just as well because he spent an awful lot of time around the house. I found his cheek annoying most times and yet, when I turned my back on him, I felt a grin come to my face. I never wanted to brake his young harmless spirit. He thought I was fat and he told me so! Anybody else saying that so outright to me, I would have belted them one!

When he was competing with Molly on the badminton court, he would often say to her, 'Now come on Molly, be active Molly, move yourself around!' You should have seen the slant of her eyes and watched her lips turn inwards; she would usually beat him solid when he got her into this mood – and she beat him often! But try as hard as I could, I very rarely beat him at badminton.

His wife was a charming little Sikh girl with a very husky voice and just a little bit tubby – not fat, I always enjoyed looking at the beautiful colour of her skin around her mid-drift. As each of their sons were born, they turned out to be great fun too, as they grew up. We loved Harbhajan's mother dearly. She was a very motherly sort of person and without as much as saying a single word, you could see a loving mother/child relationship in her face. To me, this is what life and people are all about. Harbhajan's uncle, Mr Nan Singh, was a magnificent example of a Sikh warrior; he was tall and slim with a dark but greying beard. His sparkling eyes would be highlighted by the criss-cross of his turban over his forehead. Mr Nan Singh used to have some great parties in his house, and we were invited to most of them. The brandy flowed like water from a tap. Some functions in the house were more sombre than this; they were of a religious nature. For example, his son was going to university in England so the family and close friends were called to this religious ceremony to offer the pertinent prayers. There would be about forty people there, all of them men except for Molly. She just covered her head with a Sikh scarf and sat on the floor with the rest of us and listened to the two men singing their 'hymns' whilst playing a sort of accordion, lying on its side. The floor was a bit hard on the BTM but only I complained and not Molly.

If I had my life to live again, there is one thing I wouldn't do and that is wish my time away. Most of us do it in varying degrees, especially out there in Africa. One's whole three year tour is divided up into neat chronological pockets, from when you arrive until when you go back home on leave again. The period of leave just gets lost. In

Africa there was so much worth living for, so much going on for you, I shouldn't have wished a single second to pass too quickly. It was time for leave.

5

The United States of America

'Well, Roy my boy, your blood pressure hasn't been to good lately, so you had better sit down because what I am about to tell you isn't going to help it very much! Roy, Molly is going to have another baby! Now, take it easy. If your fourth child is anything like your other three, then you should be a proud man.'

I said thank you to Dr Sailor, our family doctor in Sacramento, California. So, we were going to have another baby – gulp! And this one will be a Yank – another gulp! It took me only minutes to get used to the idea; anyway, it was poor Molly that has to do all the work.

It was during the last year of our tour in Kenya that Molly and I drew up another one of our lists of things for and against living in one place or another. We opted for the USA and can you believe it, it took a year to get all the necessary documents done. You have really got to want to go to the USA or you would give up long before you supply your final proof that you or your family haven't got VD! To start the programme moving, there was a lengthy form to fill in. This was followed some weeks later by having to get the police record from every place you have lived since you were fourteen years old. This in turn meant many trips to the police station for finger printing sessions; the police were the only people with the skill to take your finger prints. We notified the US Embassy in Nairobi that the time had come for us to leave for Canada; what did we do next? That's fine they said, you just report to the embassy in Toronto, where we will forward all your documents. Great. We went home to England first, to see my dear parents and from there we went on to my in-laws, who now lived in Toronto where they were well established.

After we had been in Toronto a week the girls and I went down to the American Embassy to collect our visa. They had never heard of us! Honestly! Well, we repeated our story to several immigration officers and I could see that slowly my situation was getting through to them. After several more hours (poor kids) things started to cheer up a bit. 'Now, this is what you have to do, Sir . . .' said the lady behind the counter, '. . . then we will see if we can't get things going for you. You must first get a VD test done for you and your wife and we need X-rays of all of your chests. Here are some more forms for you to fill in and we will see you back here in two days' time. We will give you all a medical examination and there will be further documentation.' I only just kept my temper and my cool!

Molly's mum was the house-keeper at a large Toronto hospital and many of the doctors and technicians were buddies of hers, so she was able to do a lot for us as regards to finding out where we could get these tests done. Back to the embassy, bright and early as instructed. We were interviewed and we all had a medical. I would like to tell you this: over these last two days, I could remember that every time I spoke to someone or had something done, I had to fork out dollars, lots of them! You covered the costs, believe me. Then, at nearly four o'clock in the afternoon, we were told that we would have to return next Monday morning (again!) to be sworn-in by a US judge. I couldn't believe my ears! I can't remember now my exact words but I know I challenged the whole of the United States of America to a punch-up!

Of course, I knew I was being stupid but they, the Government of the People of the United States had broken the back of the proverbial camel. I didn't think that this could be done until now. It was an uncontrollable attack of sheer frustration. I was keen to find a job and get some dollars coming in instead of going out all the time, I wanted to find us a home for we didn't have a stick of furniture. I wanted to get my little Gay into school as soon as possible. I wanted to make Molly feel happy and secure in her own home. The audacity of these impudent little gods, hiding behind a concrete wall of official power! In my defeat, I thought I was never going to get into the States; all the forms I had filled in, all the work and costs over this past year in preparation for entering 'the promised land'. It just wasn't working!

While I was suffering my brainstorm, I didn't notice that the lady behind the counter had disappeared for some minutes. Molly thought that perhaps she had gone to get the Marines!

'Sir, hurry up, if you will all come this way, the judge is waiting for you now.' All that I had thought was magic about the United States of America dramatically glowed at that moment. Surely, this could only happen in one of those Hollywood movies that I used to gloat over as a youngster. 'ROY EDWARD CHARLES GRIFFITHS AND MOLLY ROSE GRIFFITHS, RAISE YOUR RIGHT HANDS AND SAY AFTER ME . . .' said the lady judge and when all was done she said may she be the first to welcome us to our new country. We were given a large brown envelope and told to hand it over to the immigration officer at the point of entry into the USA. There, why all that fuss over this last year I don't suppose I'll ever know – but it was worth it!

We had collected our old Hillman Estate car from the docks soon after we had arrived in Toronto. We had, of course, shipped the car out of Mombasa weeks ago. Now we loaded all our bits and pieces plus loads of food that Mum and Dad had prepared for us to take. We kissed everybody goodbye and remembered to put the girls in the back of the car and then, as that well known English disc jockey, Jimmy Young, would say, 'Off we jolly well go!'

Our port of entry was Detroit. We pulled up outside the Customs and Immigration Office at the 'gate'. Molly got a large basket out of the car and filled it with bottles of orange squash, fruit, biscuits and so on for the children. We were prepared for another one of those long hang-about sessions. I must say that the children had been nothing less than incredibly good through all this. No naughtiness, no crying, no demands other than the usual that little girls make! 'Come on girls, hamburgers and ice-cream when all this is over.'

We piled through the door and made for the empty bench, the only one in sight, strange as it happens. Molly and the girls sat down comfortably and I went over to the man in uniform standing behind the counter. I handed him the sinister looking brown envelope. 'Hi!' he said. 'Good afternoon,' said I, giving him a look as much as to say I don't like you, however, let's start answering all the questions and filling in the blooming forms! He tore open the large envelope and inside there were five smaller envelopes. He looked at me again but didn't say a word. He opened the five envelopes and out of each he took a piece of paper and placed it in a file. He also took a green-looking card, sealed in a plastic cover which he put to one side. Molly and the girls were motionless as they stared across at him with their eyes wide open, because they had just come into a shady room from the bright sunshine outside. Wendy made the first move by only slightly swinging her little legs under the bench in time with a little nursery rhyme that she must have been silently singing. The tearing of envelopes had finished, The officer picked up all the green-coloured cards, tapped them together on the table and handed them to me. I took them. Still not a word. The officer just stood still, resting his outstretched arms on the counter; for coolness no doubt. 'Is that all, Sir?' I said to him.

'That's it, buddy, stop looking so dumb and start supporting yourself. Good luck.'

Without a single word of instruction from me, the girls all shot up in absolute unison and in double time they made for the exit, clearly demonstrating that they were getting out quick, before the officer changed his mind. I stood there eddying in the turbulence that they had created and then broke out in hysterical laughter. The officer caught the spirit of the moment and heartily joined in my jubilation. As we sped along the road I cast a quick glance at Molly and yelled at the top of my voice, 'We're in!'

'Yes,' she laughed, jumping up and down in her seat and rubbing her hands together in excitement. This was another one of those days. As I write, I am laughing and weeping at the same time. We never stopped feeling glad to be in the United States.

Needless for me to say, it really is a great country and it's full of great people. A land where people work hard; the hardest working people I have ever known; and they play hard. We were for ever aware that the Americans took day by day living very seriously, whether at work or at play. They had to do everything well; it was important for them to do so. It seemed to me to be their way of life to go out of their way to be liked, yes, and to be courteous too. Most people I met were attentive to what I had to say and, more times than not, would ask me questions about what I had just been talking about. Their generosity to me and my family was some times embarrassing, to say the least. If I had ever tried to reciprocate their kindness in full, I would still be in America today, trying to pay my bills.

When we were heading through Nebraska and passing through Omaha, Joy developed a high temperature and was complaining about her water-works. Of course, we sorted out the next nearest doctor. We had no medical coverage insurance, we were never going to need it! Dr Ford gave her a thorough examination and said that she must go into hospital. My God! We got her nicely settled in and assured her we would be back later 'with something nice'. It always worked and in Joy's case, especially if it was food! Off we went and got ourselves a motel room. Joy was in hospital only three days and each time we went in to see her we could clearly see that the nurses were in love with her. I must admit, she was like a little doll, a Shirley Temple type, with her blonde curly hair and blue eyes. Always a smile for anybody, even when she was so poorly. A real extrovert – and still is. The staff tried hard to get her to say something to the doctor in Swahili (which she spoke nearly as much as English!) Yes, they all loved her but she wasn't for sale! Dr Ford said we could now continue our 'safari' but, Joy would have to continue with the antibiotics for a few more days.

The doctor was very interested in our lives during those periods we spent in Africa. I guessed that by now he had come to his own conclusions about the situation we had found ourselves in. I had heard some pretty hair-raising stories about the costs of being sick in America. I felt ever so humble (I have just looked up the real meaning of the word in the dictionary, '. . . but filled with gratitude. . .') when Dr Ford said, 'I'll only charge you a nominal fee and I'll ask the hospital administration to do what they can for you. Good luck in finding a job out West, take good care of yourselves and God bless you.'

Dr Ford didn't charge a cent! God bless you too Dr Ford and perhaps one day you will come to Erbusaig. We all jumped in the car, cuddles all round and 'off we jolly well went.'

You'll never believe this. We had to get out of the motel quick because the manager told us that a newspaper reporter was looking for us. It gets worse! We had only got a half a mile down the road when a deputy sheriff's car pulled us over to the side of the road. 'It's just not true,' he said, 'a car with no driver (our car was a right-hand drive!) driving down the wrong side of the road!' Oh my goodness I thought, now what!

'Hi yer kids,' he said to my girls, through the open window of the car, 'Where are yer goin little ladies?'

Well, this opened the discussion with a little less 'heat' than I expected. Before they had the chance to answer his question, he asked me a few more formal ones. Before I even had a chance to answer, his mood turned very friendly as he crouched down by the side of the car. He started to tell us about some of the interesting things that we could see on the way to where we were going, with an emphasis on points of interest for the children. After a while he put his dark glasses back on, put his cap back straight, raised from a crouching position to a bending one, and then, in a voice about two octaves lower, said to the girls, 'Now git on yer way little ladies and tell yer Pa to keep on the right side of the road. It could hurt, sooner or later, if he stays on the side he was on!' What an incredible people the Americans are! I love 'em.

The girls were quite comfortable sleeping on top of the 'junk' in the back of the car, so Molly and I decided to get some 'eastings' behind us and keep driving through the night. At about half past five in the morning it seemed a good idea to stop in a graveyard and have about an hour's sleep before the girls were back into action. Indeed, at about seven o'clock there was no chance of getting any more sleep until the cubs had got some breakfast in them. So, off down the road we went and we didn't have far to go before we came across a transport type café. This was the first time we had experienced hash fried potatoes and we thought they were scrumptious. We had them as often as we could for the duration of our residence in the States. Whilst we were eating a very large truck pulled up and in two seconds the driver came in. He went and had a good scrub-up first, as that appears to be what all American truck drivers do and then sat down to order his breakfast.

'Hi!' he said as he passed my girls and then to the waitress, 'I'll take ham and two eggs, over-easy, toast, jelly and some coffee.' He took a quick look at the morning paper, then a sip of his coffee. This was followed by a long pause. He laid the paper down and took two bites of his ham and eggs and one bite of his toast. One more sip of his coffee and then got up and threw some money on the counter and then walked out. As he walked past us he threw a deep-set but gentle smile at the children and said, 'So long girls, have yourself a nice day now.'

'Goodness me! Look Molly, can you see how much food he has left there?' I continued my vocal astonishment by saying that I couldn't see how the world could go on like this, when one half treated the abundance of food like he did, yet when most people would consider themselves lucky if they had that same amount of food to last them for several days. I'm saying nothing against the driver, you understand. But I can't help but wonder what is going to happen when all the people on the face of the earth are going to discover that some have got everything but some have practically nothing. The way things stand at the moment, it appears to me, a person's destiny is considerably biased by where their mum is when they are born!

In this dying world, there is no room for rubbish talk and somehow, we have got to learn to live together and put Mother Earth first. We need a totally new dialogue and a new set of rules that common sense alone will make each and every one of us adhere to them. We must have a system that can be understood and handled by mere mortals. Those of us that are still alive tomorrow morning must realise that they must help to take command of the situation now, not next week. Press your political leaders to grasp the nettle while we still have a chance; the future is now. I want to write pages on this subject and put some of my ideas forward, but maybe this is not the reason you are reading my book.

Crossing the Nevada Desert produced another laugh. Our Hillman had done only 19,000 miles when we shipped her from Mombasa, so she couldn't have been all that decrepit; nevertheless, she did start to badly overheat. Eventually, we ran out of water available for that use. Molly got the brilliant idea of getting our kettle out and waving it at the occasional passers-by. The road was a very quiet one. As each car went by all the occupants treated the matter with great mirth and cheerfully waved back at her as they sped past at great speed. God only knows for what reason they thought Molly was waving the kettle! We did the same thing, one car after another – and so did they! In spite of our predicament, we saw the funny side of it too and got a good laugh out of it. Eventually a truck stopped and rendered help.

Joy was fighting fit now, as were her other two sisters as we went rolling down the sierras into California. What I was feeling at that time must have been the same feelings that hundreds of settlers before us had experienced when arriving in California. It was a very emotional experience, actually, I like to think of it as 'the spirit of California' being revealed to us. All very floral you might say, all very Hollywoodish too! Be that as it may, I felt I had entered the Mecca of life at its best, as I knew it then. We had passed Auburn and now, for some reason unknown to us, the vast motorway had suddenly spewed us out into the downtown streets of Sacramento. Never did know where or why the motorway finished! We were impressed at first with the tree-lined roads of the capitol, as well as the smart painted houses, not to mention the big offices all gleaming in the six o'clock in the morning sunshine. Then we had to cross Fourth, Third, Second and First Streets and that's when our visions were shattered. There must have been a couple of dozen scruffy-looking men either standing around or sitting down in broken-down doorways of old boarded up shops. Some of these chaps were literally staggering all over the place and some of them even had a wine bottle held up to their tilted heads. Down on First Street a Black Maria was picking up some of the poor degenerates and putting them in the back. My girls didn't like seeing this although they had seen a lot of unsightly things in their young lives but they seemed to take it all in their stride – as long as Mum and Dad were about. It's funny that seeing this put us off of ever wanting to live in Sacramento. I'll eat these words!

I lost my heart in San Francisco. I could have put my bones to rest there. In our early months Molly loathed the place. There were reasons for this of course. As far as she was concerned she was as far away from anywhere that she could ever be, if you understand my meaning. Her security amounted to about zero. She had no home of any kind; at least in Africa she had a tent! The accommodation that we had in the town was terrible, by any standards. It was a block of apartments near the Ferry Building and Molly detested the smell of the place, let alone anything else. I started to feel that I was walking on a tightrope. Nevertheless, I still found Molly a tower of strength and I was going to make things good for her – soon. That unwilting confidence or, am I just plain stupid?

'Before I can get you a job, you must belong to Local Union Number Three,' said the man at the place where you go when you are looking for a job. I couldn't understand why I, as a professional man, had to belong to a union. However, I did as I was told; I couldn't afford to do otherwise. This man tried very hard, for two whole weeks, to get me a job with no avail. He was getting as depressed as myself. He was saying the most complimentary things about me on the telephone to potential employers but it ended nowhere.

In the evenings my women and I took in many of the places that most people come to San Francisco to see. Chinatown, Telegraph Hill, Fisherman's Wharf and so on. All great stuff. We took a ride on the city's famous Cable Car at that time of day when business traffic was a little slack! The operators had turned the 'tram' around at the bottom of the hill in just seconds and we wasted no time in jumping on and then we were off. We hadn't gone very far when the operators started singing and dancing to a catching rhythm played on the warning bell. We found this top entertainment and it was noticeable that the coloured operators were focussing their attentions, most of the time, on my little girls. Lovely. Of course, the girls were at home with these chaps.

'Now man, I just can't dig it, not getting a good guy like you a job is crazy man! I'll tell you what I'm going to do. I'm going to call a buddy of mine; his office is out of town but we will see what he can do for us. Now, just sit your fanny down over there and have yourself a cup of coffee.'

Up until this 'fanny business', I liked this man! Minutes passed and I started to get those black thoughts; you know the ones I mean, when they start to hurt the centre of your chest. Panic, I think some people call it.

'Come over here, Roy, and bring your coffee with you. Now, this pal of mine, John Haight is his name, he wants to take a look at you. That's good eh? Well, it's at least a step in the right direction. Now, his company is called Packard, Muir and Train and you will find them on the intersection of 32nd and 'J' Streets. Oh yes, Sacramento that is. It's about eighty miles up the Freeway to Reno.' Sacramento! My God!

'Sacramento!' Molly cried, 'You must be joking!' And that was that.

'Well, let's sit down and talk about it with a nice cup of coffee. It is the first break that has come our way.'

There was still no change in Molly's expression. Another cup of coffee. I still couldn't sufficiently support or strengthen the case. Again, I felt that I was walking on very thin ice. Wendy was getting a little warm sitting on my lap and said, 'Oh come on, let's go. I know it's lunchtime but you can get us a hamburger on the way, Daddy.'

I felt an immediate surge of triumph, as if it was me who had made the decision and that it was me in command of the situation. I often kidded myself this way. The girls had already grabbed their respective dollies and jumped into the car. Neither Molly nor I had said a word yet. Wendy asked me to drive carefully because her dolly, Sue, had got malaria and wasn't up to scratch.

I got to see John Haight and we talked survey. Then he got around to asking me how much pay did I expect a month – so I told him. He thought my figure was a bit high but the matter stopped there. Nice friendly man was John, a big Californian as you would expect. He used to pilot one of those big bombers during the war and, in fact, he was stationed in Britain. 'Well thank you for your time, Roy, and thank you for taking an interest in our organisation. I will let you know the outcome of this meeting as soon as I have had the chance to see some of the other directors. In the meantime, perhaps you would like to fill out one of these application forms.' If he only knew how I hated these damn forms, like I hate nothing else.

At this time we were staying in a very good motel in Valajo, owned by an Hawaiian couple whose names I have long forgotten, except that his first name was Sam. They had offered to take incoming telephone calls for us, just in case something had come up for us while we had been out hunting. On the way back to Valajo from Sacramento, you would never believe what happened. The 'big-ends' of our engine went. I had never heard such a noise. This was one of the times that I wished I had stayed home and worked for Wiltshire County Council, back in England, where the only break from the routine of life was to go fishing on the River Avon on a Saturday afternoon. We took the car to a garage that advertised themselves as Rootes Agents. With all due respect, I'm sure that most of the chaps had never seen a Hillman before; they probably thought that a Hillman was somebody from the Black Hills of Dakota. That was on a Thursday.

When we eventually got back to the motel Sam came running over to us and said that a John Haight had been phoning all afternoon. Would we please give him a call at his house as soon as we got in. Molly went a sort of deathly white as she grabbed my hand and pulled me over to Sam's telephone. We had made it! Could I start on Monday? Without transport I didn't know how I could manage it but I assured John that I would be on the door-step on Monday morning. This was another one of those great days and I thanked the Lord for it. I'm sure he heard my prayer. Why? Because the next day was Friday and the telephone rang again. 'We have got your big-ends re-ground and your car will be ready tonight.' What service, what speed and what efficiency. When we got to the garage, the manager said that an Air Force sergeant had been looking for me; he was being posted to Australia and wanted to take our car with him. Just at that moment, in walked the sergeant. 'Give you 600 bucks for your wagon,' he said. 'Well, what about it?'

'You are on,' said I and with that, he put 600 dollars in my hand and without saying another word to me, he turned to the mechanic and said, 'Put a roof-rack on it,' and walked out! I didn't even know his name. I felt like a Masai warrior who had just received his pay for a few days work, standing there with his right foot wedged against his left knee, a spear in his left hand helping to prop himself up and with a piece of string tied around his private parts.

The story may become a bit difficult to keep up with at this point but please try! In the morning, we went round to one of the local car dealers and – wait for it – his name was Harry England. As we stood there talking to Harry, a car drove up and the same driver wanted to take delivery of a new Ford. Harry went over to him and mumbled a few words into his ear; he waited for a reply and then came back to us and said, 'Quick, jump into this car and see what you think of it.' I did just that. I didn't know if this was a genuine deal I was getting or whether I was being taken for a ride – pun not intended. The car was an American 3,500cc Ford, fully automatic with a V8 engine. It seemed to respond magnificently and when Harry told me the price, I took it. As it turned out, that car served me for two years without a single fault and I sold it when I had finished with it for nearly the price I had paid for it.

On Sunday we moved up to Sacramento West and took a self-catering room in the Redlands Motel. It was comfortable and very clean, we were all well and together. We had plenty of food in the fridge, we had a good car (essential) and Daddy had a job. Talking about food, this was another thing that amazed us, the big food supermarkets! We didn't have anything like this in Nairobi. Brightly lit, pleasant music playing in the background and generally a friendly atmosphere. The staff were so polite as they packed your groceries for you and then took them out to your car. As we selected things off the shelves and put them into the trolley, I could see that even the little one was sensing that they should only select those items that were essential to us. They tried so hard to turn their eyes away from those items that looked so colourful and so attractively packed; they even touched some of these items with their finger-tips. At this moment I felt very tender towards them all and I knew that I was not worthy of such love and innocent understanding. I could not have existed, if God Himself ordered it, without Molly and my girls.

My life in America, my experiences, my feelings and my interpretations would fill a book this size alone, so in a way, I feel it is unfortunate that I must reserve the space for just the more prominent incidents in my land, Africa. However, I could not finish this chapter without another important incident in America being disclosed. The time came for us all to prepare for a new member of our family who would be with us very soon. Was it to be another girl, or this time were we going to have a boy? Molly and I did draw up another one of our lists of all the advantages of having a girl and those for having a boy. No one will ever know what was contained in that list because, as usual, we tore it up. It was only a couple of hours after Molly had jumped into her bed in the Mercy Hospital, Sacramento, when Dr Sailor, dressed in those forbidding green surgical clothes, brought to me a new bundle of joy and said, 'Father, may I introduce you to your daughter. This is Jennifer.' I was a very happy man because I wanted another girl. What else could I say but 'Hi there, wee Jennifer,' as my eyes filled with tears, as they do each time Fatuma presents me with another daughter. I looked at her and could clearly see that she was one of mine. I always say that!

I could remember before Jennifer was born, Wendy would rush in from school, go into our bedroom and look into the cot to see if 'her' new baby had arrived yet. Now, she would sit in front of the TV for hours, holding the baby in her lap. Gay adopted the attitude of the responsible older sister and just kept a cautious eye on all of us to make sure that none of us would bring any harm to her baby sister. Joy just beamed, the way she always beams and spent much of her time trying to make Jennifer laugh. We all spent whatever time was left loving and caring for the most precious person of all – Mummy.

It was with great reluctance that we made up our minds that it was time to move. We had to move because we had to move. It was time to put a few thousand miles behind us. From all and varied aspects, we had certainly found much in America to interest us. I have to admit that a romance did develop between us and the States, especially California. However, the truth of the matter is we never stopped being homesick for Kenya. These interests and 'love affairs' in California diluted the yearning we had for Kenya but the feelings were always there in the background. To give up Kenya was the price we had to pay to live in America and no matter how many 'lists' we drew up, our hearts just could not find a balance to the equation.

6

The Third Tour of East Africa

I wrote to my old employers in East Africa through Crown Agents in London and asked what were my chances of being reinstated. The response was positive. They offered me a post as a construction surveyor which satisfied me immensely. So, in the summer of 1964, we sold our home in Sacramento and much of what was contained therein. We sold our car and a very good friend of ours, Jim Fitzpatrick, lent us his second car for some weeks before we finally left California. The folks at the firm made us a very demonstrative farewell card (which I have kept to this very day) and which was signed by nearly everybody in the firm. The last moments in the office were a very touching experience when all those that were in the office at that time lined up to shake my hand and say goodbye. The bosses presented me with a lovely present and a very big bon-voyage cheque. Where else would I get this? It was really too much saying goodbye to Jim down at his office when we handed his car back to him. He kissed Molly goodbye when she handed him the keys; then without looking at me, he turned around and walked back into his office. There is always a price to pay. Sometimes dearly!

We rented a Hertz-Rent-A-Car to carry us across the country to Molly's good parents home in Toronto. The car was a brand new Ford Impala. These people offered a service whereby you picked up a car in one place and then you could hand it back anywhere in North America. We certainly took advantage of this. Again, the kids were absolutely marvellous on this trip. Our hearts were truly heavy for what we were leaving behind and let me be honest, there was always an element of doubt that what I was doing was for the best. Nevertheless, we still had a most enjoyable trip.

Shock! When we arrived at Molly's folk's house, we found that they had gone away for the weekend. Jammed in the door knocker was a telegram addressed to us, which had been forwarded on to us from Sacramento. It read, 'Don't give up your job or leave Sacramento because your Post is in abeyance. Your Citizenship is uncertain,' signed by Crown Agents. Bloody cheek. There were frantic telephone calls to Crown Agents at four o'clock in the morning, I can tell you. You can imagine what Molly and I were going through. What an anti-climax! In the end, I told Crown Agents that I was on my way, come what may. Really, what else could I do? The time soon came around to get our flight to London and the whole Vango Tribe was at Toronto Airport to see us off. (Vango is my wife's maiden name.) The girls loved every minute of it. The last time we crossed eastwards across the Atlantic was by sea and that was in the middle of winter. Boy, was it rough too. We were about half way across the Atlantic and it was blowing at least a Force Ten outside. Joy and Wendy were having a great time trying to walk straight but, poor old Gay was feeling very sorry for herself and just couldn't find her sea-legs. She was lying in her bed and there she stayed for most of the trip. Well, it was time to go for lunch (excuse me Gay!), so Mummy gave the 'active two' instructions to do 'you know what'. It was whilst Joy was taking her turn when the ship gave a horrible lurch in one direction which 'de-throned' the poor kid. To prevent herself from flying across the toilet compartment, she put her tiny hands out to stop herself. Then the damn ship decided to lurch in the opposite direction. Slam went the toilet door and off came the top of the poor little girl's finger! It was horrible. She was a real brave little girl about it as my little girls always seem to be at times like this. There was all sorts of action from the Top Brass after that event. They came down to measure this and they came down to measure that. They mumbled under their breath, careful not to cast even a glance in our direction whilst they were carrying out their deliberations. Poor people, I rather imagined that they thought they were going to be sued to high heaven. Why should we do anything like that? Was it because the latch that supposed to hold the door back didn't work? Nevertheless, we all felt for our poor little Joy, Bless her. We took her to Odstock Hospital when we got back to my parents' house in Salisbury. The doctors there asked why in heavens name didn't they look for her finger and stick it back on! To this day she has a claw-finger but her issue of charm, elegance and grace more than make up for it.

When we arrived in London, we went straight round to Crown Agents, where all hell was let loose again. To cut a long story short, later that day we were on our way to catch the onward flight to Nairobi. Even though we were now absolutely on our way to Kenya, events over these last two weeks had been so unpleasant that there was no doubt about it, a lot of the pleasure that we had always enjoyed when on our way to Africa had been dampened. What made it more than a little sour for us was that because of these uncertainties our stayover in England was far shorter than we anticipated; in fact, we were in England for only a few hours! Therefore, my chances for seeing my parents were non existent. Fate has it that I was never to see my mother again; she died six months after I arrived in Africa. I often think of her and miss her terribly. Always love and worship your mother, make her happy, make her laugh, keep in regular contact with her and tell her over and over again that you love her. No matter who you are – don't dare leave it too late. If you can, phone her now – go on!

When we arrived at Nairobi I had to quickly shoot back to the plane to find Sue, Wendy's dolly, who we had very nearly left behind. Walking towards the terminal building, I had Joy holding one of my hands with a smile of excitement on her face whilst she cast inquisitive glances here and there, holding her dolly in her other hand and trying to hoist up her panties with her elbows! Wendy was holding my other hand and she was just looking ahead with a dazed but cross expression on her face. Sue was being carried upside-down, to keep the sun off her head. Gay was walking behind with her mother, giving responsible attention to her mother's needs, at the same time holding her baby sister's hand, her little sister being carried in her mother's arms. I looked around for the usual welcoming officer but, there didn't appear to be anybody who had an interest in our arrival. Oh well, he must be waiting inside. We were soon through Customs and Immigration; it was interesting to note that all the officers were now Africans, Kenya now having achieved her independence.

Whilst we were walking along the corridor to get our luggage and I was trying to convince Joy that she didn't want to go to the toilet, two men came rushing along to meet us. One of them I noticed immediately as Collin Heyes, an old Army colleague of mine and a damn fine surveyor. The other gent was my boss. Apparently, he had been my boss on my other tours too and was quite put out when I said, and quite genuinely, that I didn't know him! Anyway, he said to me, 'I don't know what you're grinning at, you will stop when you find out where I'm sending you. You are going to Makumbako!'

What a nice chap, I thought, and where in the blazes is Makumbako? Whilst I was pondering and waiting to hear what else this 'nice chap' had to say, Collin was welcoming Molly as best he could, under the circumstances, in a much more cordial atmosphere than the one I was sharing with this bloke. I would never have believed that this was not going to turn out to be 'one of those days'. What was going wrong lately?

We spent the first ten days in a Nairobi hotel, doing the things that had to be done and during this time I found out where Makumbako was. The end of the World! I thought that events had started not to go too well just lately and wondered if the gods had been trying to tell me something for these past few weeks. Because of the existing political situation Zambia had been having trouble in transporting their valuable product of copper out without it going through Rhodesia. To overcome this problem, the Powers That Be decided to put into operation a lifetime dream, a railway line from Dar-es-Salaam to Zambia. The first stretch of it branches off of an existing mainline at Mikumi (now famous for its fine game park) and, in fact, was already under construction to as far as Kidatu. There was quite a large sugar plantation and refinery at Kidatu which was operated by the Dutch. However, it was German money that was being used to build the railway. I had heard that the World Bank had turned down an advance to build this line, but it was thought that the Chinese Government were giving the matter some thought and that they might build the line from Kidatu onwards to Zambia. Be that as it may, the route was being located by an EAR & H Team. The engineer-in-charge of the team was an old gentleman who was generally known as Wonk. No, he wasn't a Chinaman! He was what I always looked upon as a typical tough White African with a deep love of Africa. He must have been in his late sixties at least and was particularly identifiable by a large scar across his face, caused by a motor car accident. He got around the bush like a young gazelle. I believe he also had a farm up near Iringa. Even though we were on safari together, I really never got to know him because he didn't allow me to! When he spoke to me he always did so by looking to one side or the other of me. I think perhaps he was a bit shy. He knew his job well and was in command; there was never any doubt about that.

The ten days in Nairobi were soon up. The best thing that happened was our meeting up with Doug Valpy again. My orders were that my family and self were to catch the train to Dar-es-Salaam and then a bus from there to Iringa. The train journey would take the best part of two days and the bus journey would take another one. I had to leave my family in Iringa when the Land Rover came in from Makumbako to collect me. And that was it. I would be allowed to come back from Makumbako every second weekend to see my family. I would arrive late on Friday night and then would have to leave again early on Sunday afternoon. We had no friends in Iringa; in fact, we would have a job to even find another fellow countryman in existence these days. How on earth did I get into this situation? Where did I go wrong? Why didn't I realise that I was not going on construction but on a route survey? When should I have seen the red light and refused to sail on that tack? What could I do about it now? The answer to the last question was nothing.

This period of time was not a very happy one and I hope you don't put the book down because of it. To illustrate my theory that I think there is always 'a price to pay', I think I have to express some of the heartbreaks which usually seem to follow some of the highlights, when things are going so well. At all of these times, I often read my state of morale and I give myself a grading by a number of one to ten. In the Topographic Squadron I learnt to use this method to measure the state of my morale: number one was reflected when there was a death in the family and number ten was the moment of ejaculation when having intercourse.

All the way to Iringa my heart actually hurt. We were going to an absolutely strange place in Tanzania; not even in Kenya, knowing we would ultimately be separated. All we had in life was each other. We were essential to each other and needed each other to share every thought, opinion and experience. After all, wasn't having the experience together was what it was all about? Together, not apart. I needed Molly and those girls as much as they needed me. A moment without Molly, under these circumstances, was a moment of torture. We never planned, not for a single moment, to be separated. What was the reason for being there at all if we were not going to be there together? As you can tell, I was pretty cut-up about this. If I had been called-up to war, then Molly and I would have managed and we would have done so knowing there was a good reason. But, in no way could I find a reason which would console myself for this current separation. The pain lasted for several months. My employers had goofed-up somewhere and I was the answer to their problems – and they held all the power. Help that was asked for in my prayers never arrived – but the Land Rover to take me on safari did! As I waved goodbye to Molly and the girls I felt terrible. Why did I ever leave California?

When I arrived at base camp, I made myself known to Wonk. He said very little more than that he needed me to get the job done. He pointed out which was my tent and then left me to it. Not as much as a welcome, let alone a cup of tea. I got into my tent where I could smell all the familiar smells of safari life. I sat down on my camp chair and sank into a depth of despair. I heard a Land Rover pull up to my tent. Into the tent burst Harbhajan Singh! He looked much older and more mature now but he still had that cheeky grin on his face as he grasped my hand with both of his and with a hearty shake he beamed out, '*Jambo Bwana* Roy.' As the saying goes, 'When one door closes, another one opens.' This man saw me over that rough period, I can tell you, and if it wasn't for him turning up at that time, I really don't know what I would have done. Was this the help I was asking for in my prayers?

Wonk had put me in charge of an independent survey party/safari, with Harbhajan as my draughtsman and two young Kikuyu trainee surveyors as my assistants. Of course, we had the usual army of bush-cutters and chainmen. Our task was to 'shoot' the topography for a hundred metres either side of the proposed centre-line of the new proposed railway line which went on and on until we got to the Livingstone Mountains. The next day, we left Makumbako Camp and went along the Great Ruaha river and set up our camp at the Saddle. This was the highest point along this section of the railway line and the chosen route would have to pass over this point – without a tunnel.

Wonk had already been along here and put in rough bush-pegs to show the survey team what he wanted surveying in greater detail. The two Kikuyu chaps were soon off working, one in charge of a team doing accurate levelling and the other carrying forward a more accurate chainage. I was following behind doing the topography either side of the proposed route. When this was all reduced and plotted up, the engineer-in-charge, Wonk, would be able to do an accurate 'paper location' of the future line. From this we could then take off quantities of 'cut and fill' and the future setting-out instructions.

I can well remember those first few weeks of that safari. Every morning we had to drive along the top of the escarpment until we reached a point adjacent to where we had finished surveying the day before. We would then have to get out and start walking the rest of the way; I should say climb the rest of the way because that is what it amounted to. It very nearly killed me! The distance was about three miles each way, over very rough country and dropped several hundreds of feet. We then had to do a day's surveying/bush cutting in between walks/climbs.

The very first few days were difficult because I felt the extra physical exertion exhausting; you try keeping up with Africans in the bush! And mentioning Africans, none of them knew whether they could trust me or not and at that time I didn't care one way or the other anyway. What a state to get in! I could never get Molly or the girls out of my mind. I was still angry. I would gladly have had my girls out here with me and I know they would have loved to have been with me, but the rules permitting this have now changed. It was said, quite rightly too I suppose, that if I could have my family with me then so could everybody else in the team. I, personally, could see reasons why my case was different and it made me mad to think the rules had changed so much. I could get nowhere by pulling rank or stressing the fact that I was an ex-patriate officer or anything else. I found no comfort by admitting that I was wrong, that I had no more rights than anybody else. Agreeing did not bring my girls out to me. I could not appeal to most of the senior officers because they were now Africans, and so they should be, and good men at their jobs too. A few of the top desk jobs were still held by ex-patriates but I couldn't appeal to them either now because I felt that they didn't want to rock the boat; my particular problem had become a new one and it may carry with it strains of racialism.

Perhaps senior officers of my race were experiencing difficulties in exercising their authority over problems created by such as the likes of me. In an effort to carry out a policy of non-preferential treatment to ex-patriate officers, I think they came to look upon us chaps as just articles, as just a number if you like or as just something that is issued or withdrawn, like a kitchen table – and about just as important. They had a difficult job to do and I would imagine that if they had taken one step out of line they would be up to their necks in hot water. So, if you meet anyone with a problem such as the one Roy Griffiths has, then the best thing to do is turn your back on him and leave the room quickly.

You could see that my whole railway world, as I knew it, had changed and I didn't like it one bit. It meant that now the cards were played differently and the quicker I adapted to the game, the better for me.

Well, the first two weeks had gone by and they were the longest two weeks of my life. It was now time to go home, for the want of another word. When I look back, if they had only let me go home every weekend, which I don't think was an awful lot to ask for, then I know I would have felt totally different about the situation. Also, if they had only given me some indication of how long this stunt was going to go on for it would have helped.

To get 'home' we first had to climb up the Mafindi Escarpment along a track cut through the bush, a little nerve-racking in places, especially when the track at the tops of some of the steep hills was only as wide as the vehicle. This is where the half-shafts of our forward control

Land Rovers used to pack up. At the top we kept on through the tea plantations to meet the main track to Iringa. At one time, on the way home, I stopped by an African's hut and bought a big white cockerel and took it home and gave it to Gay. She called it Charlie. From then on, every night, just before sundown, the cook, the ayah, Molly and the girls would all have to run around the house and garden to catch him and lock him up in the garage!

We were all so glad to see each other on those Friday nights. In front of the lovely roaring wood fire (I brought the wood back from Makumbako) we huddled together and not one of us wanted to part and go to bed. Jennifer was getting lovelier and lovelier and was the centre of all our attentions. Much of Saturdays was spent getting stores and M/T spares and carrying out safari business. It was only a few ticks of the clock and then Sunday afternoon was here and off back to camp we had to go. I was determined to get out of this situation as quickly as I could; if only I could find a way. Weeks and weeks and weeks went by.

Harbhajan Singh's wife, Bansi, and their three little boys were staying in Iringa too, at her older brother's house. We went there for one or two parties at some weekends; loads of lovely curry; as only Sikhs can make it, with a good few stiff brandies. A couple of times Harbhajan and Bansi came to our house to have a bit of fun and they taught Molly how to make 'their' curry and she has been doing it ever since.

As the route survey progressed, along mile after mile, we got a better system going for getting home on our weekends off. The dirty great Canadian Ford Galaxy car that I had bought in Nairobi had arrived in Iringa by railway transport. Molly had decided that if the ayah would lend her bike to her from time to time, then I could take the Galaxy on safari with me, as long as I could find a way down the escarpment with it. It turned out to be quite a military operation getting this huge thing down but everything worked out all right. As soon as I tidied up my camp and paid the men I was able to leave straight away without waiting for the men to load up in the forward control Land Rover. I now used to arrive in Iringa hours before the Land Rover. The other beautiful thing about it was that instead of leaving Sunday afternoons with the rest I was able to leave on Monday mornings at four o'clock. Every other Monday was a tough day, I can tell you. Harbhajan always travelled with me.

Every evening meal in base camp was a pleasant excursion. After making sure that transport and everything else was ready for tomorrow, that we had reduced all our field-books of today's field-work, we had our baths in the back of our tents, then time left was ours. One evening, Harbhajan would eat European type food in my tent and the next evening we would eat Indian type food in his. My tummy rumbles when I think of some of the dishes he produced. I always used to think that Harbhajan lost out on this deal but he never complained. Sometimes, after dinner, we would sit down and take our clean socks off and help each other to take the jiggers out of each others feet! One picked these jiggers up in the bush and they would get under the skin of your toes and the underside of your feet. When they had got themselves comfortable they laid their eggs. Some days after the eggs were laid, you would get an uncomfortable itchy spot that would flare up and sometimes even badly fester. We used to dig these out with a needle and sometimes, if in an advanced state, we'd make the little things move by applying paraffin. What we also found successful was an application of meths. When your foot is nicely soaked in this cooling meths, you put a match to it! You have to watch what you are doing because after a few moments of blazing, your foot starts to get quite warm. When the heat is no longer bearable, or you can't stand the smell of burning human hair any longer, then dowse the 'fire' with a cloth and then you'll find a riggling jigger just waiting for your attention – also a lot of cooked eggs!

Molly and I were active Christians in those days. We thought that the Salvation Army provided an excellent

Sunday School for the girls as well as meetings which we could attend as a family. The girls always enjoyed so many 'aunties and uncles' who readily welcomed them to the hall. Over the years we met a lot of fine people through the SA, both in America and Africa. Not only did we find the worshiping together gratifying, we also enjoyed the warm and loving friendship that was always on offer. Nairobi was alive with officers because the SA was doing a lot of work in schools and hospitals there. These officers came from Australia, USA, Canada, Sweden and Britain. Even though there were a large number of officers it still turned out that the band master and songster leader was a soldier. In fact, he was an engineer with the East African Posts and Telegraph Service.

Anyway, whilst in Iringa we discovered that there was no Sunday school for the girls to attend, so Molly and I took it upon ourselves to do something about it by starting one. The first week about a dozen nippers turned up and after the meeting Gay handed out lollipops to them all. The next meeting was two weeks later, when I got back from safari. We had the shock of our lives. There were so many we couldn't fit them all in! I like to think that the children wanted to hear the message from the Bible but I can't help but feel that the anticipated lick of a lollipop may have had something to do with it. Especially when I recall that some of the little souls wore turbans. In their own little ways, those children were all aware of God.

Another Friday afternoon had come around. I noticed that the air was full of smoke from grass fires that one always gets this time of year. What actually starts them I have never been able to find out but they spread over areas of several square miles at a time. However, I could see the foothills at the bottom of the escarpment and the way between looked clear of fires, so off we jolly well went. This weekend, when I arrived home, there was every sign that we had had enough. I was desperate. The time had come for me to do something about it.

'Come on, we're going to Nairobi,' I said.

Once I had said that I was absolutely elated. I felt a burden lift from my shoulders. I was very aware of the decision I had made – and I was prepared to accept the consequences. I knew that this pattern of life had to stop and stop now. I noticed the family were silent; there wasn't an argument from anybody. They just stood there motionless with blank looks on their faces – even the baby!

'Right, anything that can be eaten, throw it in the back of the car. All the clothes that you can lay your hands on, throw them in the back of the car too.'

All hopes of being able to find reasonable justice and a fair hearing was thrown in the back of the car as well. Then, late that afternoon we all jumped in the car and started off on a 600 mile journey to the big city – Nairobi.

We drove for the rest of that day and night, taking it in turns to drive (just Molly and I, that is.). The children were absolutely marvellous again; not a moan about anything from any of them; they sensed there was something very serious going on. Tiredness began to hit me at about five o'clock in the morning. This is when I am always weakest and my imagination runs riot. I've always had to watch myself when I get into this state of tiredness; I have to get a grip of myself and come to terms with the facts; keep with it. I started to think of the worst things that could happen to us and those thoughts weren't the least bit comforting. The smile of assurance from Molly was!

'Are you all right, Daddy? Is there anything I can get you? Would you like to finish the coffee that's left?' asked little Gay.

I cast a quick glance all around at them and thought, 'My God, look at them, this is what it's all about. This is why I'm here. This is why I'm doing what I'm doing.' By golly, something good must come out of this. All of a sudden I was in front of the Head Office in Nairobi. Oh dear!

'What on earth are you doing here, Griffiths? Has the engineer-in-charge given you permission to leave your safari? Come on man, what is it?' said the Big White Chief.

I had always feared this man; to me he was always so cocksure of himself; so aggressive in his la-di-da manner. The room was full of morning sunshine and it was quite hot. There wasn't a zephyr of air and he didn't have his fans on. The room was stifling with the smell of old drawings and stale cigar smoke. There were two other senior officers sitting down in the room and they were both glaring at me.

In my tiredness I think my brain must have gone on holiday because I felt absolutely no fear of this man at all and even less respect at this moment. I stood another two inches taller, pulled my shoulders back and lightly clenched my fists. In a surprisingly strong and steady voice I said, 'Good morning to you. This is my weekend off from camp. I'm here because I've not got any response from my letters regarding a matter which I consider very significant. I refer, Sir, to my request for a posting to a construction. Whilst I was living in America, you offered me a post as a construction surveyor and I accepted. In no way can I accept that my present job constitutes such a post. I'm sure you are aware of my strong feelings about this for I have written several letters to you on this subject.'

I could see by the look on BWC's face, that maybe, even if for only a minute, he couldn't handle me.

'Good Lord man, what would happen to the discipline on the railways if we allowed officers to leave their posts, willy-nilly, like you have just done? Now, you wait here whilst I go and see if the chief engineer is willing to deal with this matter this morning,' said BWC.

He was gone for what seemed an eternity. I suppose part of the treatment was to let me sweat it out, as they say. I felt that the whole of HQ knew I was here and why and that every person was waiting to see what terrible disaster was about to beset me. While waiting for his return, I spoke to one or two fellow officers who were actually rooting for me. For the first time I learnt that the bosses knew something about my posting that I wasn't aware of. Initially, I was not meant to go to Makumbako but there was a change of circumstances just as I had arrived and I became the immediate solution to the problem. I had been cheated and I felt bloody sure that they now knew that I had tumbled to it; it was clear that they had been taking advantage of my professional character.

I was suddenly overcome by a strength and yet an anger. I was now really waiting for the BWC to come back. Come back he did. When I saw his face, I must confess, I started to shrink back to size, even before a single word was spoken.

'Now I have discussed this matter with the chief engineer and we can't see why you don't stick it out until the end of the safari which is in about eight weeks' time. In any case, we are not going to be forced into a snap decision under these circumstances. You will return to your safari and we will let you know what action we intend to take in due course.'

What are you going to do now, Roy? I thought. I very uneasily took my weight off of one foot and put it on the other whilst I was looking straight into his eyes, waiting to hear what else he might have to say. I was now so overcome by tiredness I could hardly focus on the man. Only seconds passed and I shifted back onto the other leg again – not once did he ask me to sit down! I have made my point, I thought again, what am I waiting for? They don't appear as if they are going to throw the book at me, I bet they are trying to save their faces. If I were wise, I would now gracefully but proudly back out of the room and then see what happens.

'Well Sir, I'm sure you can imagine how desperate I am to go to these lengths to put my case and willingly suffer the embarrassment and consequences in so doing,' I was going to say, but I could feel that I would be talking to the wind. There wasn't another word from my senior and it wasn't hard to figure out that it was time to go.

We had left the girls in the care of Collin's wife (Collin was my old Army pal, remember?) She had given the girls a good refreshing bath and something good to eat. When we got back to them, after our 'conflict', they had an excellent lunch waiting for us. I shall always be grateful to them for their kind consideration and feelings at a time when I really needed an ally. They understood our position and helped but, very wisely they kept out of the row. So would I have done. They offered us a bed for the night, the whole six of us, which we turned down, as grateful as we were. I thought it prudent if we returned to Iringa as quickly as we could, to show that we wasted as little time as possible, if for no other reason. Up until now it had been my own time and at my own expense. This had been me against the might of the Railways HQ – getting involved in a situation that I normally wouldn't dream of doing. They had always been such fair employers and I had never found the need to employ such battle strategy. Come to think of it, what about when Gay was born, back in 1953? On the return trip, Kilimanjaro curiously looked a whole lot friendlier that evening than the night before.

It was early Sunday morning when we arrived back in Iringa, so we wasted little time in climbing into bed. We all slept through until about midday and although I certainly didn't feel up to it, I decided to return to camp with that afternoon's Land Rover. Harbhajan turned up at the truck too and was so surprised to learn that I had been to Nairobi and back. He kept looking at me very sheepishly, not knowing what I was going to say next. Later, he told me that he thought it was best to let me reveal all, if I wanted to, in my own time.

'Well, I'll tell you this old chum, I don't know if I'm fired or not. We will have to wait and see.'

'Of course you're not fired. They may demote you a couple of grades or even fine you a month's salary, but they will not fire you, Roy,' he tried to console me. 'As a matter of fact, as you asked, I collected the mail and messages from the DTS's Office and there is an urgent message from the Chief Engineers Office, Nairobi. It's addressed to Wonk and it's sealed and I bet it's about your 'little lot'!'

At camp, I didn't tell Wonk that I had been to Nairobi at first. He barely said *Jambo*; no questions, not a word. I thought I'd wait until later. Harbhajan asked the cook to rustle up something to eat. A couple of hours went by and I felt relaxed and found myself laughing heartily; for the first time in that camp, I felt comparatively happy. We had finished eating and talking about where the survey started tomorrow and I had just said that it didn't look as if there was anything in the mail concerning me, when old Wonk sent his cook to my tent to ask if I would go along and see him.

'Griffiths, I have a message here from the Chief Engineer which says you are to go on the construction of this line, back at Mikumi. They have a construction type house for you and the resident engineer has been notified of your imminent arrival.'

It was only then that the questions flowed pretty freely from Wonk but he more or less implied that it was a wonder that I hadn't been shot. Harbhajan and my two Kikuyu surveyors hugged me when I told them what had happened. Only then did I realise what friends I had and hadn't appreciated it before.

I helped out at Wonk's base camp for a few days and then departed for Iringa to collect my family and go on to my new posting. Before I leave Iringa, I must tell you one more small story of that period. We were very fond of chicken in my family, cooked one way or another. Whenever we had chicken during the weekends that I was home in Iringa I always noticed that Gay slid out the back door to make sure that Charlie was still around. It's a good job that she didn't do so on the last day that we were there. I feel bad now if I think about it too much.

We loved Mikumi from the very first moment we arrived there. It was about a hundred and some miles up-line from Dar-es-Salaam. Mikumi was the station at that time from which the new line branched off to Zambia, or would be when the line was built. There were two construction camps about three miles from Mikumi and these were about two miles apart. One camp was known as the Railways and accommodated the office of the resident engineer, railway staff and their families. The other was for the Italian construction contractors with their stores, staff and families, who had won the contract for building the line as far as Kidatu.

The house that had been allocated to us was built of timber and corrugated iron sections and we found it quite acceptable. The loo was a tin hut built away from the house because it was only a drop-pit but as long as you made plenty of noise as you went over there, most things would crawl away. I usually would go over there first and take a look around and then give the all-clear for the girls to use the place. Gay didn't think that this procedure was really necessary. One snag, however; I couldn't always prevent something from crawling back into the place after it was occupied. The bathroom plumbing consisted of an oil-drum cut in half and laid on its side outside the bathroom. Under this, the cook would light a fire; thus we had hot water. A pipe passed through the wall from the drum to the bath, the flow being controlled by a tap. 'Wallah', a hot bath! The bath water appeared far dirtier before we started than a coal miner's after he had been down the pit. However, putting lashings of Dettol in the water first seemed to kill most things. We even had a generator in the camp which was operated by our very competent Seychelles mechanic. This gave us light every night from seven o'clock until ten o'clock; eleven o'clock on Saturdays. We had a paraffin operated fridge and a wood-fired cooking stove. What more could we want?

Entertainment was performed every evening by a family of monkeys sliding noisily down our tin roof. Nearly every night we were visited by hyena which would whoop it up outside our shack and it was not a rare occasion to hear lions roar only paces from the house. Nobody wanted to use the outside loo after dark. Cowards!

The resident engineer and his lovely wife were quite young people and were indeed very pleasant folk to boot.

They had a young son too, so mother and son turned out luxurious company for Molly and the girls; they got on very well together which was essential if life was to continue happily under these sort of circumstances. Morogoro was the nearest main town and was in the direction of Dar-es-Salaam. Although very small we could get many of our essentials there. We usually took it in turns to drive there to get everybody's shopping. It was a good arrangement. About once a month each of us would try and get down to Dar-es-Salaam; this was always a welcome break and a good outing. When it was our turn, we always made for the ice cream palour as soon as we arrived, before even booking into the hotel. Gay said that when she got married, she hoped her husband loved ice cream as much as Daddy!

Thirty miles or so up the new line was Kilumbero. This place was primarily a sugar plantation together with its own refinery. It was run by the Dutch so, therefore, it had an air of productivity and efficiency about it.

It didn't take long to get into the swing of things, both at work and with fitting into the community. The first Saturday after our arrival the RE gave a Welcome To Mikumi party which we thought was very friendly and great fun. Circumstances certainly turned a little better for us now. The song that was a great favourite that night was 'Yellow Bird'; do you remember that one? It went down well with the moonlight and surroundings. When the party was going great guns one of the members of staff wanted to have a word in my ear. By this time I was laughing and dancing like a coastal tribesman. 'Yes, yes, go on, what do you want to tell me!'

'You know Roy, we expected you here ages ago actually. We were told that we had a new surveyor coming here from America and that he was bringing four children with him. It was all right because he was 'an old timer.' I had to go to Morogoro and buy some more mosquito nets and things, post-haste! What in the hell happened to you?'

Would you honestly believe it?

There were lots of activities going on for at least half the evenings of the week. Every Wednesday night there was a film show at the contractors' camp (there being no TV of course) and us railway people were always invited along. When we arrived we were always made very welcome with a smile, refreshments and a friendly chat. There was always the news from Italy and Britain. Happy hours. Sunday was the only day we had off and that was mostly spent at the sugar plantation. They had a swimming pool, cool beer and they always gave a luscious Indonesian style Sunday lunch. This may have been because most of the Dutch there had been to Java or nearby. Some had even been prisoners of war of the Japanese – even some of the ladies. The Dutch had a reputation for being able to make anything grow.

The girls absolutely loved it here; every moment of life was fun to them. They still had to do their schooling however. Molly took them every morning for English, history, reading and general knowledge. I took them in the late afternoon for maths and physical training. Between various missionary friends and ourselves, their religious tuition didn't get overlooked either. We always prayed together every night as we did for many years to come. Regardless of the range of years between our ages, we always made PT a fun time, even though we usually worked hard – well at least I had to! This consisted of about five minutes of twists and turns followed by a mile and a half of jogging and walking. Jennifer would watch a lot of this from her playpen, making loud gurgling noises, pulling face distortions and shaking the living daylights out of the sides of her playpen. Mummy would often be restraining me by reminding me not to treat the girls like a squadron of sappers. One day, when we were jogging through a new railway cutting, we had to do a very smart about-turn because as we came round the curve we came face to face with a herd of elephants.

The only person who was getting any trouble, health-wise, was myself. I had a tropical infection in both ears, right down to the eardrums. This was painful and turned out to be a nuisance. I learnt, very quickly, the trouble Mr Thompson must have had at Sultan Hamud. Let me illustrate. On this occasion the RE was a little anxious about the size of a certain culvert he had to put in. He asked me if I'd go out and do a survey of the area that had to be drained off and passed through this culvert. The area turned out to be about a mile across and about two and a half miles away from the track. While I was performing a compass traverse along the top of a ridge I required more bush to be cut. On issuing instructions so to do I suddenly realised that I was talking to myself. There wasn't one of my chaps to be seen. Where in the blazes had they all gone? What on earth were they doing? This was most unlike this particular bunch of chaps. I moved to the right in search for them when, my God, right in front of me was a lion. He looked at me straight in the eye. Although very scraggy, I thought he had a very intelligent face. At that moment I was shocked but not a bit frightened – honestly. I just felt that I wanted to have a good look at him. He was about ten paces from me and now I started to feel very frightened as it dawned on me what was happening. I started to freeze to the spot I was standing on. It was only seconds, I suppose, that we were looking at each other. My sense of smell had only returned to me a couple of weeks before so I became very aware of a strong horse stable sort of smell and now and again I got a whiff of his disgusting breath. About twenty seconds must have passed by now and for the first time, I started to think, 'God, what do I do now? No wonder I can't find any of my chainmen! I bet they shouted at me but I wouldn't hear them because of the medication in my ears.'

The lion made the first move by letting out a sort of belch-cum-growl and then doing a half jack-knife backwards. He ran for about twenty feet and then retired to a slow stroll, away from me. He then let out one colossal ROAR! The bottom of my toes were sore through gripping the soles of my shoes. In spite of my tan I noticed that my fingers were white. I had experienced what must have been deep fear for the first time in my life. Water came into my mouth again and I could feel my blood start to circulate around my body as at about fifty paces away he disappeared into the bush. I started to make my first movement backwards. I started to turn to make a quicker retreat and just as I did so he shot back into view again, half skidding as he came to a halt at only about thirty paces away. He just as suddenly turned away again and disappeared into the bush. I'm sure I did better than the four minute mile back to my Land Rover and when I got there, there were my six chainmen locked in the vehicle! They said that they had shouted at me as soon as they saw the lion but, they had to run. Because of my ailment I had not heard them. Shows you how loud that lion must have roared! Back in the camp nobody was particularly interested in my story.

About the same distance from the station to our camp but in the opposite direction were a couple of tents known as Mikumi Game Camp. I believe there is a hotel there today. Well anyway, in our day we used to spend many a pleasant evening down there. Somehow, the men running the place always managed to put on a good meal, all things considering. Oddly enough, the prices were very reasonable too. As soon as it was sundown, they used to have to light a large wood-fire to keep the lions away. As we drank and ate, we could see them lying down, in the firelight, casting all their attentions in our direction. Sometimes they would get awfully noisy and even make angry thrusts towards us but we would disturb their 'war-dance' by throwing some firework bangers at them. When driving back to our camp, at about midnight, they would be really ready and waiting for us. We were often forced to stop and we had to toot them out of the way. It was no time to get a puncture or for your engine to catch fire!

I can remember one day when a bunch of our young engineers decided to go down to the Game Camp for a Sunday lunchtime drink. They enjoyed their well earned Tusker (or six) and were now in a very happy and relaxed mood. Be that as it may, they realised it was time to get back 'home' and try and retrieve as much of their Sunday lunch as they could. They were driving an open Land Rover with two of them in the front and two of them sitting in the back. Young Alton and Mike were the back seat occupants. Just as they were negotiating a very rough part of the road, a lion started to make a chase and, it didn't take very long to reach them. No matter how much speed the Rover picked up, the lion was always just a few paces behind. Can you picture it? The two backseat-riders were being bounced and thrown all over the place as they tried to grip the floor with their finger-nails. Yet, all the time their eyes were fixed on their attacking marauder. Can you imagine for one second being in their position? For a brief moment, when the breath wasn't being knocked out of him, Alton yelled out, 'For God's sake put your foot down and get a move on! We are about to be eaten alive here!' The gentleman driving the 'doomed vehicle' answered, 'Stop shouting at me, I've got to watch these springs, we haven't got a replacement and I doubt if we could get any for ages.'

They got away with it but it was very touch and go there for a while. It has just occurred to me that the typewriter I am using at this time, was the one I bought in Dar-es-Salaam that very same weekend!

Months went by, months of staking-out centre-line of railway track, staking-out top and bottom of cuttings and embankments, staking-out of fences and turn-outs, computing quantities, being petrified by lions, computing curves to the left, curves to the right, sweating, film shows, parties and Molly and the girls were managing very well indeed. It was during this time that I got the sad news that my dear mother had passed on. She had died and was cremated by the time the news had filtered through to me. Another price to pay. This was something that you had hoped would never happen. I shared my secret with the elephants and I am sure that they understood my deep sorrow.

One day I received another message, only this time it was a happy one. I was to return to Nairobi within these next couple of weeks to help to carry out the chief surveyor's duties, whilst he himself went home to the UK on leave for a period of six months. Molly and the girls were equally as happy to hear the news. This also meant that the girls would be able to get a spell of 'formal education'; the thought of this didn't seem to bother them at all. After surviving the farewell party and saying all our farewells to the good people at the Contractors Camp, the Kilumbero Sugar Refinery and the Game Camp, we drove off to Nairobi. We stopped at Moshi for the night en-route, allowing us to arrive at Nairobi at a respectable time in the evening of the next day.

We stayed at the Queens Hotel for the customary ten days, during which time we were able to get schools, accommodation, electricity, water and sundries sorted out. The three oldest girls were in at St George's School and to see them walking down the road in their school uniforms made them the pride of my life. One of Gay's schoolmates was Elizabeth Kenyatta, a lovely kiddy and, my goodness, how like her father she looked!

The railways put us into a very attractive flat overlooking Nairobi; we were all pleased with it. Anyway, with the kind of places we had had to live in during our past service, we were easy to please. Our neighbours were all tip-top folk. There was a middle aged couple in the apartment below us. He was English and was employed by the railways as a stores superintendent. His lovely wife was of Spanish origin. She absolutely adored Jennifer and had the peculiar habit of biting her every time she saw her – I used to wait for the yell of agony! She was such a good-hearted lady and always seemed ready for a laugh. She would always seem to appear at Jennifer's lunch-time and would love to feed and chat to her. The first words that Jennifer ever spoke were strongly flavoured with a Spanish/Swahili accent! This was the time when Jennifer was struggling with her first words. For days she had kept on saying 'Fa-Fa'. 'What is it, darling? What is it that you are trying to say?' we all asked. There were times when Jennifer was nearly blue in the face with exasperation as she repeated 'Fa-Fa' over and over again. I cannot recall which one of us was clever enough to identify the meaning of this strange word. The little cherub was trying to say 'Jennifer' and to this day the nickname 'Fa-Fa' has stuck.

To me, Molly seemed more at home in Nairobi than in any other city of the world. I believe she loved Africa and its people in spite of the hardships and diseases she had to suffer. All the Africans that she was associated with, men and women, those that worked in her various offices as well as her own domestic staff, clearly demonstrated what could only be called an affection towards her. Apart from opposing some of my perhaps scatter-brained ideas, Molly never belly-ached. As years went on I learned that she always found me overpowering and very strong-minded; she was even a little frightened of me. Often, when we were larking or horsing around, I received a wallop from her which soon made me toe the line and it wasn't very apparent then that she was frightened of me, But there, I guess that was different. The door to her innermost thoughts and feelings was very rarely open to me. Nevertheless, I did believe she loved Africa – and I believed she loved me too!

Because of my job I still had to go away on short safaris for field inspections from time to time. But even so, I was mostly in Nairobi and our lives were very happy. When not working or at school, most of our time we were either at one of the two drive-in cinemas, visiting old and new friends, having folks visit us for a meal or going to very happy meetings at our church.

Whilst working in Tanzania, I was walking down a steep slope which was covered in high elephant grass. I could hardly see where I was going. I had a heavy tripod on my shoulders and I was walking down the slope almost sideways letting my downhill foot hit the ground rather heavily, as one does on that sort of terrain. I didn't see the 'pig-hole'. Down I went and it didn't half shake me up! I limped for a year after that. Every time I went for a good walk or played badminton, my ankle would swell up and become very painful. So, whilst I was stationed in Nairobi I thought I'd get the ankle looked at. I was admitted to Nairobi Hospital that day and they operated on my foot the next morning. How dramatic! Apparently, I had broken open the 'ball and socket' joint and subsequently, the 'cement' had slowly leaked out and formed 'knuckles' around the perimeter of the socket. This in turn was making me rather club-footed. Well, the surgeon knocked off these knuckles and put a zip down the front of my foot. I had only a few days off of work but it took a very long time to heal. The posting in Nairobi lasted another four months, so that helped me immensely.

The chief surveyor came back from UK leave which meant that I had to move on to where I was needed most. This was Jinja, Uganda. The EAR & H were building what was known as wagon ferry terminals at various positions around Lake Victoria. Jinja was one of them. Basically, the ferries and the terminals were designed to allow whole trains to be driven onto them. In turn they would be transported across water from one terminal to another. The purpose of this was to cut out hundreds of miles of travelling by rail to reach the same points. They were extremely interesting things to build and required very careful setting-out. Another interesting and pleasant thing about this posting was that the RE from Mikumi had now been posted to the job as 'RE Jinja.' He was quite a hard task-master but he was very professional and a pleasure to work with.

We soon had our gear packed and were off. We stayed for ten days in the Falls Hotel in Jinja and without losing very much time I got stuck into my job and Molly got the girls into school. She also got our accommodation sorted out. She was able to get the girls into the Victoria Nile School which the girls settled into in about ten days flat. It turned out to be a very good school so we were all lucky. Jinja is a very interesting place really. It is one of the main camps of the Uganda Army. It has a very impressive dam which holds back the whole of Lake Victoria. And there is a very productive and successful cotton mill. The mill is run by the English and in fact, they have quite a number of English people living there. Over the years Molly had developed a 'nose' for finding accommodation and it didn't take her long to find out where these English lived and that not all their flats were occupied. The management of the mill very kindly let the railway rent one of these flats; that was ours. Again, this kind company allowed us to use the other facilities that their staff enjoyed: club, swimming pool, etc. When using their club on film-show evenings we were always confronted with the problem of hippo coming between us and our cars.

We met a lot of good people who worked for the Jinja cotton mills and we became warm friends. Thinking of these dear people brings a story immediately to mind. In the middle of one night we heard and felt an awful rumble. It was an earthquake. Molly, in a state of absolute terror, ran to get two of the girls from one bedroom and I ran to get the other two from another bedroom. Then we tried to congregate back in the main bedroom. I got there all right with Gay and Joy but whilst Molly and the other two were coming towards me there was one almighty shudder. Gay and Joy clung to my legs and screamed for their mother. As hard as we tried, Molly and I couldn't get to each other. The thought did flash through my mind that this was it. Molly and I were not taking our eyes off of each other and I wondered, until this day, if I had as much fear showing on my face as she did. I can remember I tried to smile whilst those tremors were happening but I felt so inadequate and feeble. I was desperate to have them all around me where I could hold them tight and perhaps they could at least find comfort in the strength of my arms. I loved them all so much and this, I found, were the terms of reference used when death seems pretty obvious. Down went the lamp-post outside our flat – crash! Our hands were just about to reach and grasp each others when there was sudden silence – an absolute deafening silence. . . It was over. . . The house-lights came back on. It seemed ages before any of us moved or even said a word. I think, in fact, we were waiting for the final collapse. Again, a thought went through my mind: 'Did anything happen, or was all this just a horrible nightmare?' The girls stared at me, searching for my reaction, for this maybe would tell them what would happen next.

Next morning I was eager to share news and experiences with others, but the only mild interest they showed was by saying, 'Oh' Was there a quake last night? We often get them!' Be that as it may, a whole village between Jinja and Entebbe was swallowed up that night.

Lake Victoria has a beauty and interest which is quite unique. Whilst we were there we seemed to have thunderstorms every other afternoon. On one such afternoon I had to walk along the shore of the Lake to put in a survey control point. I climbed onto a large boulder to gain an advantage. The sky was full of dark grey and black clashing masses; it was a spectacular sight. There came a sudden and strong breeze causing ripples to cascade along the shore, It was only four o'clock in the afternoon but yet it was getting darker and darker. A blinding flash of lightning was followed almost immediately by an almighty crash of thunder, Still no rain yet. As I surveyed this tumultuous upheaval, that great Salvation Army song went through my mind: 'How Great Thou Art.' I've never seen such an effect, not even at sea. The memorial to John Hanning Speke (1827–64) looked on.

We had another small problem at Jinja, the shallow waters, often not much more than puddles, which were infested with, schistosomiasis. As a result, you dare not let your feet be exposed to the water for fear of infection. Apparently, the situation was made more critical by infected persons urinating in local waters. I have known several people who had got infected and became very ill before the fault was diagnosed as bilharzia and the cure took a long time.

We had a lot of trips into Kampala, which was a lovely little city, to get our bulk provisions. The Uganda Army was a little menacing at times, we thought; they liked to search women, especially white women. It seemed clear to me (1965/66) that trouble was brewing. Never mind, you could still get a good meal in Kampala and purchase most things you required from the shops. As we motored along the road from Jinja to Kampala we could see that the tea, coffee, sugar and sisal fields were all looking healthy indeed. I often feel that these developing East African countries would have had a more impressive economic picture if they hadn't been clobbered so heavily by the high oil prices that the Arabs imposed on the world. Unfortunately, this happened at about the same time as all these countries became independent and could have done without this price hike, Hardly fair.

For the last few months of this posting life was quite interesting and happy, The girls were doing well at school and Molly always seemed to have plenty to keep her happily busy. We would often meet at the swimming club at lunchtime for a bite to eat and a swim. The job was reasonably interesting and was going well. We were a hard working bunch of guys but had lots of parties at each other's houses. We would always meet at the twice weekly film shows as well as at other visits to the club. Molly and I would often go out and around Jinja, on our bikes, in the cool of the evening; we really used to enjoy that. Then, as I said, there were always the trips to Kampala and Entebbe. The girls were so entertaining too and they always enjoyed going for walks or a ride on their bikes with me. And there were their dollies with their cases of malaria and bilharzia!

During the last couple of weeks, I had a tropical infection in my 'rear part' and for a while it was thought that I could have something else. We did have a surgeon in Jinja and he was an African of huge build. He looked an awful lot like Amin actually; they could have been brothers! Anyway, he said I looked the picture of good health but he would like to take a more detailed look at me but this could only be done at the operating theatre. He said that he would see me there tomorrow at about ten o'clock. You should have seen the Op. Room! It wasn't much more than just a shed at the back of the hospital somewhere. To get there, you had to pass a dead looking tree with hundreds of bats living in it. When I got to 'the shed', I watched birds flying in one window and out the other. I was approached by a male African nurse who was in green and covered in blood. He asked if he could help me. I told him who I was and that I was to meet the surgeon here, He shouted out, 'Doctor, Mr Griffiths is here and he said that you wanted to see him.'

A reply came from within 'the shed'. 'Hello Mr Griffiths. I am just finishing an amputation and I won't be long. Wait for me and the nurse will show you a seat.'

I was horrified. There was a second half to this shed and the nurse asked me to follow him into it. The nurse pointed to a chair in this dark cool room and then asked to be excused. My eyes very quickly became accustomed to the dim light and there, lying on a bench, next to me, was a dead Asian gentleman. He had a smock loosely draped over him and a label was tied to his big toe. He was very clearly staring straight at me. His face was full of shock and fear. His hands were an unforgettable yellow in colour. This, together with what I thought I had wrong with me, put me in a proper state, I can tell you!

In burst the surgeon, fully dressed in green including a green cap, but he had pulled down his mask. He wasn't covered in blood so I could only presume he had been wearing a rubber apron and he had taken it off.

'Good morning Griffiths. Get on the bench over there and I just want to take a look at you. It won't take long but I have to use this instrument.'

The 'other gentleman' was still staring at me, even though I had changed my position! As it turned out, I had no more than what was first diagnosed – a tropical infection.

A few months later, knowing that my tour was near its end, we started thinking on the lines that we would like to take in Canada again. Molly's family lived there now, so this should make moving a lot easier for us; for a change. I took a chance and wrote to my old employers, the St Lawrence Seaway Authority, because I had read in one of the engineering journals that the Seaway had another big project coming up. They replied and said that after I had been through the normal immigration procedure etc., I could call in and see them. We wrote to the Canadian Immigration Service in London to get things started.

We decided that Molly and the girls would go home to UK by sea and I would go by air. There was such a lot for me to do. The plan was that I should go to England by air, stay with my Dad for a couple of days, deal with the Canadian Immigration, fly to Canada, get a job and then find a home. When Molly arrived in England, she would go and see my Dad and then fly to her parents in Toronto, In theory, I should just about have everything organised by then.

I got Molly and the girls on the train at Jinja and Harbhajan Singh met them at Mombasa and put them on the *SS Uganda*. The day that Molly got on the train at Jinja I caught the flight from Entebbe to London. Molly would be at sea for the best part of three weeks and it would be about five weeks before I would see her again. Could I live that long without her?

7

Home for a Spell

My late father was a War Department policeman and was stationed at the MRE, which of course was at Porton Down in Wiltshire. I arrived at his house but it was locked. As I turned around I could see him coming up the road in his police uniform, carrying his raincoat over his arm. He looked a lot older. He was still a fair way down the road and I don't know why, but my mind went back to 1939.

Before war began he was stationed at Frome Road Barracks, Trowbridge. He was an artillery sergeant-major and often, as I went to school, I could hear his voice on the parade ground which was over a high wall. My school was also in Frome Road. Soon after war was declared, his field artillery regiment was sent over to France. As I stood outside his front gate and he was drawing nearer I could remember going down to Trowbridge Station with my mother. As each train load of soldiers from Dunkerque stopped at the station, I would walk the length of the train, if I could, asking the men if anybody knew or had seen Sergeant-Major Griffiths? I was twelve years old then. Two men knew him but hadn't seen him since they were firing at the Germans with their guns at Lille. That was about two weeks before. I remembered his face vividly when I woke up from my sleep about two days later and found that he had arrived home during the previous night. I first saw his uniform jacket on the back of the chair; three-quarters of the left sleeve was missing; on the dining table was some loose change and a .38 service revolver.

He had almost reached the gate and I stepped forward to meet him. We heartily shook hands and I said, 'Hello Dad,' and he replied 'Hello boy, you're looking fit.' He had such a beautiful Welsh accent. It was lovely seeing him again but once we got inside it turned very emotional because we didn't have Mother any more and her absence was very deeply felt.

After being home for a day or two and tea was running out of my ears, I went up to the Canadian Immigration Office in London.

'Where is your family? We can't give you the all-clear until we have seen them. They must have a medical too, especially because of where you have been!'

I couldn't believe my ears! I would not see them for nearly three more weeks yet. The Canadians were polite but remained very sorry. What on earth did I do now?

This was early summer 1966. Although I had been home only a couple of days, I had noticed some incredible things going on. Britain was alive and kicking. We were about to build a tunnel under the English Channel. We were going to have a third London Airport at Maplin Sands. We had got new motorways and were building more, all over the place. There was construction going on at every corner you turned. And, you could get hamburgers (just like America) at Wimpys, which had a branch in nearly every town in the country. I thought things were looking good – really good. TV programmes had improved immensely, and in the afternoons on the radio we had an excellent young man named Terry Wogan.

Well, to pass the time away as much as anything, I thought I'd look around and see what the employment situation was like. Through the press and contacts, I had eight interviews and subsequently I got the eight jobs! Mind you, this had its embarrassing moments. Three of the companies I had an interview with were called Westminster Dredging, Land & Marine and James Shipping & Contracting and they were scattered far and wide. However, they all belonged to the same parent company – Boss & Kalis of

Holland. One day, whilst I was out, one of the directors came to my father's house and said to him, 'Would you be kind enough to ask your son which one of the companies does he eventually intend working for?' I was subsequently very embarrassed when I met this man at Southampton.

There was a bit of a problem when the time came to meet Molly because the dockers were on strike. However, I was able to meet them on the Tilbury landing stage after panic inquiries. I could see the shock on their faces when they saw me standing on the pontoon. I drove them down to Salisbury for we were staying with my father and they too were both so pleased to see each other. While driving I had to tell Molly, in a little more detail, why I was in England and not Canada. She described the shock she had. I very slowly talked about how things had changed so much back home now. Then I got onto the subject of employment opportunities. And then, how lucky I had been because I only had to accept the job of hydrographic surveyor in what was probably one of the biggest dredging fleets in the world. What that poor girl had to absorb in the few hours since she arrived! Of course, she had already worked out her plans for Canada. No doubt at all that she had been looking forward to seeing her family again. Then there was the problem of where were we going to live if we stayed in England. Accommodation had never been so easy to obtain here as in some parts of the world. What would be the best for the children? What, in the long run, would be the best for us? The item that had come forward over these past months and now required our utmost consideration – and it had to come sooner or later – was the girls' education. They should not have to suffer because of their father's nomadic existence. Did we ever intend to go back to East Africa again? The next day, Molly revealed her feelings which appeared to be in sympathy with mine. As regards the job she said, 'Go for it!'

The dredging company, not surprisingly, was at Southampton so it wasn't too difficult for me to commute from Porton every day for the time being. It would only be for a couple of weeks, at most. Naturally, I was keen to learn where the company intended to send me and wanted to be on my way as soon as possible. God, I'm an impatient man! Gravesend! That was where it was to be and that suited us fine. It was only a few weeks more before we were in our own rented house in Longfield, near Dartford. We had got Gay into Gravesend Grammar School For Girls and the next two into Longfield Primary. The penny had dropped; I knew the time had come to stop travelling around for the next six or seven years and give the girls a chance of a good education. The first three girls all went through Gravesend Grammar and did very well. I didn't really enjoy my years in Longfield but it sure gave me ample reward as far as the girls were concerned, if you know what I mean. Mind you, for a great deal of the time my work was interesting enough but I missed the foreign smells, sounds, sights and new horizons.

My work incorporated a sea environment and consisted of performing hydrographic surveys for mostly dredging activities. There was also the 'sweeping' of channels to prove that the seabed was deep and safe enough for shipping to use. The work involved the use of the latest equipment and techniques. There was some land survey involved too on the land reclamation jobs; land being reclaimed by pumping sand and water ashore and then draining off the water. A lot of this meant working with clients, or their representatives to calculate and agree upon the amount of work done – for payment. Work took my section to the Thames and Clyde areas as well as up and down the East Coast mainly. We did a lot of 'remedial works' on the North Sea oil and gas pipelines too and this required us to find the pipeline, examine the adjacent seabed for scouring and then 'burying' the pipeline with hopper loads of gravel. We did the same treatment for the legs of rigs too.

As well as carrying out the duties of a hydrographic surveyor, I was expected to train young men to perform some parts of these duties. This task brought the usual amounts of laughs and mischievousness that you expect when you get a bunch of young men together. It also meant that I had to tolerate their bad moods and frustrations and often their unwillingness to bend to professional discipline – and I don't mean the 'Yes Sir, No Sir' type of discipline either! Generally speaking, they were a good bunch of chaps and worked hard when called upon to put their shoulders to the wheel. I quickly adapted myself to the system where I had to be careful how I administered my authority and presented my orders in case of complaint to the management, or even union activity; let alone a biff in my ear! I feel I managed all right because there were plenty of signs I could pick up when I attended management meetings, office parties or when having a pint in the pier pub with the men. It was all a far cry from being chased by some buffalo in some obscure place in the Kenya bush. Often I would feel like throwing my towel in when staff were being a bit bolshie or after worrying in the middle of the night if the dredgers were dredging in the right place and to the correct depth or when management told me that they couldn't understand how I computed such a low quantity in my interim report or if, when I got home, the girls had declared war on me for some incomprehensible reason. Fortunately, the family cat Smokey, was always friendly – until I tried to get him indoors at night. I'm sure we all suffer these things! A lot of my young men have moved up the ladder over the years into responsible and in some cases, high-ranking jobs. Most of them keep in touch with me until this very day.

I had to spend a lot of time away from home, surveying. This gave me the time to think about taking a further professional interest and that was when I was elected to full membership of the Guild of Surveyors. A year later I was elected secretary of the London and Home Counties branch. Another year later I was again elected to be chairman of that branch. I enjoyed this extra work and my employers liked me doing it too and they helped me in many ways. One significant thing came out of all this. It was whilst I was chairman that my friend and colleague, a senior hydrographic surveyor, paid me a visit. When we were having a drop of lunch in Gravesend, we both expounded our feelings on the training facilities, or the lack of them, for young up-and-coming hydrographic surveyors. When I was a young man it seemed to me that the only way I could get good and valued training as a land surveyor was to join the Army; more specifically the Royal Engineers. The same thing applied to hydrographic surveyors, except you had to join the Royal Navy. We didn't think that a good feasible idea today. During the next few days and after this 'meeting', I sounded out some of the senior surveyors across the country to find out what they thought. At the next General Council Meeting of the Guild of Surveyors at Kings Cross Station, London, I brought this subject of training for hydrographic surveyors to the attention of the Council in 'any other business'.

The Council of the Guild finally agreed that I could call a meeting of some of the most prominent surveyors in the land. The venue was my company's London board room in the City. Those attending were Port Authority surveyors, surveyors in the teaching profession, head surveyors of companies and surveyors representing our national professional institutes. My own president was there and I chaired this first meeting. From this meeting the Hydrographic Society was born. Today, its membership consists of survey personnel from navies all over the world as well as those from commerce, together with hundreds of associated disciplines from within the industry. It is a very special and important forum. It covers a much wider field than ever Peter Gadsden or myself ever thought possible when we had that drop of lunch in Gravesend. May the Hydrographic Society continue to grow and its members benefit from its so doing.

The years between 1966 and 1973 went very quickly for me and yet I was never completely happy. Life in England seemed so very much more complex than my life abroad. Is this a good enough reason for feeling so unhappy? Why? It's hard to put my finger on it. It's a consequence of a lot of little factors, all complex. Of course I had to stop roaming for a while and that was one factor. Another was that, like a lot of other people, I and my family had to make do without a lot of things because the equation between cost of living and my income wasn't very well balanced. Accommodation, although very modest, took a much higher percentage of my income than it did when I was living abroad. Yet another factor was that I didn't enjoy having to be so involved, for the first time, with trade union activities: having my electricity cut off; not having my dustbin emptied; having to queue for bread and not getting my mail. I knew in the back of my mind that there must be good reasons for these nuisances but I didn't want them. It seemed that it was the accepted way of life to be suffering with one catastrophe or another. I worked hard and paid my taxes and yet!

To illustrate another factor, I was talking to an American visitor who said to me: 'Do you know what, Roy, I have just been up to Birmingham to see an old great aunt of mine. After seeing her, I got back to the station ten minutes before the train was due. I thought it very odd because there wasn't a soul to be seen on the platform. Something very strange here, I thought. Half an hour went by and there was still nobody around. The station was deserted. All of a sudden, just like a cotton-pickin' ghost, a uniformed man shot out of one side room and continued into another. He looked important because of all that silver stuff around the peak of his cap. I went over to the door he had just entered and banged on it. Out came the uniformed man. "Good morning Sir," he said, "what can I do for you?" For a while I didn't know how to answer that, Roy! Where was the train? I always thought that one could set their watch by the punctuality of you guys! However, at the moment the station was empty, so where was the train? "Sorry Sir, have you not heard that there is a strike on? There won't be any more trains today, I'm afraid." "But we have a contract for you to transport me back to London – and I have completed my side of the contract – I've paid you! You have my money!" "Sorry Sir, but that is the situation." God damn it!

I followed some vague instructions and walked around town, with my suitcase, and found a coach going to London. In the hotel, I told my story to the maître d'. I added onto my story by telling him that on my way to the hotel I saw mountains of black bags of rubbish – up every side street. Looking the maître d' square in the face and shifting my legs to hold a firm and steady stand and putting my head back and to one side I said, "Tell me, aren't you really a bit pissed-off with all this behaviour? God has given you the gift of this lovely country and yet you folk give us visitors the impression that all is not well. What's wrong?" The maître d' raised his eyebrows and gave a quiet gentle cough, tidied some glasses on his tray and then pulled his shoulders back. He put his empty hand smartly down the side of his trousers and then looked me square in the eyes. With an air of grace, dignity and a little boredom, he said, "Never mind Sir, summer will soon be here!"

Another factor that I was constantly aware of these days, was that executives were looking younger and younger!

Crying in the wilderness wasn't getting me anywhere, so I gave up my job, together with its pension and started my own survey consultancy; Griffiths Land & Hydrographic Surveys. It was 1973 and my troubles and sleepless nights had only just begun.

I have always loved Bath. Who hasn't? As a boy, when I lived in Trowbridge, it was a mere eleven miles away and made it possible for my buddies and me to cycle there and back hundreds of times. I can strongly recollect going down Limpley Stoke Hill with little or no brakes. It's amazing, when you are at that age, broken arms or legs or even death itself, is as far away as the moon. I always think that Bath has a lot of class and style and as do its citizens. As a young Royal Engineer I used to visit Bath quite often because it wasn't far from my unit, the School of Military Survey, Longleat. I used to wonder if there was such a thing as an ugly girl in that city.

The morning that Molly, Jennifer and I were in Bath was a typical February morning; cold but sunny. Bath looked a picture from Warminster Road hill; I wished I could have stayed there for another month. We walked into the city and had coffee in the Pump Room and listened to a lovely trio on piano and strings. Oh, lovely Bath. After a walk around the excellent shops we walked back to our B&B to collect our car. We then drove as far as Melksham and pulled over into a side parking place to get some Bath buns out of the back of the car. We were hungry because we hadn't eaten for the last three hours. Now, I can't remember which one said it but one of us said, 'Wouldn't it be lovely to live here!'

That statement started something I can tell you! I was brought up and schooled in this area and I can't ever recall thinking about whether this was a beautiful area. When I took another purposeful look at it, I had to admit, yes it was a beautiful spot. Mind you the sun was shining and nearly everywhere looks nice in the sunshine! No, it wasn't only the sunshine; I was convinced it was a lovely place.

Now there was another big event coming up in our lives; we were going to move to Wiltshire! Actually, as a surveyor, it doesn't matter where I live, I still have to travel around to do my work. Not so my family! So, why not live in a place that you and your family find most attractive? In my case, I felt extremely lucky to be moving back to the lovely countryside of my early years and to know that this was the choice of my family and not mine alone.

In the days that followed our trip we were swamped with pamphlets on houses for sale. Every morning Jennifer would go downstairs as soon as the postman had called and bring the letters up to my bedroom. We would have a look to see what houses were on the market. Jennifer would then take all the pamphlets into Wendy's room for studying. One house in particular suddenly interested Wendy. So attractive was this possibility that it prompted her to get out of bed and jump into mine for a 'conference'. 'Look Daddy, it has a peach-house, a stable, a conservatory with productive vines, two garages with adjacent Parking Area and nearly an acre of ornamental gardens! The thought of it already made my back ache! All right darling, we'll put it on the pile with the rest of the possibilities and we'll go and have a look at it this weekend. We looked at Inmarsh House and we didn't need to look any further.

We moved into Inmarsh House on 28 August, 1975 and the big black grapes were waiting for us. Smokey, our cat, took to the house straight away but he never did figure out what the cows were that looked over the garden wall at him. I enjoyed the apples, Victoria plums, greengages and soft fruit, all products from the well-established garden. I noted that we even had edelweiss growing near one of the greenhouses! On the opposite side of Inmarsh Lane we had seven large oak trees which must have been hundreds of years old. Which reminds me, the house itself was over three hundred years old – it was built (or part of it was) about the time Columbus discovered America. It was at the bottom of the hill . . . therefore an overcoat warmer . . . and Seend Village ran along the top of it. The house was surrounded with park-like grounds with horses, cows and wood pigeons. When the hunt was on the fox used to hide in my stable which I found acceptable – and he got away with it. There were 400 roses of different kinds in the garden and one day, when I was returning from duty in the North Sea, I could smell the garden a good half mile away.

Work was pouring in and keeping my four survey teams and myself busy. We not only stretched ourselves from the North of Scotland down to the South Coast, but we incorporated Ireland, Pakistan, West Africa, Tahiti and the Arab countries. The stables were soon converted into offices under the watchful eye of Gay. The fox would have to find another bunker when the hunt was on.

8

The North Sea World

This is really a continuation of the last chapter but I think that my life in the North Sea was so different to my general pattern of living that it warrants being put in a compartment on its own. At this time may I offer my most sincere apologies to all my professional seamen readers.

An amusing thing happened one day in 1972 when I was working for Westminster Dredging; my vessel was a Dutch salvage vessel. We were not alongside the rig at the time but hove-to very close to it. On top of the platform of the rig several welders were working. Suddenly, the adjacent surface of the sea was ablaze! Can you imagine what it looked like? The skipper gave a string of orders – in Dutch – and two deckhands climbed up to the water cannon (fire hydrant) on the starboard side and the chief ran down below. The chief quickly reappeared and joined them at the cannon. The skipper was well fitted into the shoulder-harness of the cannon and was leaning into it with his legs apart, preparing himself for the terrific pressure which I presumed this cannon would have to cope with. The two deckhands had their hands on the cannon barrel to help steady it and the whole atmosphere was electrifying. I could do nothing except stand there look and feeling pretty useless. I wasn't even too sure what was hoped to be achieved with a water cannon in this situation! However, I just watched with intense interest and in case there were any orders. Up until now, only a small trickle of water came out of the end of the cannon but the crew were certainly ready for action. All of a sudden the young cook came out from somewhere shouting at the top of his voice, 'Stop! Stop! Stop! You're sinking the boat!' The engine room was filling up with water. The chief shot down below; he had apparently opened or closed the wrong stop-cocks! Up on the rig platform, a man casually walked out onto the catwalk and looked below and without appearing to think much about it he pulled what looked like a lavatory chain which released what I thought was a powdery substance – the flames went out almost immediately. The chief was kept busy for hours afterwards.

Each time I did a stint in the North Sea it usually lasted about three weeks at a time. I have never been sure whether that time passed quickly or not. I do know this, however; each time I went out I would have to write off those three weeks of my life. You and everybody else worked all the hours that God sent. Certainly on a survey vessel you worked until you collapsed and then often you had to go on some more. There weren't any spare bods out there. There was little time for a chat so you rarely got to know anybody. Every time you went near a lay-barge or a rig, there was always the feeling that your hours were numbered. There were many ways you could die and on-board food comes to mind! Sometimes the food would be good but more times than not, it left a lot to be desired. I found it very easy to lose weight during my stints. Often your meals would be continental and I could never get on with a Dutch breakfast. You didn't think of your wife and family as often as you would have liked but that was only because you were so busy and often very worried about the job. The projects were so big and yet almost any one man could bring the job to a grinding halt if he made a mistake – then he would be in for it. In 1975 all surveyors seemed, strangely, Englishmen. Other than us, every rig I went on I would find Americans, Canadians, French, Dutch, Italians, Welsh (riggers from the old dockyards) etc. I personally never met a Scotsman although I'm sure they must have been around.

Another thing I must tell you is that I found that after only a week at sea I started humming the tune, 'There ain't nothing like a dame.' I became very aware that this item was completely absent. When I am working ashore I take very little notice of ladies but when I am at sea, as each week passes, I miss them like blazes. One gets to feel absolutely randy. Poor Molly! The second night of one of my return homes, I had a bad dream and woke up when I found I was pushing Molly out of bed and was saying to her, 'Molly, what in the hell are you doing up on the bridge? You'll get me hung if this is found out!' That was the state I got into after three weeks on a survey vessel. How did Captain Cook's crew manage? You see, it's not like just an ordinary mariner's life where you go from A to B; we left port and then went about 180 miles north to the Frigg Field and there we stayed, just bobbing up and down, never being too sure when we would be going back to shore again. It's a good job I was kept busy.

Another time I went to the Frigg Field was in 1975 when I had my own survey firm. I was commissioned by Decca Survey Ltd., to take 'hydrographic command' of one of their survey vessels. Of course, the captain had the over-all command of the ship. However, while surveys or survey work were in progress the vessel was put at my disposal, for the want of another expression. At this particular time, I was to join the *Decca Scanner* which was out there working for the *Lay-barge 27*. A helicopter was supposed to have taken me out to the lay-barge from which I would be transferred to my vessel. However, the weather was too bad for chopper flight so I had to utilise whatever other resources were available. The information offered to me by the agent at Aberdeen was that there was a tug, *Rigmate*, leaving Peterhead at 14.00 hrs – it was then 13.30 hrs and Peterhead was thirty two miles away! What a drive and what a driver that turned out to be; he was absolutely mad! We got to Peterhead by 14.30 hrs and the *Rigmate* was still alongside. The *Rigmate* was a brand new service vessel and she looked very smart indeed. We eventually left Peterhead at 15.00 hrs and arrived at the *LB 27* at 18.00 hrs. How busy the North Sea looks nowadays with all these clusters of oil rigs; mile after mile after mile!

The *LB 27* was owned by an American company and she was an absolute hive of industry. Her job, as you can no doubt guess, was to lay pipelines. This was done by welding one section to another and then paying them out over the stern. She had a crew of some 400 men and yet she had no engine; she relied solely on tugs for her propulsion. She worked twenty-four hours a day so there was always a large number of her crew asleep. She had a cinema on board showing films all day and all night, although I never had the chance to visit it. There were popcorn and ice cream machines all over the place. A T-Bone steak at any time you desired one; but again, I didn't get the chance to sample such luxury. Getting transferred from a vessel onto the LB, or vice-versa, was something else different again. It's done on a basket. The crane of the LB hooks on a piece of equipment which looks like a large lifebuoy with pieces of rope tied around it at equal distances and all joined together at a common apex – this is called the 'basket'. When the crane operator is ready, you stand on the lifebuoy and hang onto the ropes. The crane then lifts you up quite high and passes you out over the sea to your waiting vessel. The next part is definitely quite tricky. The survey vessel is rising and falling with the swell, the amount depending on the weather, of course. You can generally rely on a vertical movement of six feet – if you are lucky! So what happens is, at least two deckhands are waiting on the deck of the survey vessel so that when you and the basket come down closer to the deck, they get ready to grab you. You just have to trust the crane operator and the two deckhands; when they say jump you just had better do that.

If the first described was tricky, then it's a hell of a lot worse going the other way. The basket comes over to you and sometimes just pounds the deck! The trick is to jump on the basket when the vessel is at her highest point and for the operator to start lifting you straight away. Most times they have got you away before the vessel rises again and pounds the basket once more. The duty deckhands won't usually let go of you until they know you are safely away. Oh yes, you had better wear a Mae West too, just in case the wind catches you or your foot slips or the deckhands don't like you or the crane operator doesn't like you!

The monster *LB 27* was kept in position by no less than twelve anchors, the total weight of which came to many tons. She was able to pull herself on two forward anchors at a pace she wanted. There was another tug which was kept busy just moving these anchors twenty-four hours a day. These two forward anchors had to be positioned by a surveyor because of the existing pipeline which was running parallel to ours and only seventy metres away. If one of these anchors had been dropped on the existing pipeline it would have smashed it. To repair the broken pipeline would have cost a million pounds sterling. The purpose of our ship being here was to look after all the survey and setting-out requirements of the lay-barge.

There was very little darkness up there in the summer time. After what little darkness we did have the sky started to look bright and friendly once more and then one radio after another would come on the air with some guys impersonating the early morning rooster. No doubt Americans. It started the day off with a much needed human touch. Quite often you would hear some wit mingled in with the radio message which I couldn't help but laugh at. The Americans again were particularly good at it. One evening we were just hove-to having a cup of coffee and the radio came on for us. '*Decca Mariner* – *Decca Mariner* – this is *LB 27* – do you read me?' said this American voice which I so often had heard.

'Go ahead *LB 27* – I read you loud and clear,' said I.

'OK *Decca Mariner*, will you move up ahead, we want to move our for'ard anchors.'

'On our way *LB 27*' I replied.

We checked our Hi-Fix against the reference buoy and found that was OK, so, with both engines 'full ahead' we turned sharp to port and 'sounded off'. We had one of those cheeky sirens; I'm sure you know the sort. You could almost play a tune on it. We were bristling like a battleship. We had been hove-to about a mile from the LB and even though it wasn't quite dark yet, I thought how warm and friendly the LB looked all lit up. It didn't take long for us to move into position and when I was ready, I gave the customary radio call, '*LB 27* – this is *Decca Mariner* – we are three-quarters of a mile ahead of you – we are on line and we are all attention.'

On came the Yank. '*Decca Mariner* – this is *LB 27* – Hey, who is this guy with all the tension?' Blighter!

Normally, when the LB shifted her for'ard anchors, she liked to place them three-quarters of a mile ahead. While we were moving into position to do this deed the tug was picking up the anchor from the old position and then he would come steaming up to us at an alarming speed and say, 'Where do you want this, Mac?'

'Come right up to me and touch my starboard/port bow and then let it go when I give you a toot', I usually replied.

In the meantime I was checking the other pipelines for position to make sure of my distance off (with my side-scan sonar), my bearing fore and aft and my 'distance off' the LB with my radar. Assuming all read well and the tug was now on my bow (on the correct side) I gave him a quick blast on my siren and away the anchor went – too late if I had forgotten something! The tug didn't hang around to find out!

'So long Cap'n, see you in court!' and he was gone. Another blighter! You have got to have nerves of steel.

LB 27 was laying a pipeline for Total Oil Company and I suppose, quite naturally, they had to have a representative on board; in this case a Frenchman. I was surrounded with hi-tech equipment, echo sounder, Decca Hi-Fix, Decca Navigator, 'Fish', ORE equipment, side-scan sonar, radar, radio and goodness only knows what else. On top of this, I was surrounded with a Dutch captain, a Portuguese mate and a French rep. *Mamma Mia!* At times it was enough to try the patience of Job. Thank goodness my assistant and equipment operators were all English. Don't get me wrong, I loved 'em all; not too sure about the Frenchman! Things could and did get worse. On 4 July, I had two French representatives on the bridge!

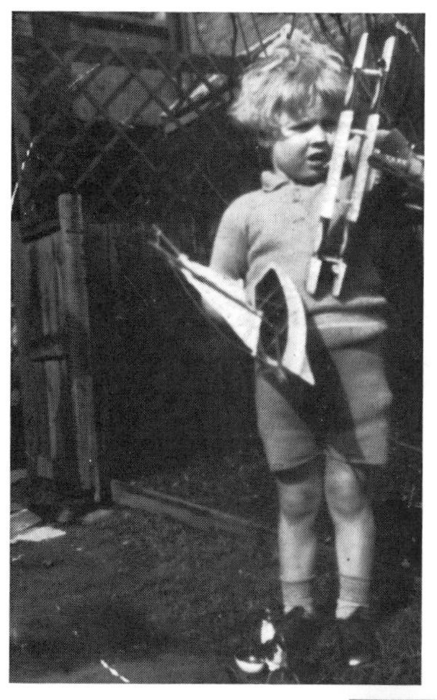

The Author, 1931. Even aged three I dreamt of travelling!

The Author, 1948

Working. Topo. Squadron R.E.s in Ma'am, Jordan, 1949

Name collecting (for maps) in Jericho, Jordan, 1951

Working at Fort Bayir with legionnaires, 1950

Instructor, School of Military Survey, R.E., 1952

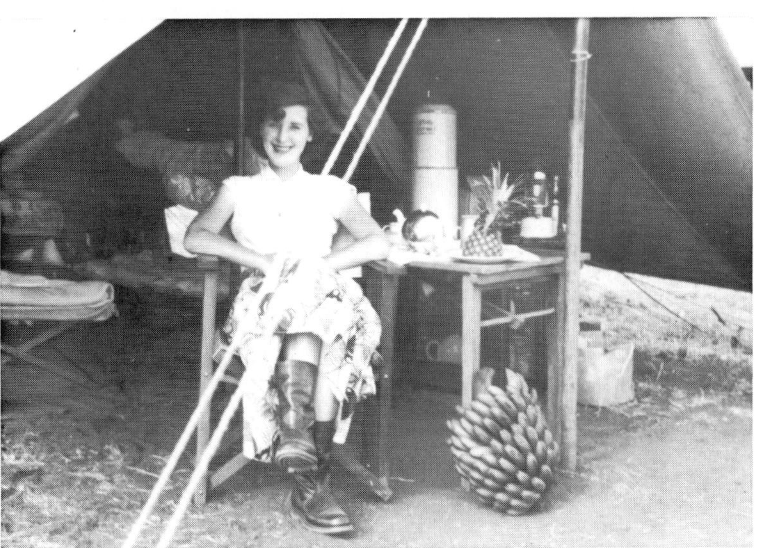

Molly on Kenya safari, 1953

Roy and Molly off to Nairobi. Mwea Tiberi, Kenya 1960

Author and Harbhajan Singh, 1956

The author 'at home'. Saltan Hamud, near Nairobi, 1953

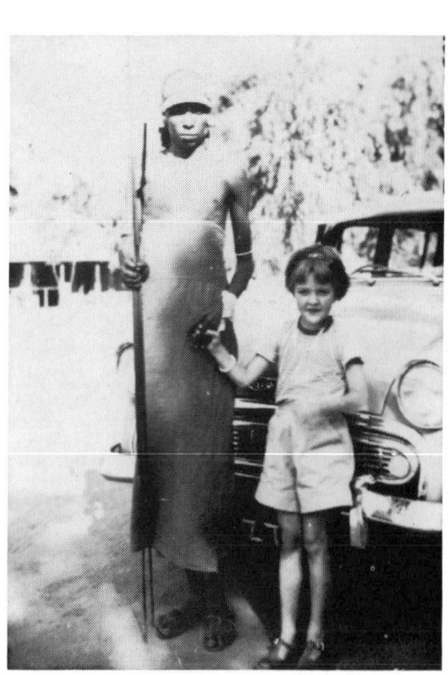

Gay on safari with me with Samburu tribesman friend, 1959

Safari – Thompson Falls, 1958

My ‘home’ being built at Mwea Tiberi, Kenya 1959

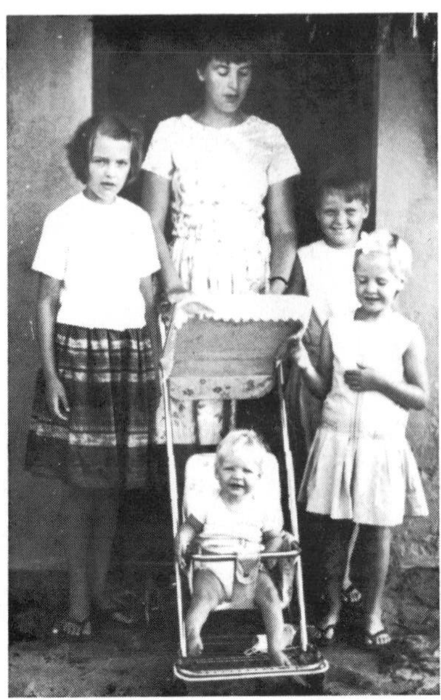

The family. Dar-es-Salam, 1965

End of the line so far. Molly, Joy and Jennifer. Mikumi, Tanzania 1964

Harbhajan Singh and Author, 1958

Landslide, Tanzania 1965

The author with 'Princess' Fatula, Isle of Makatea, Tahiti

And then there was Maggie. Wedding 1988

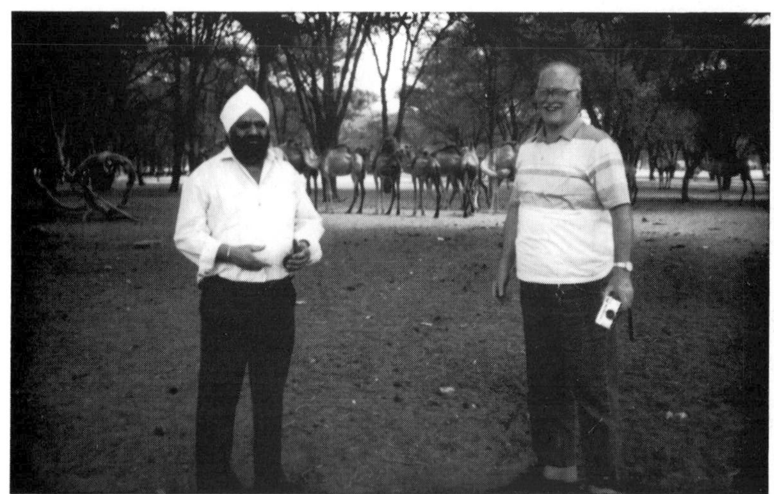

Author and Harbhajan visiting Kenya in 1991

Author and Harbhajan in far north India, 1991, 'Mount!'

9

A Taste of Travel Again (Mauritania/Tahiti)

Before I go any further with this story, I feel a re-cap would be in good order. It was now in the later part of 1978. I was still living in Inmarsh House in Wiltshire and I still had three or four survey parties working all over the place. Fortunately, the jobs hadn't stopped coming in and most of us had been kept in full employment.

Just lately, Ian Gordon seemed to be spending most of his time working overseas. I've never actually told you that the work of my firm was primarily land and hydrographic surveys and the setting-out of civil engineering works. This meant that all my eggs were not all in one basket. My policy was to train my staff to be as versatile as reasonably possible. This didn't always make me very popular with them but it did keep us in work! Often there was little land survey for us to do but plenty of hydrographic. Sometimes, it was the complete reverse. There were times when there were neither types of work but plenty of setting-out of engineering works. We had carried out most aspects of our work for Sheerness Steel in Kent and that was where I was working at the beginning of July when I had a phone-call from one of my favoured clients, Keith Murray.

Keith was one of the senior civil engineers with that old and famous firm of consulting engineers, Crouch and Hogg. Keith knew me first as a hydrographic surveyor with my old employers and he gave me my first chance a few years previously when I went into private practice.

'Would you like to think about coming with us to do a job in Mauritania?' asked Keith.

'Sounds interesting to me, I'll see if I can fit it in,' said Roy.

That was the beginning of a lot of preparations and planning. For a long while I thought I would never work abroad again; always a depressing thought. But here was my chance. The opportunity filled me with an exciting happiness; I couldn't believe it. But there were feelings of apprehension too. I would be travelling without Molly and the girls. Supposing something should happen to anyone of us whilst I was away? Would Molly be able to continue running the business without anything 'horrible' happening? It was no good, I had to go.

We travelled on the Air France Airbus and we were impressed. As a bonus, I always enjoy a glance at Paris; one day I'm going to spend a long holiday there. When we landed at Dakar we were horrified by the heat and humidity; the sweat just rolled off. The other three were slim and fit but it rolled off of them as well. What must it be like in the middle of the day? I thought. As the night wore on we learnt that the terminal was air-conditioned. What on earth was it like outside? We landed at Nouadhibou at eight o'clock in the morning; it was very hot but there wasn't a drop of sweat between us! I don't think I perspired once during my whole stay at Nouadhibou. There wasn't that much difference in latitude with Dakar and yet what a difference in humidity. We cheered up considerably, I can tell you.

On the face of it, Mauritania didn't look very prosperous, which isn't totally surprising, when you think that two thirds of the country is rocky, sandy desert waste. It seemed to me that the only place you could see life and anything green was along the Senegal River and in some of the oases. I don't think it rains much at these places, if ever. I think they get their water from flooding from areas of precipitation further inland. I understand that about three quarters of the population are roaming cattle herders, some years the cattle outnumbering people by as much as five to one. Off the coast, they have the cold Canaries Current which is ideal for the rich fishing ground. This is the creator of the fishing industry there and the reason for us being there. At that time, I believe there were about 30,000 tonnes of fish coming into Nouadhibou. The country earned most of its foreign revenue by exporting copper and iron ore followed by animal products, gum arabic and dates. This meant that although the 30,000 tonnes of fish a year were valuable they weren't the main source of income. I feel that because of the gorgeous climate and trips into the Sahara, they could, with a bit of work, have a thriving tourist industry. I loved the climate, but to me Nouadhibou as it was then, was a one-off sort of place. It was noticeably very quiet for there was very little traffic. The whole town smelt very strongly of drying fish, for that was the town's main industry. This would be a problem for the tourist organisers! My clothes smelt of drying fish for weeks after my visit. The food was mostly strange to my palate but I could survive. As I write I can't remember if I saw any women; I must have done but I guess they were dressed in yashmaks; there certainly weren't any women in the hotel. Nightlife was absolutely non-existent unless you were a local and had between one and four wives!

It was a great day when having got the echo-sounder and gear all set up in the boat, I switched on and it all worked. Everybody, including the Mauritanian deckhand, held their breath and crossed their fingers when I was about to switch on. Echo-sounders, all of them, are an occupational hazard! A hydrographic surveyor's nightmare, but we have to have them. Some are more temperamental than others; no two are alike; but you get to know most of their idiosyncrasies. Their troubles are caused mainly by the way they are transported and by the damp sea-air environment. Every day there are dozens of reasons why a hydrographic surveyor cannot do his survey that day but the competent surveyor knows how to prevent this or quickly overcome the problems and get the job done.

I can't really say much more about this trip except that it was over in fifteen days and I flew home on the sixteenth day. I reported back to Sheerness Steel for work only two days later. Did it ever happen? I worked at Sheerness Steel for the next few months and having had a taste of overseas travel again, I had dreadfully itchy feet. I could remember one time last year when I got awfully depressed thinking I would never work overseas again; mainly because I thought I was too old. In no way could I remove Molly and the girls from Inmarsh House and I certainly wasn't going to separate them, or leave them.

You know, strange as it may seem, my heart has always been in Kenya. Never a single day goes by without me thinking about her. I find that over and over again I compare this or that against Kenya. Everything is better or not so good as it is in Kenya. Sometimes, I miss her so much it hurts; I feel that I shall never see her again. However, this last little excursion helped me no end even though the only thing I could compare with Kenya was the call to prayer every dawn.

On Monday, 4 December 1978 I was working at home computing some of the Sheerness Steel job and tidying up my grape vines when the phone rang. It was Andy Christie, a splendid fellow who went to Nouadhibou with me. I think he was phoning from Paris. Would I be interested in some work in Polynesia? What a silly question! The second call that day was also from Andy. Would I be able to go to Tahiti with Keith Murray on the 12th, have a look at the job and hopefully to be back on the 22nd? Again, what a question! To cut a long story short, the three of us left for Tahiti on 29 January, 1979. In the short time between the first calls and our departure, there was a great deal to be done: visas, inoculations, checking out electronic equipment and making up survey stores; it was all a sort of game of Russian roulette. To give you some idea how much stuff I had to take, the air freight charges for my equipment alone came to £2,400, so I am told.

To help capture the magic and spirit of Tahiti, I'd like to refresh you on some of the historic background of this haven.

Captain James Cook (1728–79) was a master in the Royal Navy, an explorer and a hydrographic surveyor extraordinary. He was an Englishman born at Morton in Yorkshire. He didn't join the Royal Navy until he was twenty seven years old! I believe there are still Charts published which originated from his command and still bear his name. I can remember being taught at school about Captain Cook, but I seem to recall learning about him in the vaguest terms. I think I was merely told that he surveyed the east coast of Australia, naming New South Wales and Botany Bay. England's later claim to Australia was based on this voyage. I definitely recall my ill-informed teacher telling me that the captain was killed by an Australian and he wasn't – it was an Hawaiian. They didn't tell me that he thoroughly explored and charted New Zealand on his voyage of 1769. Nor did they tell me that this Britisher made a voyage of 70,000 miles in 1772–75 in the *Resolution* and the *Adventure* with a total crew of 193 men. Another extraordinary detail of that cruise was that because of proper hygiene and diet, he lost only one sailor, scurvy being avoided. During this cruise he discovered New Caledonia and located precisely many little known South Seas islands. In 1778, when he was on another voyage with the ships *Resolution* and *Discovery*, he discovered the Sandwich Islands (Hawaii). I wish I had a pound for everything named after Captain Cook. What a man!

When I was living in Sacramento, California, I tried to help Gay with one of her homework assignments. She had to find out what was the name of the state song of Hawaii; what was the state emblem; what was the state flower and describe the state flag. We visited the Sacramento County Library and I shall never forget what I read that night. In one corner of the Hawaii state flag is the Union Jack: the flag of the United Kingdom. This was in memory of Captain James Cook. The people of Hawaii insisted on retaining this respectful memoire and their insistence caused a lot of friction in political circles at that time – but the people won! The other strange thing was, before venturing off to the County Library, I phoned around to a lot of friends and asked if they could describe the Hawaiian flag to me – and they couldn't. No wonder!

Tahiti was another one of the islands visited by the captain. There is ample evidence today which indicates his strong association with that island.

Tahiti was probably first visited in 1606 by the Spanish navigator Pedro Fernandes de Queiros and there is a good chance that several other explorers visited Tahiti before James Cook, but it was the captain who gave the world the first detailed description of Tahiti. The very name of Tahiti brings magic into my life. I never thought that one day I would visit it.

Molly and the girls came to Heathrow with me, where we met Keith and Andy. I think it was Keith who said, 'We've got to stop meeting like this!' We said our farewells and away the three of us went. When we landed at LA we had a couple of hours to wait before the next part of our journey, so I took the opportunity of phoning some of my old and dearest friends in Sacramento; Jim and Sylvia Fitzpatrick. They were as shocked to hear me as I was pleased to hear them. I said that I would try and visit them on my return journey. We didn't venture far from the airport front door, but what we did see looked excitingly prosperous.

We arrived at Papeete Airport, Tahiti at five o'clock in the morning. I felt the magic of Tahiti as soon as I got off the aircraft. We flew in an Airbus again so there were plenty of people to get off. The terminal building was a fairly 'open' sort of construction but it was still very hot in there with so many people. Because of the heat and the equipment we were carrying, we rather stood back a bit and just let the 'mass' disperse. We commented on how slowly the queue was moving; the officials seemed to be doing a thorough job on checking everybody. Nobody was getting through very quickly. The passengers seemed to be equal numbers of Tahitians, French and New Zealanders – and then there was us. They closely examined passports, health documents, bank affidavits and all sorts of bits and pieces of paper. The sweat was running off us. Now, at last, it was our turn.

Keith went first. They asked him what exactly was he carrying and looked at his passport but didn't open it and then waved him on. This took only one minute. I was flabbergasted. The small-built uniformed man with the Errol Flynn moustache, then looked at me and said in a mere whisper, '*Bonjour monsieur.*'

'*Bonjour monsieur*,' I said; this being the only French I knew, and handed him my passport with one hand and a load of documents with the other. He looked at the cover of my passport and immediately passed it back to me, waving me on at the same time. How come I thought, all this trouble with all the other passengers and yet, with us, we were just waved on. To my mind, we looked a very suspicious looking mob with a very big question mark hanging over us. Andy got much the same treatment as me. This was too much for one of us – no names, no packdrills – who went over to a very tall French-looking policeman, standing near the exit and said to him, in French, 'Excuse me please, but we have been standing and sweating in this queue for over an hour, watching how long it took for them to check-out each person, but with us, they passed us through without hardly a word. Why?'

'May I see your passport, monsieur?' said the Charles De Gaulle-looking policeman. My friend handed over his passport. The policeman put on a deep frown, shrugged his shoulders and pointing the fingers of his empty hand half way to heaven he said, 'Common Market monsieur!' I suppose it was common sense but not one of us realised it as we stood in the middle of the Pacific Ocean!

I would like to read the entry in my diary for Sunday, 28 January, 1979: 'It's now eight o'clock in the morning. This is my first impression. I have never seen such beauty in all my life and I am deeply moved. We didn't have to travel very far to reach our hotel, The Royal Tahitian, before we saw beautiful long-haired ladies dressed in sarongs and their heads, wrists, necks and ankles covered in flowers. They also wear such soft and serene smiles too. I was greeted in my hotel room with the happy songs of strange colourful tropical birds. The sun is bright and welcoming and the temperature is in the lower eighties. Truly Heaven! I thank God for letting me witness this moment.'

I could write a book about our visit to Tahiti and it would be the same size as this one – it would have to be! For reasons given before, it will have to suffice to enter just a few notes. Our job was actually on the island of Maketea which is about 150 miles north east of Tahiti and the vessel that took us was an old Japanese hospital boat called *Moana No.2*. She had long ceased to be a hospital boat and was now converted to goodness only knows what. The accommodation was dreadful – non existent. You went to the gents in Papeete and then 'hung-on' until you got to Maketea. All day we had noticed about a dozen men with their suitcases or little bundles of belongings, hanging around the quayside. Just before we were about to depart they made their way on board and made themselves comfortable in any little cranny they could find. We learnt that they were our men. Everything was so casual in Tahiti. These chaps had been hired from a local survey firm. They were all such colourful men and most of them had colourful names as well. Tu Tahaai, Pierrot Tepa, Max Tuanea, Antoine Arutahi, Jean Paul Atin, Philippe Taarea, Andre Potatevatshi, Terii Virassamy, Michel Garnier, Jean Lois Metuarea, Miltou Metuatea and Jean Claude Lemaire. You will notice the mixture of French and Polynesian names. Does your spirit not travel momentarily to Cook Bay and sit under a coconut tree and listen to a distant strumming of a ukulele? Another interesting thing I noticed about our survey crew was that they all had the same coloured skin, a sort of olive/tan, and at least half of them curiously had blonde hair and blue eyes. Some people said that this was a throw-back from the days of the *Bounty* – I find that a pleasant thought and I like to believe it.

Now it's time to 'let go for'ard – let go aft' and off we jolly well go. I've never been so sorrowfully sick in all my life. Pacific Ocean! The swell was absolutely horrible. We had not long left Tahiti Lighthouse behind when I knew Griffiths was in for a bad time. It was a living nightmare. I had only the deck to lie on and I couldn't do that unless I wedged myself between two immovable objects. Can you imagine trying to stop yourself from being flung around an open deck in pitch darkness and periodically trying to feel something to hold onto whilst you are sick. We won't even talk about sleep. I looked at my watch and it was only a quarter past nine. I made up my mind, there and then, that when the time came to leave Maketea, I was going to swim back. No way could anyone get me back on this torture chamber.

The locals didn't amount to very many. There was one very Polynesian looking lady, quite rounded but very pretty, named 'Princess' Fatula. I think she was one of the descendants of the one time royal family and she was certainly 'the boss' of this island. There was her husband who I understood to be the chief. Then there was the Princess's sister, even a little tubbier than the Princess but I liked her very much. She had her husband who was a very slight built man and a son named August. They all lived together in one large three or four storey, very tropical house. There was another sister and her husband that lived in another house in a different part of the island. This lady had very few teeth but a lovely figure and was known as the Postmistress and Radio-Operator. These had a very young son and a daughter. The daughter was about sixteen and I would often see her running around the island, scantily dressed and athletic-looking. In a small shack in the north of the island was another man living with a much younger Frenchwoman. They never spoke to any of us. That was it – ten local folks plus us fifteen visitors – making twenty five people in all – men far out-numbering the women. I understand that in these islands it's a matriarchal society that prevails.

Andy and I were sitting on an upturned boat under a mango tree, trying to enjoy what shade there was. The smaller boat kept very busy going to and fro to *Moana No.2* and now all the survey crew were ashore but it would be hours yet before everything else arrived. Keith was talking to the 'locals' under some palm trees. They were speaking in French but even so I understood him to say that he would be staying there for about a week or at least until the *Moana No.2* came back again; which could be a different thing. He also referred to me as Monsieur Patron and this was in connection with who should have the best bedroom – the Princess's – I'm not always this lucky!

When the day's work was done and all the survey gear was safely in the house, it was nearly dark so I thought I'd have a shower. No water! On these islands every house was so arranged that the rainwater was collected off the roof and was guttered into a storage tank. From there it was circulated under gravity to various parts of the house. Sometimes, it didn't rain for several nights so some people had a problem. On the floor below me nearly twenty people were accommodated and every one of them knew, except Andy and myself, how the water supply was obtained. From then on, in spite of the heavy demand on the water, I got my shower every day before the water supply was exhausted. In any case, sometimes I would have a swim in a lagoon but this never substituted for a shower because I would always have to walk back up the cliff to get home. I would then be just as wet from perspiration as I was with water from the lagoon.

On Wednesday, 31 January we started survey work proper. I realised that I had to get us all working as soon as possible, all pulling in the same direction with an end result of detailed plans that would prove of immense value to the consulting engineers. While washing myself first thing (it rained the night before) I asked myself the question, What could each and everyone of us do? What are their talents? The more quickly I found out the better. It wasn't very long before the job was going very well. About a week later, when I was going to bed, after a hard day's work, the very last thing I heard was Princess Fatula's chuckling somewhere over in the palm trees below my window. There was also the sound of a ukulele and all the men singing a Polynesian song softly and in complete harmony. Good-night Molly and good-night my children.

On the second day I got one team to start the survey of the 'port area' and a second team to cut bush along the top of the cliff. I then had to wait for Keith who had gone over to see the Postmistress to make a radio call (or try to) to Papeete. I thought I'd get on with some notes for the time being. As I sat on the shady verandah I stopped for one minute to watch the palm trees dancing in the light breeze against a backdrop of the most blue sky. As I started to write again, two white birds of paradise were playing in the top of a mango tree right outside my bedroom. Somewhere in the bamboo growth I could hear an agitated cockerel crowing as he was disturbed by the sound of a coconut falling from a tree.

My diary entry for Sunday, 4 February, 1979: 'Keith left today and before he did so, he handed over to me a list of his survey requirements, about four weeks' work. It was very hot last night and this together with the men 'living it up', we had very little sleep. They must have brought their own booze with them! It was nearly three o'clock in the morning when I heard Keith's voice above the din of the ukulele and singing to tell them to 'shut up!. . .'

It was Andy's birthday on 6 February. I'm sure he was thinking of his beautiful wife and lovely son and daughter, but he said nothing. I couldn't buy him a pint of 'heavy', not even a 'wee dram' but, I tried to share his special day with him as best I could. Mind you, after I sang 'Happy Birthday To You' for the tenth time, he told me to 'shut it!' Nobody else said a thing during the day but what a surprise when night was upon us! We went downstairs for our evening meal and to our surprise everybody was in the dining-room. Andy had to hear it again 'Happy Birth . . .', but this time everybody was singing it! I felt happy for Andy for he was truly a fine chap. The next thing, one of the men came forward and put a headdress on him; it was a customary thing made in the traditional way with leaves and flowers; I still have a photo of him. The ukulele then started a special chant and everybody joined in with the singing, in their own tongue. The moment was solemn, sincere and sweet. The ukulele and singers changed their tempo in absolute unison and then in came Princess Fatula. She was dressed in floral headdress, flowers around her neck, wrists and ankles – and wait for it – a grass skirt. She was stunning. Money could not have bought this moment. She danced and danced and danced – and so did the men. One dance was performed with only one woman and ten men and I must say, they looked very beautiful – and sensual. Another dance that she did, on her own, was by performing fantastic gyrations of her hips, making a distinct rustling of her skirt. Just in passing, I think that had there been any booze, then the Princess would not have danced for us the way she did. Anyway, the Chief only turned up temporarily, which was kind of him. That's one birthday Andy will never forget – I certainly will not.

A reminder to do the hydrographic survey was entered on the top of the page, in capital letters, in my diary on Thursday, 15 February. It was something that could not be avoided any later than that day. The time had come to grab the bull by the horns. We started the day off bright and early by getting the echo-sounding gear transported from the house down to the wharf. I had these two small row boats at my disposal, so the first thing I had to do was put them in the sea and see if they leaked – and one of them did. We repaired the leaking boat and then nailed the two boats just eighteen inches apart. To do this we found all sorts of planks and pieces of timber lying around the old abandoned buildings. We fixed a strong cross-bracing between the two boats and hoped that was the carpentry side of the job done. We had two outboard engines belonging to the islanders; one was fixed to a false transom and the other was carried inboard. I set up the echo-sounder and thank God everything worked. It was lovely to hear that E/S motor start up and then the tap-tap-tap-tap of the stylus hitting the paper and then, a few seconds later, a picture of the seabed appearing. It doesn't always happen! At about eleven o'clock, I started to get really adventurous and decided to sail the lot out towards the reef, to get the feel of the thing. But just before I set off I went ashore to 'powder my nose' and when I got back, somebody had nailed a very smart name-plate on the side of our 'craft'; it read '*THE QE III*' !

I said to Raymond 'O.K. Raymond, start the engine and go astern.'

I promptly untied the painter and jumped aboard. The boat and crew responded well. Now things were looking up.

'Now Raymond, out towards the reef,' said Monsieur Captain Roy.

About ten minutes later, we had rowed the thing back to the wharf because both engines had conked out whilst we were at sea. The rest of the day was spent repairing engines and reorganising the ship with more carpentry. The next day I got the hydrographic survey done. What a sigh of relief. I still have a photo of the *THE QE III* which you need to see to believe!

On 23 February, we loaded the boat and said all our farewells to one and all. At noon, the *Mahini* started full ahead and we were off. You will notice that I'm very quiet about my previous experience with these boats. Time is a great healer; I was hoping that if I put that dreadful journey into the back of my mind, perhaps it wouldn't be so bad this time. But as it turned out, the journey was even worse than before. My poor body was absolutely pulverised. I wasn't sick but I thought I was about to be throughout the whole night. Every time I was about to be ill I bumped my head or knocked a kneecap or fell down the blasted companion way. When we arrived at Papeete at eight on Saturday morning I was amazed that I could remember my name. What a nightmare!

I needed at least a week back in Papeete to get my plotting done to a reasonable stage; even then, a lot of work would have to go back to Scotland for completing. I had to press hard for that one more week and what followed was a week of rumours about when we were actually leaving – today – tomorrow – the day after tomorrow? I just bashed on with the job. One way or another I got my week but it was only just enough. Monsieur Brodier, the proprietor of the Tahiti survey firm, was extremely helpful in meeting our heavy space and staff requirements. Within an hour of walking into the office we had a lot of people working on our plots. It was lovely to be back in Tahiti.

There seemed to be plenty of nightlife in Papeete but I imagined you would have to have plenty of money, that let Andy and I out! The truth was, we just didn't have the time; we never saw the downtown area after sundown. Our only entertainment was for about twenty minutes when we had finished work, at about six o'clock in the evening. We used to go into the bar next door to the office for a quick ice-cold beer with some of the lads and lasses that worked with us. After a beer it was a matter of getting a taxi back to the hotel, having a refreshing shower, another beer and then dinner. It would then be nine o'clock. After dinner, I strolled along the beach to feed the romantic side of my character. I'd listen to the ripple of the sea running over the sand against a background sound of ukulele and singing, coming from the hotel. Everyone staying in the hotel seemed to be in transit, either on their way to New Zealand or on their way to the United States. There were a few on tour, who were staying for just a few days. From which side of the ocean the young, suntanned and bare-breasted girls came from, I suppose I'll never know. Did you know that the beach sand in Tahiti is black? The only explanation handed to me was that it was volcanic.

Diary, Saturday 3 March: '. . . sat and had breakfast on my own; the hotel appears empty. I guess they all left on that early flight this morning; I can't remember whether it was going to New Zealand or the other way! The waitresses always look so pretty and fresh in this early morning sunshine. The flowers around their neck and behind their ears looks so fresh; I'm sure that the flowers make their eyes look brighter and their teeth whiter. Bali Hai looks magnificent this morning and if possible, the sea looks bluer than it did yesterday. The chatter of the surf is trying to tell me to stay! I think that Tahiti so fits in with my personality and that is as a worker, not a holiday maker!

On the way back from Tahiti my plane touched down in Los Angeles at half past six in the morning. It was about 55°F and promised to be a nice day. I said goodbye to Andy as he caught his connection to Paris and Scotland. I already missed him. I didn't have time to phone Sacramento because I took too much of it to see Andy off, having another breakfast, listening to that stupid tape just outside the airport door at the main entrance, telling you to shift your car and then booking my flight to Sacramento. It was already time to go to my gate because my flight was due to leave at 08.45 hrs.

I flew upcountry by Western Airlines, 'The Champagne Airline'. I was impressed by the efficiency and outstanding courtesy of the staff and was physically overwhelmed by the beauty and grace of the stewardess. She was waiting at the top of the ramp with a glass of champagne and a smile for me. I fell up the top two steps! My flight arrived at Sacramento at ten. Coming in to land, I noticed that all the tomato fields were under water; they must have had a lot of rain lately. Significant, as a point to remember if ever I decide to come back for a holiday. Indeed, I'll be back! I phoned Jim and Sylvia as I arrived at the terminal and they appeared soon after.

This was one of those Red Letter Days. It was so wonderful to see them both again. No, they didn't look noticeably older but they did think I did. There was so much news to exchange; our jaws were going nineteen to the dozen. Just being with Jim and Sylvia played havoc with my emotions; I was so deeply happy to see them again and so sad that I ever left. It was very nostalgic driving through Sacramento out to Citrus Heights. We even went through a residential sub-division with its young mums in their Bermudan shorts (and rollers in their hair!), out in their gardens mowing the lawns. It seemed only yesterday that these homes were on my drawing board shown only as a farm and some orchards! It was one of my designs. My friends' home was exactly the same as I remembered it, except I couldn't see my children playing in their garden and helping their Uncle Jim to get the barbecue going. Gosh, that must be all of ten years ago now! Liz, their daughter, was resident at Davis University so I was able to have her bedroom. As it turned out, she was skiing up at Squaw Valley the day I arrived, so she was able to call in and see me on the way back to her campus. She was growing into such a lovely woman and that red hair of hers! She wanted all the latest news on her playmates, my girls. The two boys I met earlier, smart young men.

I would like to show you my diary entry on the second day I was there. Monday, 5 March 1979: 'Jim and I took Liz back to Davis University first thing this morning. She seemed so proud to show her Dad and I around and introduce us to some of her friends. Afterwards, Jim and I made it back to Sacramento via the 'Capri Trailer Court' where my family and I once lived. It hadn't changed very much; the pool looked spotlessly clean and the court generally looked smart and in good shape. Why shouldn't it? I didn't try to meet anybody; this life has passed away now. We had lunch on First Street. I couldn't believe it, First, Second and Third Streets have been done-up and turned into a sort of museum! It looked good too. There were many restaurants to choose from and the one we chose was first class, the service and food were excellent. Spent the rest of the day home with dear Sylvia.'

Let me transcribe the entry in my diary for the next day: '. . . First thing this morning, Jim and I paid a visit to his accountant. Whilst Jim was dealing with his money, stocks and bonds (!), I went to a place which was very nearly next door, a 'Do-it-yourself' store and had a look around. I was delighted with what I saw; gorgeous materials, tools, gadgets and items of furniture. I fell in love with a red shower cubicle – I could just imagine Molly in it! We then went off to Foulsom Dam and Village for a look-see and a spot of lunch. We travelled a little way on the freeway and it was unbelievable to see such huge cars doing only 50 – because that's all the law would allow! Jim's rifle club was very near so we called in to see what was happening. We spent an hour at home to get all spruced-up for the evening and then Sylvia, Jim, Jimmy, Paul and self all took off to Davis to collect Liz. 'Dad' then took us all out for a really big 'nosh-up'. We went down towards San Francisco to a magnificent restaurant called Nut Tree – oh boy, what a feed that was.'

The next day, I already had to say goodbye to everybody and I didn't like it. Jim drove me down to Sacramento Airport to see me off. We never liked saying goodbye to each other. Very sad. As I sat in the plane, I went into a world of deep thought. Sacramento is also a place I could put my bones to rest. Ah! There was Hollywood, it would only be seconds and we would be landing in LA. Once down, I checked my flight times.

10

Kenya

I got off the plane at half past six on Sunday morning. It was cold, damp and dark. Molly, bless her, was at Heathrow to meet me; at least one ray of sunshine!

'Hello darling, how are you? Don't tell me, we are going to Tahiti aren't we?' she said.

I loved her. Of course, the answer to that question took a lot of thinking and talking about. First, I wanted to know how everybody was and what they had all been getting up to. And, of course, Molly wanted to know all the news about the Fitzpatrick family and about what I had been getting up to in Tahiti.

Returning to her question about where we were going next, I think Molly had already given the question a lot of thought before I came back, in anticipation that something like this would crop up. There were a lot of things in favour of going to Tahiti but there were a lot of things against it too. At the top of our list, when extracting the significant features from our discussions, was that we are not talking about 'our little girls' any more; three quarters of them were grown up now – one of them was married. Molly's parents, who were very important to us, were now much older. I was in my late forties. I had already been diagnosed as a mild diabetic and at one time, I had suffered with kidney failure. And what about Jennifer's education? In the late and nervy hours of the night, (what is jet-lag?) Molly more or less summed it up by saying, 'Tahiti is a long way away. It costs an awful lot of money if, and when, anybody wants to come and see us. We haven't got anybody there or even know anybody there. We can't speak French; not yet anyway, and supposing any of your equipment should pack-up, or even any of our domestic things?'

If you think that Molly put a damper on things, think again, because she didn't. She continued, 'Now then, Kenya is your country really, isn't that the case? You said you've always wanted to go back there again, isn't that true? How about opening a branch of the firm there? What do you think about that, eh? It's no where as far away as Tahiti; therefore, it is not as costly for travelling. We have friends still living in Kenya and we know the locals and their way of life. Shall we at least think about it?'

Well!

To venture to Kenya to conduct some market research took a lot of planning and organising, for a lot was at stake. I could see no problems getting Ian to stay in the country for the time being and looking after the work of my current clients. However, I was kept awfully busy at this time doing between ten and twelve hours on site and then three or four hours of writing or answering letters in connection with the potential branch in Kenya; whatever time was left was for eating and sleeping. A lot of the time I was working away from home. Molly wrote to twenty-eight potential clients in Kenya of which twenty-six replies were most encouraging. Then there were the letters to various Kenya government departments that were, or would be, concerned and involved in any plans connected with Kenya. As it worked out, at this time, my daughter Joy was completing her time at Bath University and was prepared to stay at Inmarsh House and look after the office side of things while we were away. Now I had to book flights to Kenya for myself and for Molly; how could I go to Kenya without her? We decided that 10 June was to be the Big Day.

We arrived in Nairobi with a most beautiful dawn. We hired a car and booked in at our old favourite, the Norfolk

Hotel. Although very tired, once we had settled into our hotel room, we went for a walk down the road to Nairobi town centre. I was home. Our first impression was that we didn't think Nairobi looked quite so clean as we remembered it but our hearts were full of happiness just being in Nairobi. Food was a heck of a lot cheaper than back home but our car, petrol and hotel costs were quite expensive.

The next day, we were up bright and early with sabres at the ready. I had two portions of paw-paw with quartered limes with my breakfast because I absolutely love paw-paw. When we were tucking into our Kenyan bacon and eggs we looked around and then at each other and we both felt Kenyan again. We felt a great peace and contentment and that's the effect that Kenya has had upon us. It was bright and sunny outside but it was cool in the dining-room. The tables looked so pleasant with their white table clothes and polished cutlery, every one of them highlighted with a vase of colourful Kenya flowers. The whole room had the aroma of fresh Kenyan coffee. The waiters were very smart too in their white uniforms and all of them wore a happy smile. We were welcomed with 'Good morning Madame. Good morning Sir,' and when I responded with '*Jambo Bwana, habari gani asubuhi*?' the waiter's face lit up and you would have thought that I was his long-lost closest friend.

Back in our room we got out our list of the first twenty telephone numbers that we wanted to call. It didn't take long to realise that the phones didn't work most of the time. We just had to keep on trying, one call after another and then back to the first call again, until we got satisfaction from our efforts. The second disturbing thing that happened was that many of the people we were phoning, those who had responded to our original letter, were not on the other end; they were in England on holiday! However, we were able to make enough appointments to keep us busy for the next few days.

I don't want to bore you with a blow by blow account of our activities, but I will tell you about the pertinent details because they help to make up my story and in any case, you might find them interesting. We called in at the Railway Office and found that it is now called Kenya Railways because after Independence, the EAR & H system was disbanded and in Kenya itself even the ports had been separated from the railways. I found this very sad. While we were in there, we met quite a lot of people that we had known over the years. Mr Waweru was one of them. He was the DTS in Iringa when we were there and was Molly's boss at one time. He had now been promoted to quite a high office at headquarters, but he was still the same very pleasant man. Then I met the chief engineer. He was put in my section at Mombasa for surveying experience but that was a good many years ago. In those days he was a young African cadet engineer, one of the first; there weren't many of those around. Because Molly and I were visiting HQ as 'old officers', they gave us free return passes to Mombasa. While I was in HQ, through a chain of contacts, I was offered some work in Uganda but I declined the offer because I knew that at this time I could have landed up with a bullet in my earhole. We walked back up the road towards the centre of town and called in to see a Mr 'Digger' Hemsworth (obviously an Australian) who was the head of an insurance concern and he said he was able to take care of all our insurance requirements. He first came to Kenya at the beginning of the Emergency as a Kenyan police inspector. He was now a nationalised Kenyan citizen, had a lovely home with a swimming pool out at Karen and a successful business in Nairobi. He had a son and daughter who were as Kenyan as they could be. Our two families became good friends as time went on.

That evening we drove out to the Thika Road drive-in cinema and saw *Close Encounters of the Third Kind.* We had some refreshments on our car window tray and I know I was going out of my way not to think of our children. The film hadn't started yet. All of a sudden their absence hit me like a ton of bricks – I missed them, I missed them so much that my chest hurt. But they weren't little girls any more, so there was no way I could have them with me anyway. This drive-in could never be the same. This . . . this was my first experience, my very first, of feeling the tragedy of getting older.

We didn't waste much time before we visited one of the school options for Jennifer. It was called Hillcrest. Both Molly and I were impressed with the school, its surroundings and, what was more important, the headmaster. He wanted Jennifer to take a small test back at her school in England to see if she was acceptable and if she was, where she could best be fitted in. The fees were quite expensive but she was worth it and I only had the one girl to find funds for now. I wished it were four! We called into several house agents that day too and they all assured us that we would have no problems in finding rented accommodation in Nairobi. I had a look at a few places that were on offer and, as a result, I felt quite happy with this aspect. We had a critical look at the supermarket and there was no doubt about it, the price of imported food was very high but if we balanced this against the cost of the much cheaper local produce, then we were no better or worse off than we were in England.

On another day we called in on the British High Commission and I must say how surprised we were to find that they had so much interest in us. They gave us the names, addresses and phone numbers of all the British firms that were connected to my profession, including those that were only vaguely associated. They also gave us the name of a man who was our contact 'should the need arise!' One of the most pleasant events of the day was meeting Collin Hayes, my old Army pal again, and his lovely wife, Stella. We had a very pleasant couple of hours together when they came to the Norfolk and had dinner with us.

The pages of notes were piling up now and one thing they clearly showed was how one thing usually leads to two others. If any of my readers wanted to start a business abroad, no matter what the business was, I think they would have to go through the same procedure as I was doing. Anyway, perhaps I have given them some useful tips, I wish them loads of luck. I will say this to them however, you must have something to sell that people will want to buy, be it goods or a talent. By the way, I can't imagine how you could manage without a fair knowledge of the language. Always observe local customs and be generous with your good manners and politeness although other peoples can be very trying at times! Accept it that you are not allowed to make mistakes, even though at times you can't help doing so. Be patient and understanding and to be a little humble at times can give remarkable results.

Digger had introduced me to an accountant and he consented to taking me on his list of clientèle. Another job done. Someone along the line thought I should meet the Minister for Industry, which I did and it was an occasion that I will long remember. He, in turn, wanted me to meet the Vice President the following week. It was at this point that I thought that things were beginning to get a bit out of hand and I had to delicately decline the invitation. I had little time to waste and I'm sure that Mr Vice-President was in the same situation. It was kind and thoughtful, however. I filled in all the forms pertaining to the new name of my firm and submitted them to the Register of Companies. More forms! This time it was a work permit for the Chief Immigration Officer. Sometimes we were finding that we had to take some forms from one office to another and we knew that some trips could have been avoided if some offices had given us the correct advice when we had visited days earlier. This was frustrating. But you had to carry on with the procedure or you knew what the alternative would be. I met the Chief Surveyor of the Survey of Kenya to discuss the business of acquiring a professional licence. He thought I was too old to take a land surveyor licence and suggested I confine myself to only non-title work and there was plenty of that. On our rounds we were very happy to meet our old friends Sheikh Mohammed Yaqub and his charming wife Khalida; remember our badminton club in the Mombasa days? I went to the General Post Office in Nairobi and acquired a post office box.

Mr Gordon Melvin, an esteemed Nairobi architect, told me 'to get off the streets' before they ran me in. To do this he really took me under his wing. He gave me a delightful office in his Fourth Ngong Avenue and, you must admit, it put me in very prestigious accommodation should I start up in Nairobi. The fight was only half over; this I realised only too well when I visited the Central Bank and the Provincial Trade Officer. The reason I had to go to the Central Bank was to do all the documentation that was required to import all my equipment.

On 19 June we caught the train down to Mombasa. For both of us this was the most exciting, entertaining and luxurious trip we have ever made and we have made this trip many times. The booking arrangements were still the same and when the time came to catch the train you had to look for your name on the seating Arrangement Notice Board which was on the platform. When you found your numbered compartment you would find your name again on the window. There was all the busy activity on the platform for about an hour before the train left. There was still the same excitement when the engine has taken its first tug and everybody was making their last waves. There was still that great joy in watching your steward pour your first ice-cold 'Tusker' before you had hardly left the station! As you tilted your head back to get the last drop of that gorgeous nectar, you couldn't help but look out of the west window and see that famous and friendly landmark, the one that Baroness Karen von Blixen loved so much, the Ngong Hills. It wasn't long before the first dinner-gong sounded, but all this I have described in another part of the book. These days I often sit back in my quiet study at Whitecraigs and go through the whole drill again, even though I realise that the Number Two Down is thousands of miles from me!

We had arranged for a hired car to meet us at Mombasa Station and I'm happy to say that it was there right on time. We had quite a good night's sleep on the train and a good wholesome breakfast, so we were refreshed enough to enter straight into an energetic inspection tour. We were a little bit disappointed with what we saw at first and this was mainly for two reasons. The first was the terrible state of the roads; you really had to keep your eyes open and make sure you drove round the potholes, or you were very sorry if you didn't. The second reason was that it was very noticeable that there was a shortage of paint. I don't think that anything had been painted since we last lived in Mombasa? Thank goodness the people were just as lovely as they ever were. Mombasa people! They are the best. Europeans, Asians, Africans, Arabs and all the mixtures. Great folks. I felt I knew every nook and cranny of this town.

Just before lunch we pulled ourselves away from downtown Mombasa and headed out to our hotel, the Bamburi Beach Hotel. The hotel was magnificent, the palm trees were dancing in the breeze, the sand was gleaming white and the sea and sky were blue, blue, blue. Lunch was excellent. The rest of the day, we talked about everything. Not only was my wife an ardent lover, but Molly had always been my best friend and counsellor; we always enjoyed conversing on the thousands of topics we would often whimsically choose.

Oh no! The very next day I was so ill. I felt like death warmed up, if there was anything to warm up. Molly couldn't get into the bathroom. The hotel manager called the doctor out to me. Apparently, he was used to such incidents. Dr Dhillon was a very welcome sight. He diagnosed acute gastro-enteritis. He said to Molly it was no good giving me anything by mouth because I would only throw it up again. Instead, he said he was going to give me an injection first and when I had settled down a bit, he wanted her to give me this, and this, to swallow. I should feel a lot better in a few hours. I did.

The next day was Friday the 22nd and I wrote in my diary: '. . . Molly and I were up bright and early this morning and shared the dawn of this day sitting together on the beach, listening to the love song being sung, in duet, by two sweet little birds to the background boom of the waves breaking out on the reef. In my prayer I thanked Him for letting me pass through this discomfort quickly. I also thanked Him for letting me have this treasured moment with the one I love above all others and in this land that owns my very soul.' The next day, Molly also came down with the very same ailment but Dr. Dhillon soon put her in much better comfort.

On Sunday, 24th, I wrote '. . . Molly felt a bit better today. Myself, a little better too, but tummy still a wee bit tender. I guess it is the price to pay for being in such a paradise. After sunbathing we drove down to Mombasa and had another look around. The campsite at Bamburi where Wendy drank the paraffin; the lighthouse; the two leading lights that I located to guide the super-tankers in; the Cosy Cafe; the Fontenella; Roy Cook's old house; Harry Proctor's old house; 'the tree'; Ken and Pat's old house; the Causeway; what was The Port Rietz Hotel etc., etc. Handed back the car at Mombasa Station and the train left Mombasa for Nairobi at 19.00 hrs and we were on it.'

It hurts to say anything more.

We had a few more days to go in Nairobi and we used up every second of them doing all the things that had to be done. Many of the offices we had already visited once or twice before and now we had to visit them yet again. The Ministry of Works said that they were sure that they had plenty of work for me. Gordon Melvin wanted to know when I would be back because he had a couple of things that he wanted me to get on with. A big British construction company also had work for me and there were about another two dozen possibilities of work sooner or later. I think we had now covered most aspects – all the significant ones anyway – should we decide to come to Kenya. And, I hadn't burnt one bridge; there was still one thing not yet resolved. I didn't have my trading licence in my hand. I called in to see the Provincial Trading Officer again, and was told that he was on safari. However, I told his charming secretary that the time had come when I must return to

England so I left my UK address and phone number and said I would be grateful if all future communications could be sent there. With as broad a smile as I could muster, I said my farewell and left.

On 30 June we spent the whole day trying to sort everything out. We even had the purchase of one or two vehicles organised with Vic Preston, who was also going to organise the financing. Vic Preston, from whom I had hired the car over these last few weeks, was a well-known name in motoring in Kenya and his name was all over the place when, each year, Kenya held her safari rally. One of his young managers at one time, Ivan Smith, was an absolute credit to Vic. Ivan, in his own charming manner, wouldn't hesitate to give a helping hand if he could, and he seemed to be known and liked all over Nairobi. He was born a Kenyan citizen and had hung onto his citizenship, which made him an asset to that country. Building and flying airplanes was one of his interests. Today he has a drilling company and seems to be doing well. Good luck to him. That evening, we went to the drive-in cinema after which we drove out to Kenyatta Airport, handed over our car and then caught our flight to London. To our astonishment, who should be getting on the plane but Yaqub and Khalida. It was a good job that they were there too, because I had completely forgotten all about the new airport tax and I didn't have a penny on me. Poor Yaqub came up with some assistance.

On the plane, we had just finished eating our dinner and were drinking our coffee. I looked at Molly and said, 'Well, that's that, darling. We have certainly had a busy time. But still, we know a lot more than we did a month ago. Now then Molly my love, what do you say?'

She took her coffee from her lips, briefly looked out of the window into the darkness, then turned and looked straight into my eyes and said, 'Go for it! Go, go, go!'

11

Griffiths Engineering & Hydrographic Surveys – Nairobi, Kenya

We arrived back in England safely but the flight was awful. The air-conditioner had packed up and I must have lost five pounds. The first thing I was confronted with was a new 'job list' as long as my arm of all the things I had got to get done. In one hour I listed 149 jobs, ranging from those that would only take a couple of minutes to execute to the bigger ones which could take a couple of days. They included a visit to Jennifer's school to discuss the required 'test' and her transfer; a visit to the vets to arrange Smokey's health requirements as well as his future Health Clearance Certificate; a visit to the travel agents to book air-tickets and to arrange for the shipment of my VW Camper; a visit to the bank manager re required references; contacts with British Airways about the cost of freighting my equipment; insurance and all it entailed; photocopying of various documents and their forwarding to Central Bank, Nairobi; arranging for the letting of my house to the Canadian Navy; arranging for a gardener; ordering packing cases; arranging for Ian to take over management of my UK firm; notifying all valued clients about what was happening. Not to mention jobs related to 'the books', VAT returns, jobs to the house, vehicle servicing, professional work in hand, future jobs, the men's pay, PAYE payments, family attentions and so on and on. Every now and again, I had to sit down and pull myself together and remind myself that there was always a price to pay and that in this case, it was worth it. Molly was an angel through all this.

On Wednesday, 11 July, 1979 I twice phoned the Provincial Trading Officer, Nairobi and when I eventually spoke to him he said, 'Your licence has been refused because we know there will not be enough work for you.'

I couldn't believe it! I again told him my side of the story, that I had work out there waiting for me and a non-ending list of work. I knew that first I had to study the market and I also knew that if I thought that after a fair period of time, things weren't working out then I would have to return to England. We had already discussed this at previous meetings. He told me to put all this into a letter and send it to him. Help me! How frustrating! We were so upset about this we phoned the Kenyan trade attaché in London. He made a note although he said of course he could do nothing from London. On this very day I had to drive to Scotland to do a job up there. It wasn't a very pleasant drive, I can tell you. I could see that officer's face all the way up the M1 and M6.

I worked twelve days in Scotland, got the job properly completed and then drove back to Inmarsh House. Still no news from Nairobi. By the 24th it was getting more than I could bear. For the whole of my plans to work things had to run smoother than this. I again phoned the Provincial T/O at Nairobi and was able to speak to him. He said he had not received my letter. But he had thought about my case and still couldn't see the urgency for my services. I could have spit. On Monday, 6 August, I phoned this officer again but I could not reach him, which was a pity, because I now had to accept a commitment at Sheerness. As luck would have it, I was subsequently admitted into St Martins Hospital, Bath, with suspected malaria.

There is more. When I was discharged from hospital I phoned the Kenya High Commission for advice, or perhaps even help. They said it was clearly evident that it was time for me to go back to Kenya because this was a domestic problem and they were sure that it could be resolved if dealt with there. Right, that was all I wanted to hear. Molly got me a ticket to Nairobi and I was on the plane and off. The plane never actually left the ground – it had engine trouble. Was this price that I was having to pay really worth it? Kenya Airways put me in a hotel near Heathrow and from there I phoned Molly. After the original shock of hearing my voice, so soon after leaving me, only an hour ago, she burst out in laughter; my, how she laughed; she just couldn't believe it!

Diary entry, 28 August 1979: '. . . TODAY, WE HAVE BEEN GRANTED OUR LICENCE! I tried to phone Molly all day, but she must have been out . . . Told the Nairobi accountant "It's on!" Told Digger to commence my insurance coverages . . . Got a rubber stamp made . . . Had a lovely lunch at the railway station . . . Called in on Gordon Melvin and asked him to get the "Welcome Carpet" ready . . . Immigration gave me the gen on what I'm to do next . . . Completed the deal with Ivan Smith on new transport . . . Finally phoned Molly and told her it was "GO, go, go." '

The next few days things went on and on and on. Every night was a sleepless one, for I worried like I had never worried before. I'm sure it was reaction. By eleven o'clock every morning I wondered what in the hell I was worrying about the night before. The very next evening I started the process all over again. This was the biggest step I had taken in my life – I was on my own, the results of my actions were completely on my own shoulders. There were no employers to share my load or responsibility or face the bills. What a state to get myself into! I think these feelings helped to stabilise me in thinking through each and every move, One night I wondered what would happen when I got my family out here and settled down and then if I died. What would Molly do then? That kept me going for a few hours, I can tell you. Yet you know, I would only have to hear Molly's voice on the telephone and my heart would be filled with joy and confidence and I would then feel as strong as a lion. When things got really bad I would have another shower, no matter what time of the day it was, then I would put on another clean shirt, dig out my regimental tie and put it on and then I would say to myself, 'Come on Serg, brace yourself and remember, it's for the Firm!'

Madness.

On Thursday the 6th I flew back to England and on the 12th I was back in Nairobi with Jennifer, Molly and Smokey. There was no way I could have got Jennifer out to Nairobi without the cat! And so it should be.

Happy times but even now my feelings were tinctured with a little sorrow. At the same time as we left for Nairobi Joy left for Sri Lanka, to take up her post as teacher with the VSO. No matter where I lived, when Joy left for Sri Lanka my heart would have been just as heavy for her. She had been such a great help to me over these past few months. Fortunately, she didn't try to reorganise my firm while I was away. She was so strong and independent. Since she had started her life at the University she had slowly grown away from me, more and more as each month went by. There was many a time that I wanted to give her a little cuddle; I needed such things, but she didn't want to know. That's life!

Within a very short period of time we were in our own furnished apartment situated on State House Hill, very smart and very secure. Within a few days of arriving Jennifer was in school and was enjoying her first Saturday off with one of her new schoolmates. In the end she went to the Loreto Convent and I was very lucky to get her in to that excellent school. We had brand new transport and Daddy had a couple of jobs to start him off. All the things that were planned and organised over the past weeks were now in full operation. The hard work of planning paid off because the first few months of our new lives ran very smoothly. Smokey was soon out of quarantine.

Freddie Muchene came into our lives in Kenya in a very big way, so I think I'll tell you a bit about him. While I was staying in the Jacaranda Hotel, during that time I was alone, I met a smart young chap who was a receptionist there. Going in and out of the hotel, I passed the time of day with him. I knew I would be wanting new staff and with this in mind he appeared to be just the right age and had the right personality and education to train as a surveyor's assistant. I approached him at a convenient time and made him the offer of a job. He wanted to take the matter home with him and discuss it with his family. Fair enough. The next day he agreed to come aboard whenever I was ready. It was a happy day when he joined our firm. As time went on Molly and I were able to go out to his house at Kiambu and meet his sweet wife, a Kikuyu girl, and his two children. They enjoyed making us tea and listening to our tales, especially of California. We also met his dad who could well remember Lord Delamere, his one time employer. He too told some fascinating stories. They had a pet cow on their property and it was a great day when she delivered a calf. She kept us all waiting – it was long overdue – and all the family and friends had a great celebration when she finally delivered the goods.

My first job was for Gordon Melvin and it was a nice tricky little number, the construction of a 'bridge' across the tops of two large Kenya Coffee buildings down near the Railways HQ, above all places! When you go to Nairobi, keep your eye open for it! On 25 September, my birthday, I started my second commission and that was the setting out of works for John Mowlems at the thermal power station at Olkaria, which is out near Lake Naivasha. Beautiful spot. It was a pity to have to leave the girls on this particular day; we had always enjoyed celebrating our birthdays. It was necessary for me to get closer to the job so I moved out to the Safariland Hotel. Even that was an hour's drive from Olkaria, over very rough tracks, but it was a heck of a lot closer than Nairobi. At the site they were harnessing the natural steam geysers to use as the source of energy to drive the generators. Very clever and advanced stuff. (I noticed that some of the technicians were from Iceland!) The drive from the hotel, which was right alongside Lake

Naivasha, to the site was very interesting because we passed acres and acres of fields of flowers which were being grown by Europeans and the flowers were flown to markets all over the world. A big breadwinner for the country.

We were settling in nicely and personally I felt that I had never left the country and my two girls seemed to have plenty of smiles. On 9 October I received a letter from the Ministry Of Works, Kenya Government, appointing me as a survey consultant to the Kenya Government. We couldn't celebrate this happy event because that evening I had to catch the train to Mombasa to collect my Moonraker VW camper, which had arrived from the UK. It was lovely to see this old friend again and she certainly looked smart. The shipping agents had her serviced and all polished up for me. I drove her back to Nairobi the following day, feeling very proud of her indeed. The distance from Mombasa to Nairobi is 306 miles and is now tarmacked all the way. It took me seven and a half hours, with stops, and it didn't seem all that long ago when it was an earth track all the way and on a good journey it would take me at least twelve hours. In those days I used to bump into lion, elephant and rhino all the way and on every trip, but, this day, I couldn't admit to seeing anything accept maybe a few giraffe and an ostrich or two. However, regardless of that, the whole atmosphere was still full of that African magic. Long may it live and we must help it.

My next job was for the Ministry of Works. I had to do a detailed land survey of Embu Hospital for the purpose of having the hospital upgraded. I was able to give Fred Muchene a lot of training on this particular job. Embu. What can I say about Embu? It was an odd sort of little town, built on hills with a wide road reserve running up through the middle of it, although the 'actual road' was a very narrow tarmac strip running through the centre of the road reserve. The whole area was covered with good trees. Shoeless ladies, wearing very coloured dresses and with huge piles on their heads and usually towing a young child with another one in her arms, seemed to dart left and right all over the place and appeared indifferent to being ran over. Some of the best looking buildings consisted of government offices and staff quarters and these too were scattered around a bit. Next were the strong built but scruffy looking dukas. Some of these were owned by Asians and the rest by local Africans. Today, of course, you say they are all owned by Kenyans and quite rightly too. There was a police post and a hospital. This was a large hospital and in the process of growing had spread out all over the place. This was one of the reasons I had turned up. The next door neighbour was what used to be called the Tribal Police Lines but was now called the Administration Police Lines and was to be included in my survey. In these lines you can find some of the most beautiful flame trees I had ever seen.

You must think that I am a bit of a walking 'sick-bay' when I tell you that all the time I worked in that hospital I had a shocking cough. In the many years I spent in Africa I used to get the most terrible coughs and throat infections for some reason. I wonder if any of my readers know the reason why? Gay always seemed to get chest troubles too. One day, the Matron, a lady of good Kikuyu stock, rushed out onto the grounds where I was working and demanded to know who was that with a terrible cough working 'in my hospital'? Oh dear I thought, I'm in for it now!

'Me Matron,' I owned up, feeling as though I'd just been caught stealing apples!

'Then you had better come and see my doctor. You are obviously doing a lot for us, maybe we can do a little for you!' she said.

I did what she said because she heaved me in by my arm. The first thing the doctor did was to order me a cup of coffee. Straight away I thought that this was a good doctor. He sounded my chest and gave me a lot of medication which did help but didn't cure. From that moment on, whenever I had one of my coughing fits, I would hear the Matron's voice coming from some seemingly hidden corner: 'Good morning Griffiths!'

She was lovely.

It seemed to me that no matter where I went in that hospital, I always had to pass the maternity ward. This ward was overcrowded – and that was the understatement of the year. There were always two mothers to a bed! While they were waiting 'for things to happen' they used to sit out on their verandah and knit, sew or do each other's hair. When I walked by them I would cheerfully sing out '*Humjambo Watu Wote*!' which meant 'Good morning everybody!' They would all stop what they were doing and in very high pitched voices would shyly say, in absolute unison, '*Jambo Bwana*'; saying it very slowly. How sweet they looked and sounded. Gosh! The smell of disinfectant was overwhelming, though.

There were hundreds of trees in the hospital grounds and I had to survey every one of them. I had to accurately show their position on my plan, state their height, girth, spread and name the species. Another feature of this survey was that I had to show every manhole together with the pipes going in and coming out of them – and there were over a hundred manholes. I couldn't believe it when I started looking for them! Well, manholes was where my troubles started. Because of where my equipment was set up, it was convenient to start surveying manholes in the area of the maternity ward and the next building down from it, the mortuary. Of course, I had to go into the mortuary to examine the manholes as well as measure the details of the building. What a morbid shock that little exercise turned out to be.

The technician let me into the building because there was an inspection chamber right by the side of the 'dissecting-table'. Just for a start, this 'table' was made of concrete and I don't suppose that mattered very much – but the concrete top was badly crumbling. How on earth could they keep it clean? The technician agreed with me and now that I had got him in a critical mood, he went on to tell me what else was wrong with the place. He said, 'Look at this so called "cool drawer", the refrigeration unit doesn't work.' Without any warning he pulled open one of the drawers.

Inside the drawer there were a woman, a child and three or four babies, all wrapped in ugly, old, badly stained bed-sheets, the string tied around their necks giving them grotesque forms. I said that I would report it to somebody who could get something done about it quickly. I shuddered. Now I did what I had come in to do, I lifted the inspection cover so that I could survey the height of the invert level of the pipe going outside of the building. There were bits of human stomach and lungs and other parts floating around inside. I lifted the inspection cover, which was broken, just outside the mortuary and the one about a hundred feet down the slope towards the Hospital Native Staff Living Quarters and found the same type of contents in each! The thing was this: in the last inspection cover that I lifted – it too was broken – the outgoing pipe was blocked and the 'fluid' was leaking out of the top of the cover and continued its run downhill to within feet of the living quarters. Some children were actually playing in it! While we walked back to the mortuary I couldn't help but notice about ten cheap coffins all piled one on top of the other; it portrayed an unkind lack of reverence.

Freddie cast me a very worried expression. I was surprised at what I saw and yet not surprised. I thought that this 'store' of coffins could have been concealed from the public view and if that wasn't disturbing enough, I noticed that a dead body was being wheeled along the verandah of the maternity ward and down to the mortuary. That was enough! As best I could, I 'closed' the mortuary and reported my findings to the doctor and within the next twenty four hours I was visited by several important people, including a government minister. I noticed that nobody was telling me to mind my own business or that I was being over-imaginative and over-reacting to the situation. Within the next few days, new inspection covers were placed, trees were planted around the mortuary building and I heard that a stainless steel table had been installed. A shed had been added to conceal the empty, or otherwise, 'boxes'. I felt that no single person could be blamed for this situation;

it could be lack of funds but it had been overlooked for a long time and as far as I could see, it had got out of hand. From that time on, for many weeks, I made sure that all my chaps, myself included, washed our 'wellies', feet, hands, arms and the bottoms of levelling staves in strong disinfectant whenever we thought we had been possibly exposed. In spite of this incident, I thoroughly enjoyed the commission. I was able to get home weekends and the girls paid me several visits. Even Digger paid me a visit once. They were all very impressed by the display of flame trees at the Tribal Police Lines. The hotel was very old but efficient and very 'Kenyan'. The food was simple but excellent. A fire was needed at night and I loved the scent given off by the firewood. I still wonder what kind of firewood that was.

On Friday, 14 December, Wendy came out to Kenya to have Christmas with us. Unfortunately, because of work demands, I wasn't able to stay at home for the duration of her visit; this has always been part of the price I've had to pay to do the job I love. However, Molly was able to bring the girls out to Embu at least once before Christmas.

Wendy assured me that she had a whale of a time out there in Nairobi but it was particularly wonderful having her with us for Christmas. Only a short distance from where we lived was the Milimani Hotel with its excellent swimming pool and friendly staff; they knew we were locals and not tourists. So, the girls and, I suspect Mother, were able to spend a lot of their slack time there and managed to have a good many lunches there too. Then they went down to my sports club for swimming, sunbathing and eating. The evenings were spent at either one of the two drive-in cinemas or visiting friends, etc. Sometimes just a walk down to the Thorn Tree for a cup of coffee would pass away several pleasant and happy hours. Wendy also went down to the coast for a few days with Digger and his family. She enjoyed herself. It was heart-breaking to say good-bye to her when the time came to see her off. She looked so forlorn and small as she left us to go through Customs. It consoled us to think that when she had finished her training in the coming year, she might want to try her luck back in Nairobi with us. It took all my strength not to say, 'Don't catch this flight, Wendy, stay here with us.' I knew I had to let her go, but my heart was asking why.

Before I left England I had arranged with Ian Gordon that we should send a report to each other every two weeks. These kept us both in the picture about what was going on in both places and it gave us a chance to exercise our sense of humour. He would often ask how Smokey was getting on. I would have to tell him that Smokey didn't like Nairobi at all; I believe he could smell the big cats that lived not very far from us! He was slowly losing weight as well as his zest for living. He was all right, it seemed, as long as he had Jennifer around to keep him company. He stayed by her side every minute that she stayed in the house. She was very loving to him as all girls are to their pet cats. I'm sure he missed the farm next door with his cream and Marmite sandwiches! I wondered if Ian was really interested in all this. I began to realise that although I was more than willing to pay the price, if I had to, I was expecting other people – and creatures – to pay also. Did I have the right? Perhaps I'm not the only one who needs to think about this.

1980 was a busy year and it was the year we got a foothold in Kenya. The saddest news of the year was that my father, Edward John Griffiths, passed away on 28 January. He was to have visited us in Nairobi for an indefinite period starting six weeks after his death. He passed away peacefully in the night, which was all right for him but played havoc with his family. He left a cavity which I know will never be filled. I'd always had Dad – but no more. He was always that valuable counsellor standing in the background, should I need him. Now the buck stops at me, as they say.

The firm was growing and a lot of work was coming in my way, so I had to increase my staff. They all accepted that Freddie was my senior party chief and were ready to accept orders from him should I not be around. Now I needed a head chainman. A labourer that I took on at Embu, some months before, turned out to be a bright penny, so I made him up to head chainman. This was a rank that an African was proud to hold with dignity; he was like a sergeant-major and he was 'a big noise'. Mike Muthui knew how to handle men and get the best out of them. We increased our transport by purchasing a Toyota Land Cruiser, custom-adapted for our use. Molly loved to drive the vehicle. So we now had the Datsun trade van, the VW camper and the Land Cruiser. Slowly, over the following few weeks, I took onto my stores list two officer type tents, three bush tents, a portable generator and all the camping gear one needs to make up a safari, for myself, my surveyors and my permanent chainmen. Mike always used the awning to my Camper, cheeky blighter.

Embu was coming to an end but the plotting turned out to be much more than I originally anticipated. There were so many more manholes, pipes, buried electricity cables and water mains than anybody in the Ministry had knowledge of, but there, that was why they called us in. While I was doing the plotting and fair drawing, I started at four thirty a.m. and finished at half past seven p.m., unless I went to the drive-in. This went on for weeks and weeks. I got Embu finished and tucked away in the middle of March and by all accounts the Ministry were satisfied with their new boy!

We went into another interesting job at the Tana River Power Station. There wasn't one day to spare from one job to the next! This power station had recently been considerably extended. My job was to establish permanent reference marks so that the effects of any future earthquakes could be monitored. A high standard of accuracy was required which always made it interesting work indeed. It paid well too. One morning I could clearly see Mount Kenya in one direction and Kilimanjaro in another, both at the same time. What a magnificent sight! Because of natural atmospheric conditions, Kilimanjaro had disappeared by eight thirty. Whilst doing this job, on Saturday, 16 February we witnessed a ninety six per cent eclipse of the sun and you don't see that very often.

At the beginning of this Kenya dream, I promised that Molly would go home for a holiday at least once a year. When you add up all the people in Molly's family and add them to the other people that love her, you are talking about a lot of people. Most of these people wanted her back in London as often as she could get there! My greatest desire, was to have her by my side for as many seconds in the duration of my life as was sensibly possible. However, there were two people in this partnership and she had her desires as well and there were people in her life that were very dear to her; her daughters for instance. So, it seemed fair to be an active and reasonable participant in this partnership and arrange for her to go. Inwardly, I looked upon it as the price I had to pay for having her with me most of the time. I wasn't that successful yet that I could afford for Jennifer to go home too – not this time anyway. Jennifer stayed with me and because her school holidays had started, she was able to get her first taste of safari life. Jennifer gave me somebody else to think about other than myself.

Molly left on 29 March and at the airport I wished her a happy and well-earnt holiday. Our house servant missed her too, but he tried to keep us happy by keeping the conversation about her on the light side. Poor old Juma also had to work hard on Smokey because he was walking around the house with a face like the map of Ireland, looking everywhere and crying at the same time. To make matters worse, Smokey completely disappeared on 7 April. Oh my God! Juma, Jennifer and myself spent hours and hours trying to find him. Had he gone out to try and find Molly? One afternoon, I used all my staff and accepted the help of two constables to search for 'Lord Inmarsh'. Another problem was that we had to go on safari in another two days. We still didn't find him but I left instruction for Juma that he must continue the search. I suddenly realised that Smokey was eighteen years old by now.

I had been successful in getting another four months' work from another big Nairobi consulting engineer – Howard Humphries. The job was very near Kericho, the well-known tea country. I was looking forward to my first visit to this land of miles and miles of tea estates – an Englishman's dream! The job was called the Capsoit Water Supply. It consisted of a couple of hundred miles of proposed water mains to be located and surveyed, starting at a pump house on the river, then up to a high tank reservoir and then all the gravity lines running down from the reservoir to various parts of the countryside. It meant that I had to do miles of traversing, levelling, detailing and plotting. Thank goodness, at this time another graduate surveyor had joined us. His name was Josephat Kogera, a fine-looking married man.

To start this job we left Nairobi at eight fifteen a.m. on the 9th and arrived at Kericho at quarter past one which made a good start; tarmac all the way. We set up our camp in the grounds of the Capsoit School, but this was only after a lot of palaver from the DC. The headmaster wasn't too pleased with us either, but there came a time when I had to think of my safari and its needs and then take very positive action. As it turned out, we had only just got our last tent-peg in and down came the rain; in buckets! Before we lost daylight the men were able to drive off to the bush to collect fire-wood and water, unpack work equipment and generally settle in. Also, my surveyors and myself were able to make our first reconnaissance so that we would know what to put our men about, first thing tomorrow morning. *Mboga, nyama, maziwa, mayai, ygai na mkate; kile Kitu iko indani duka.* (Vegetables, meat, milk, eggs, corn and bread, all available in the shop.)

We were now in tea country, as I've said, and that meant we could expect a lot of rain. Our expectations were not denied us; I guess it rained at least once every twenty-four hours. Even though I usually lose money over rain, I must admit I do like to stand and watch it – especially if it's tropical rain and I'm standing under an umbrella, or in a tent – I love the sound too; it makes me daydream!

Kericho District was a sight to behold. The rows and rows of tea bushes looked so attractive as did the flower-covered shrubs that lined the tracks that passed through the estates. Every day you saw hoards of people working in one part or another of the estate. They wore these big baskets or bags tied around themselves into which they deposited the picked leaves. They picked very rapidly with both hands at the same time – it's an art – and only the young leaves of the young shoots were plucked. The bushes were heavily pruned and you could always see a team doing this aspect of the job. They kept the bushes to about five feet high.

In the town there was a very old and large hotel called the Tea Hotel! It was an impressive-looking building for this part of the world. Many famous people had stayed in this hotel but many of the records of the hotel and the town were hard to come by. I would like to see a gigantic effort to get together all the records available of East Africa and see them under one instrument; otherwise, it's all going to get lost and to the pity. I had the pleasure of staying at that hotel on many occasions.

That first night I suggested to Jennifer that we eat in the hotel but she didn't want to; she wanted to go for this safari business quite seriously! Even though I hadn't employed a cook yet, she decided we were going to have sausages and beans for dinner and she was going to cook them. I felt this was going to be another one of those jobs where I lose a lot of weight! Actually, she did very well and they went down fine. I knew she was missing her Mum but nevertheless I was witnessing loads of jokes and laughter. We had torrential rain that night; enough to wipe out many telephone lines; but not a single member of my crew got one drop of it. Good tents. We survived the initial battle and then were ready for work. Having said that, it rained like blazes on the first day and I went on panic stations. Was it going to rain like this all the time? No; I soon had Fred and his party out levelling. Joe and I met the consulting engineer and off we went to mark up the route of the pipeline for the first half of the job.

Operations were soon into top gear with Joe on traversing, Fred on levelling and myself planting the concrete traverse stations and keeping the ten bush-cutters preparing the route ahead. When I passed the men's tents I could see a couple of very attractive girls cleaning the men's pots and pans and brushing out the tents, so the men were being 'looked after', in more ways than one I suspect!

On 12 April, Molly and I had been married twenty eight years and I celebrated the day by cutting my way through heavy bush, down a steep slope to a point on the river where the pump house intake would be built. The fact that I reached the site in only one day was an achievement – better the day, better the deed! It looked hopeless at first, but once we got the first two hours' cutting done, I could see the end of the tunnel. We had several heavy showers during the day and it was so humid, at one time I perspired just by standing still. Jennifer was lining us in with ranging rods and thought the whole thing was great fun. In a few days later the detailing started and this was the drill for weeks and weeks to come. I was very pleased with Joe and was even more pleased when I could see that he and Freddie got on like a house on fire. I was frankly surprised at this when I thought of the different tribes they were from. All the time I was in Kericho I can't recall ever seeing another white man. Once I had convinced myself that the job was running smoothly Jennifer and I went back to Nairobi because Molly was due back in two days.

As soon as I got back and said *Jambo* to everybody we went out to look for Smokey; I was determined to at least find out what had happened to him. No luck.

The 19th was a great day. Molly was safely back with us again. She wasn't in the house very long when she got up from her armchair, combed her hair, put her shoes on and without saying a word, headed for the front door! I asked her was she going somewhere? 'Yes,' she said, 'I'm going out to see if I can find Smokey!'

Would you believe it?

'I'll join you!'

Across the small valley, at the back of our house, was quite a large school and we even went over there and called for Smokey under all the raised classrooms – to no avail.

On the following Monday I got up to make the girls a cup of tea before Juma came in. I heard Jennifer run into my bedroom and jump into bed with her mother. When I had made the tea I picked up the tray and headed back to my bedroom, exuding a loud yawn en route. All of a sudden there was a hell of a din outside my front door. I immediately recognised who was making the row. I opened the door and in ran Smokey! He gave me a look that said, 'Don't you care about me? Why didn't you come and look for me? I'm angry with you!'

The two girls came rushing out of the bedroom and oh my, what a carry-on. He looked so thin and almost dead. Mother warmed up a saucer of milk for him and Jennifer was brushing his coat when the maid from downstairs came rushing into the house; all protocol blown to the breeze. 'Was that Smokey I heard?' she said.

Some guys get all the luck! It was lovely to see our dear, dear friend again. The bond between Molly and that cat was nothing short of incredible.

I arrived back at Kericho again on 24 April and found that the men had moved base camp to the chief's office at Alimoi. I had brought a letter with me for Freddie, promoting him to party chief, which I thought he had already well earned. Drinks that night up at the Tea Hotel. A few days later the engineers and myself traced the route for the pipeline from Ainamoi Crossroads to the High Tank. This would give the team plenty more work to bash on with. At last I met another white man, Father Hayes, who invited me to dinner at the Kipchimchim Mission. He was a great conversationalist, very entertaining and a fine chap all round. God bless him.

On Friday, 2 May I had to go back to Nairobi because I had to be at the Ministry of Works in the afternoon. They gave me another hospital job, this time at Marigat. This was a good bit further north in our President's own constituency. I worked home all that week-end, sixteen solid hours a day. Lump sum contracts were always very shaky. The policy that took shape with me was: always estimate how long I thought the commission would take, add on a percentage to cover bad weather, loss of interest because of late payment (always an important factor with some clients) and add a figure, in time, to cover incidentals. Multiply this by a factor of the cost to run the firm for that period of time. The last factor was made up of my and my staff's salary, profit, cost of transport, insurance, cost of equipment, etc. After estimating an acceptable figure the only factor I could play around with and not upset the balance was the extra number of hours that I worked alone. I always estimated that I would give my client a number of hours gratis; it couldn't be avoided really. Mistakes and the wrong original estimate would turn out costly and a loss. This didn't happen too often, thank goodness, but I wish I had a pound for every hour that I have given my government at the time and to clients gratis!

It's worth recording the public holiday that followed, which was because of the visit to Nairobi of the Pope. We all thought what a lovely man he was.

The day after the Pope left I went to Dandora to John Mowlem Company to discuss a future survey course that they wanted me to conduct. This wasn't a course where I would go back to basics, but a course where we could get a number of mature engineering staff together and touch up the finer points of setting out works and deal with the most common source of mistakes. This company was big enough to recognise the value and need for such a course. There were other companies, just as big, if not bigger, which did not acknowledge this need and they employed batteries of pneumatic drills to dig out that concrete which had been poured in the wrong place.

I was to start Marigat Hospital on the 28 May 1980 and to do this I needed yet another surveyor – and fast. I interviewed a man who had been in the same class in university as Joe. When he turned up at my office I thought, what a scruff! However, I thought that if he had trained in the same place as Joe and on top of that had once worked for the Survey of Kenya, underneath there somewhere there must be a good surveyor. Anyway, I took him on. On 28 May I took off for Marigat and took this man with me. I had a good look at the job and decided that it was straightforward except that the future hospital wanted to steal a part of the land belonging to the adjacent school! However, I instructed this man to carry on with the topographic survey of the site until such times as I had got this property line sorted out. I'd always thought there was one way to find out what a man could do and that was, leave him to it for a spell. I know that I am a very overbearing sort of man – larger than life so some people say – so I always tried to make allowances for myself when dealing with new staff, male or female, by keeping out of their way as much as I could. I even did this for my wife sometimes. I stayed in Marigat for a couple of days for there were things for me to do. The man stayed at the Marigat Lodge and I drove on for another couple of miles and stayed in the Baringo Lodge.

Marigat was like the inside of a steelworks, hot, hot, hot. Temperatures well over the hundreds. When there was a breeze you wished there wasn't for the breeze was always too hot! The man couldn't work in the middle hours of the day; in fact, if he tried I think he would have died. I would have done! But we were surveyors and we were notoriously coupled with hazardous conditions and we had to get the survey done; there were always cooler hours during a day.

While staying in the Baringo Lodge, I thought how unique this place was. To get there from Marigat I had to drive on an unkept, untarmaced road, across some dried up river beds whose large concrete bridges had been washed away during some past rainy season, cut through the masses of 'wait-a-bit-thorns' and 'desert cabbage plants' until I got down to Lake Baringo – and there it was. Yes, it was a 'bush-type' hotel but a lot of effort had been put into it to make it as comfortable as possible. All the bedrooms and towels had that musty smell about them, a smell that took me back to colonial days. I noticed over the last couple of miles that there were camels all over the place. I got there at about five o'clock in the afternoon and I was so hot. My head was burning because, quite stupidly, I wasn't wearing a hat; so were the lower parts of my arms. My feet were aching, they were swollen, they were on fire. The steward took me to my room and told me where the small swimming pool was. He asked me would I like a pot of tea and if so, where should I like it brought, in my room or perhaps by the swimming pool? I sort of stuttered and then said, 'By the pool will be fine, please.'

I quickly took my clothes off and put my swimming trunks on – I sometimes wore them to work in – and down to the pool I went. I was surprised with what I found. Yes, it was very small but very deep too. It was surrounded with attractive hammer-dressed stone and three-quarters of the edge was overhung by bougainvillea. It was spotlessly clean everywhere. Enough, I jumped in. My body felt like a red-hot horseshoe being dropped into a tub of ice-cold water, if you get my meaning. I twirled and swirled in the water, down to the bottom, held it there for a while and then came back up for some air. I felt the cold water under my chin, under my arms and down my groins. Two deep breaths and down to the bottom again. I thought I'd love Molly to see this. While on the bottom I suddenly thought that I'd like to live a little longer, so with a panic kick I came up to the surface again.

'Here is your tea. Sir, and I've brought you some cake which will see you through until dinner. Where would you like it?'

I took it right by the side of the pool. I ate my cake and drank three cups of tea; I didn't get out of the pool! I then wallowed like a hippo for the next thirty minutes. I was the only one staying at the lodge. Back to my room and then into a nice warm bath for another thirty minutes. I love the smell of medicated shampoo; it smelt so clean against the musty background. While on the edge of slumber in my bath I thought about my surveyors, my equipment, my transport, money and then my wife and children; but not necessarily in that order. I also thought about what this same safari was like back in those days of the early fifties. On with a nice clean shirt and a clean pair of white trousers. Over to the bar where I sat in an old wicker chair with an ice-cold (you guessed it) Tusker and a Willem II Cigar. All around me were paintings of fish, drawings of fish and stuffed fish in glass containers. That night life was kind to me. A nice piece of talapia fish, some curried chicken followed by a cold tropical fruit salad. To top it all, (you guessed it again) a nice cup of good Kenyan coffee. And then to bed. Amen.

When I started at Kericho I took on a young man by the name of Fidelis Langat, of the Kipsigis tribe. He had a good face and often wore a smile and dressed clean and smart. I could tell that he came from a good family. I knew his uncle casually; he was the postmaster at the Kericho GPO. Fidelis was waiting to go to teacher training college and for this reason he could only take on casual work. Day by day he became more and more useful and helpful and my surveyors used to have words over whose party needed him most on that day. Freddie, being senior party chief, got him most days. When the time came for us to leave Kericho he asked if he could come with us. I don't know what happened about the plan for teacher training college! It was OK by me because he had already learnt to do levelling as well as many other surveying duties. The family liked him.

Monday, 23 June was the day I started my two week course on surveying at Mowlems. If I remember correctly, I had about fifteen students which I was pleased about and quite a real mixed bunch at that. Some were still very studious and were able to keep up with me through the whole course. Others had a bit of a rough time. I tried to create the situation where every man gained something by doing the course. To some of the chaps the course showed where they might be a bit weak on some academic subject; well, I would try and find which book would help them on that subject, or which colleague he could turn to for further help. There were others who were not quite with it as regards use of certain equipment. In that sort of case I was able to bring it to the attention of their employer, thus assuring the gent that he would have access to this equipment in future.

There were others who were not *au fait* with certain terminology and had always been pestered by it. I was able to get this cleared up once and for all. They were all taught how to build proper 'profiles' and 'batter boards'. And, above all else, they were taught a reliable method of setting out works by the application of co-ordinated geometry, oblique – radiation and change of zero.

My old army pal was one of my guest speakers on 'Basic Accuracy and How To Avoid Clangers!' Their directors were able to deliver valuable words to them and Wild Heerbrugg, one of the world's largest survey equipment manufacturers, were able to show some of the latest and best equipment and show us some very interesting films demonstrating the use of this equipment. These films were shot on some very attractive Swiss sites!

During the course I got Report No. 22 away to Ian Gordon and this reminded me how fast time was passing. All the time the course was going on the crew were bashing on with the Kericho job and 'that man' was bashing on with Marigat. However, I had to fire 'that man' because there wasn't any alternative.

Since I have been in private practice I have had to learn to incorporate my joy for living with my work. After I became my own boss there was never a time when I left the office and then went home to have fun; well, not a fixed regular time anyway. My hours were much longer and my work became my life. To mould all aspects of my life into one molecule (I use the word lightly) didn't come easy at first; I had to work at it. Whatever, I always tried to keep jolly and because I was nearly always happy I'm sure some people thought I was some kind of nut; they didn't like my cheerful disposition and would wrongly think that I didn't have a care in the world. You see, I always knew that with the kind of life I led I could die a lot sooner than most – accidents, diseases, game, terrorists, jealous husbands or, just laughing myself to death!

A nice thing happened when I was charging around Nairobi one beautiful cool but sunny morning; I bumped into Ron Marshall. Do you remember him? He was at Mwea Tibere with me. He had left the Ministry of Works and was now working for United Nations; lucky blighter. Before we parted company he asked me to bring Molly and Jennifer out to his place, over at Karen, to see Liz. This I did and we became very good friends for a long time and saw each other often. Ron and Liz had a gorgeous swimming pool in their garden and it created much fun between the families. I was amazed, though, when I learnt how much hard work it was to maintain a pool – in Africa. So now, when I was away on safari, the girls would often drive over to Karen and stay with them; a whole weekend sometimes.

Actually, social life for the girls was for ever improving. As well as Ron and Liz, they had Yaqub and Khalida and loads of school and club friends. And, sometimes they had me! I always enjoyed being back in Nairobi with them and we had lots of fun. Mind you, Jennifer was seeing boys now; however, I still saw her a lot. Molly and I always enjoyed our morning coffee down at the Kenya Coffee House or at the Thorn Tree. Come to think of it, we had several favourite coffee haunts. In the evenings a visit to the drive-ins or cinemas was always entertaining as was visiting friends for a meal. And the three of us used to delight in creating an evening when we had friends home for a meal. I can remember several lovely girls who were Jennifer's personal friends. I was always able to live it up a bit to make up for all the loneliness and graft I suffered when on safari.

12

Garsen/Garissa Road and Mufindi Paper Mill

On 1 September 1980 we started a big project which would employ all of us for at least a couple of months. The German Aid Programme was going to build an elevated road from Garsen up to Garissa. The existing road, as it stood at that moment, was just a murram track and every rainy season it became impassable. A good deal of it got flooded if not completely washed away. The first task for the Germans was to get the route surveyed. Concrete monuments (concrete blocks four inches by four inches and eighteen inches long with a half inch reinforcing-bar running through the centre of them) had to be almost completely buried at every half kilometre and these had to be traversed and levelled, (determination of height above sea-level.) The traverse and levels had to be tied-in to Survey of Kenya Triangulation Stations which were located at every so many miles. (Griffiths has forgotten how many miles!) When all the monuments were in and weather permitted, they had to be marked with white-wash 1 m × 1 m crosses so that they could be seen on air photographs. These photographs were flown as part of the process for producing contoured topographic maps – a common technique these days. The distance from Garsen to Garissa is 125 miles. Very wild and sparsely populated country but loads of big game.

As nearly always happens, there was a slight problem. A good part of this road ran right through Shifta country. I never took in the complete history of the Shifta movement other than that there was a band of mostly nomadic people in that part of the country, who didn't like being ruled by the Kenyan Government. They were mostly Arab-looking people with long black hair. Suddenly, I found myself very much involved in the scrap, be it no more than trying to protect the lives of those of my safari and myself. There were periodic outbursts of activities from these people and the end results were always the same – a lot of people got slaughtered and far too often many of them were innocent civilians. A busload of people would get shot up, a carload of travellers would get shot up or a Land Rover of civil servants. Often, when the Shifta themselves came up against a bit of opposition they too would be lying around, all over the place, in pools of blood. Generally speaking, up there people would move around in groups with their camels and there was no way of identifying Shifta members until they started shooting!

We left Nairobi at half past seven a.m. and arrived at Garissa at four o'clock, after collecting some stores in Thika. Distance 234 miles – some tarmac and the rest murram roads. There was a curfew in the area and if you were caught on the road after that time you not only had trouble with the Shifta but you would get the Kenyan police after you. I was never sure which was worse. I was quite impressed with the Tana River at Garissa; the whole area rather reminded me of Egypt, and there were just as many armed soldiers too! I reported to the DC there and he welcomed us but told me that I couldn't go out to work every day without taking at least four armed Administration Police, armed soldiers or Kenyan police! These were to act as our bodyguards and I was responsible for their transportation. That was a big one. I could see that for the first few days I would have to play it by ear. The whole time I had the feeling that a shoot-out was imminent and death was standing right by my side. How in the hell did I get myself into these situations? I had to earn a living, was my answer. All my men, without exception, just took the situation in their stride, with no demands for danger money or any such things. They wanted the work as much as I did. One of my men said, 'We are safe with you Mzee, nothing is going to happen to us as long as you are around and with us!' I looked at him – twice! This must have been a throwback from the colonial days, because I can assure you, I thought they, the 'Shifta', would come after me and leave them alone. (Oh I see, perhaps that is what my chap meant!)

We made our camp in the Administration Police compound. The next day was very hot and we all confessed that the mosquitos didn't half bite up here! We found sand and ballast so Mike, head chainman, got around to manufacturing the first fourteen monuments. I found a place where we could get our Distomat batteries charged. That was the morning over. In the afternoon we collected two bodyguards; and took off to find the Survey of Kenya Trig Point from where my traverse was to start. I stopped my van and we all piled out. The two police cocked their machine guns and walked over to the big tree, which was quite a distance away from us, one looking in one direction and the other the other. I wished they had stayed a little closer to us but I could see that they had a better overall command from where they were. After a bit of bush-cutting, we found SKT No.12, very near the road actually. My diary entry for 3 September: '. . . The day War was declared 41 years ago!. . . . . . collected three armed bodyguards first thing and went out and planted our first 14 Monuments, each ½ Km apart. Got Joe acquainted with the Distomat and then he observed the first four legs of the traverse; that's a start. Decided not to start Freddie and Fidelis on levelling today – enough is enough! I'm also not sure how to share the bodyguards yet! Left Mike in camp today and he turned out another 45 monuments. Couldn't help thinking how the whole place smelt like one huge Public Toilet!. . .'

I very soon had a daily routine going: recce, 'planting' monuments, two levelling parties, traversing and 'tieing-in' to Survey of Kenya Trigs (SKT). I had good crews and they were well trained now, which was just as well because on 9 September I had to leave them to it. Mowlems had won a huge contract in Tanzania, Mufindi in actual fact. Do you remember when I was at Mufindi with Wonk back in 1964? In those days we were looking for a route for a railway line and now this new contract was a natural follow-up development. First the railway moved in and that opened up the country and then development followed. It happened when the West was won in the United States in the past and now it was happening here. The Government of Finland were contributing a paper mill and Mowlems had won the contract to build it. At this stage Mowlems had set out and completed the initial earthworks; they now wanted me to go down there and cover the area with concreted brass co-ordinated monuments, in pre-selected positions. The purpose for these was so that they could build on any part of the site and know that in the end the whole thing would fit together.

Mowlems had their own private twin-engined Beechcraft which flew often from Nairobi to Mufindi, Tanzania. Bob Higgins was their competent pilot and I said *Jambo* to him on the morning of 11 September, loaded his plane up with my equipment and declared I was ready for anything. Fifteen minutes later, at ten forty five, I had said cheerio to Molly and off we went. We flew right over Kilimanjaro and what an experience that was! I sat in the front of the aircraft with Bob and we chatted about this and that and by the time the journey was over we knew each other fairly well. En route he made some alarming little comments. When we were flying over Kilimanjaro, for instance, he said, 'God! I can't remember whether I put any gas in this thing last night!' Further on, he got on the radio and called 'Zanzibar Tower . . . Zanzibar Tower . . . etc etc. Now, I thought, what in the blazes is he up to now? It seemed like only minutes had passed and he was on the radio again 'Zanzibar . . . Zanzibar, I have you in sight!' He wasn't kidding, he really was going to land at Zanzibar! With all the jargon going back and forth on the radio I was almost frightened to speak, but nevertheless, I did say, 'What on earth is that smell Bob? It smells as if one of your instruments has broken and that is the spirit contained inside it!'

'No, it's not,' said Superman, 'this is Zanzibar so, therefore, what you can smell is cloves . . . they grow a lot of them in Zanzibar!'

Whooff . . . bump . . . whooff . . . bump . . . bump . . . bump . . . We were landed at Zanzibar. The good man on the radio told Bob what time he landed and to park in number twelve.

'Everything all right, Bob?'

'Yes, thank you, Roy.'

'Good. Then I wonder if you would be a good chap and tell me what in the hell are we doing in Zanzibar?'

Apparently the thought never entered his mind that I didn't know what was going on. 'Ah! You see Roy, Mowlems have a big contract in Zanzibar, which is now coming to a close, but there is still an English inspector of works here; he and his wife are resident here. I bring them their mail, his personal supplies and odds and ends he needs to complete the job. He still has a labour force here so I have to bring their pay too. Also, Zanzibar is a lot less busy than Dar-es-Salaam as regards to getting the landing documentation done. Later, we have to land at Dar-es-Salaam too, but that's easy if we've dealt with the formalities here first.'

'Oh!'

The IOW was there to meet us. He left his house to come down to the runway when he heard us on his radio. We went to his house to meet his wife and have a cup of tea. 'Mrs IOW' was an absolute charm, very extrovert, good-looking, had done her hair and had a pretty dress on. She seemed very happy and very contented and above all, she made lovely cakes! I couldn't believe all this! After about an hour of this lovely haven, we said our farewells and took off for Dar-es-Salaam. It was only a matter of about fifteen minutes or so and then we were down in Dar. Before I go on, I must tell you this: whilst staying in Zanzibar, I definitely felt some strange vibrations. I could feel the spirit of all past sultans and could feel the ghosts of the slave traders of long ago. Maybe the perfume of cloves was intoxicating! When we were coming into land, I could see the palace of the one time Sultans of Zanzibar. Whenever I went to Zanzibar I never got the chance to visit the 'town' or some of the haunts and always regretted it.

Another surprise: we stayed the night in Dar-es-Salaam. Mowlems had quite a big office there and not surprisingly, a lot of English staff too. We stayed with the bachelor accountant and don't let me forget, he was a Scotsman! A great guy. A dinner party had been organised for that evening. Quite a lot of folks had gathered for dinner and they made quite a party out of the occasion. We had quite a lot of beverage before dinner and the dinner turned out to be an excellent meal. I have always enjoyed this sort of party in the past – in Africa. I suppose one of the reasons is that we need each other more living in these conditions than we do, say, in England. I also have a theory that folk tend to drop their guard more when living in the tropics. The ladies looked tanned and their teeth sparkling white and their hair seemed to bounce in the moonlight. Two of them told me that they had heard all about me and that I surveyed the route of the railway all the way to Zambia years ago. They thought I 'looked the part' or whatever that meant! I kept a very wary eye on all the young and handsome husbands, I can tell you!

Next day, we took off at seven forty five a.m. It was a lovely time of day and the weather was super, especially for seeing the game, and there was plenty of that. I saw a lot of country that I had walked over at one time in my life. It brought back a lot of memories. What you fly over in just minutes in a plane seems a never-ending worldiness when you are down there on foot! There was one place along the course of the Great Ruaha River; we were flying so low I felt I could almost touch the hippo below. I had to look upwards to see some elephant walking along the top of the river bank! At nine fifteen I looked below again and there was nothing but miles and miles of bush. I could see the Mufindi Escarpment in the middle ground and then, coming up from nowhere, there were the new paper mill earthworks and a row of new houses, houses that were just being built. On top of the hill, close to the camp, was the runway which was no more than just a field where a 'scraper' had run over it. Bob flew around the site once more to let everyone know that we had arrived. Just as suddenly we were down.

This was the beginning of a successful visit. First, the electronic equipment worked. Secondly, I had lovely weather with loads and loads of good sunshine. I planted sixty-nine monuments in their close positions, securing them with just a little concrete, leaving the additional concreting to be done whilst I was away. I'd come back at a later date and punch the accurate position in the top of the brass-plate, which was part of the monument. My accommodation was quite acceptable; it was only one of those round aluminium huts, furnished with the bare necessities and a comfortable bed. The roof was covered with palm tree fronds to partly insulate the hut from the sun; it also made the structure look more picturesque, a touch of Vincent Van Gogh! I slept like a log here. There were half a dozen Brits resident and their job was to receive stores as they arrived by road or rail from Dar-es-Salaam, ready to start the construction proper. It was a good plan to get into the site to put my primary control in before they started drilling and banging and pouring concrete all over the place. The food was plain but I thought good for a construction site. There were a couple of ladies present but I didn't see very much of them, not even on 'film nights'. One of the Finnish consulting engineers was married to a lovely Indonesian lady and she too lived on the site with their little son. She was absolutely charming and I think he was a very lucky man. Her Indonesian-style cooking was really scrumptious and I was able to indulge in her art on several evenings.

The plane came at least once a week now, sometimes twice, bringing more personnel and equipment and always a film! In camp life, I don't know of a better morale booster than a film night. We would have a couple of beers followed by our dinner and then – the film. Great stuff! The price I had to pay for this luxury was to produce a good day's work! In passing, there were a few days when I would have to find some office work between ten o'clock and half past three because 'heat shimmer' prevented me from getting the accuracy my client expected from me. I was surprised to see that the atmospheric correction alone was 60 mm for 1200 metres! I had to take notice of this.

On Friday, 19 September Bob Higgins arrived at eleven o'clock, had a spot of lunch and then took off with me at one thirty for Nairobi via Dar-es-Salaam and Zanzibar, arriving at Wilson Airport at five forty five. My lovely Molly met me as always. The first and second days home I really needed time to reflect, to meditate, to think how far I had come and where I was going from here. Was I working too hard and not spending enough time with Molly? Was I working too hard for too little? Were my clients paying me enough for my services? Could I charge any more and still get paid? Did I have to go on paying such a price for living in Kenya? Did Kenya really mean this much to me? Why did I always have to fight so much to get people to pay me the money they owed me? You sent them an invoice and you wouldn't hear from them again unless you personally pressed them over and over again; all of them. My costs, rents, staff pay, transportation costs, cost of materials, all had to be paid as soon as they were due – there was no getting out of it – or you'd be in trouble. I did a lot of work for the Government and they were the worst payers of them all! I thanked God for my sense of humour. I always needed to stop and think things through, but the tide wouldn't wait for me. I had to bash on, couldn't fall back; everybody was wanting the answers yesterday!

While I was away the men had been getting on very well down on the Garsen/Garissa Road job. I was needed there very soon, very soon, for at least one reason; it was time to move base camp. I got to Garissa on the 22 September and reports were generally good. At least nobody had been shot! The men had completed seventy kilometres of traversing and levelling but transport was giving a bit of trouble, mainly because of the bad roads. I had recently taken on a new surveyor, James, and he joined us that day. Freddie kindly gave me a nice cup of African tea and we all sat around the camp fire, not because we were cold but to talk over our next move.

The next day we struck camp and were loaded by nine o'clock and, in a way, we were all a bit glad to be on our way to Hola. We arrived at Hola at half past twelve and noted that parts of the road were diabolical. We all noticed that it was even hotter than Garissa. We had two armed bodyguards with us and I had to arrange for their return to Garissa. Anyway, on our initial drive to Hola one of the bodyguards was in the back of the Datsun van, which I was driving. Like I said, parts of the road were diabolical and as a result, some of the equipment and some of the chaps were bouncing around a bit in the back. Suddenly, I heard three automatic shots fired, almost in my ear; they momentarily scared the life out of me. One thing was for sure: with the road being as bad as it was, I couldn't make a run for it! I stopped and without getting out I looked around. Strangely, it was fairly open country just there and I could see all around. I waited a good twenty seconds before I jumped out of the van. I went round to the rear of the van and opened the door and I was met with a mixture of comments and exclamations – and that's putting it politely! The bodyguard had a very embarrassed grin on his face as he pointed to the roof of my van which now had three new bullet holes in it. He had forgotten to put his safety catch on and with all the bumping around, had fired his own gun.

On arrival at Hola I reported to the DO and he made us very welcome. He was amused at my story about my bodyguard. He said that the DO Garissa had informed him that we were coming. We set up camp in the chief's compound; it was a bit public but we had water and the *dukas* were very near for the men. There appeared to be quite a few pretty girls around in no time and most of my men had smiles on their faces; I have learnt by now that when on safari the men like to have someone to wash their pots and pans and clean out their tents! They only ever seem to use two or three girls and I understand that they all share them. In actual fact, I suspect that these girls are usually related to the men; daughters, cousins or daughters of friends.

In a way, I liked Hola. It was a very small township and was what I call 'very coastal'. It has a strong Arab influence. When I use the description 'Arab', this includes the beautiful blend of Arab and African blood. The whole content seems to me to be neatly bound by the marriage to Islam. Sometimes the Arab blood comes through and sometimes the African; either way, it produces handsome and well-balanced people. And of course, where the marriage to and influence of Islam comes into it is by the perpetual appearance of the conspicuous mosques where the faithful pray; they are a constant reminder of where they belong, if I may put it that way. I love to hear the call to prayer as dawn breaks and the sky takes on its first tinges of red. I find sincerity in these Muslim men in their kikoys and beaded hats. Yes, this is how I feel about Hola. Just a minute, it didn't take me long to find out that I couldn't get Super Blend Petrol there!

Now that we had moved to Hola, we had about thirty-five miles to drive back towards Garissa to start a day's work. Hopefully, this would become five miles less each day; however, it meant long hours for the next few days. I couldn't set a camp between Garissa and Hola because it was too dangerous; we couldn't get protection and the DC wouldn't allow me. We collected our bodyguards from the DO's office next day, then took off to where we started work. The journey took just over an hour and a half. The three askaris went each side of the road, took their helmets off and examined their firearms. We got set up on the next monument, put a prism on the back monument which was half a kilometre down the road towards Garissa and a prism on the next monument towards Hola – a leapfrog effect – and started observing. I decided to stay in the van for a bit and let them get on with it; I'd do the taxi driving from monument to monument; it speeded up the operation considerably. Also, I could more usefully occupy my time by getting on with some computing. The askaris were a little out of sight of me but they had a clear view of the whole crew.

About a quarter of an hour went by so I thought it must be getting near time to move the back prism up forward and so on. I started my engine and just eased the clutch out to move slowly forward. I instantly stopped again because I noticed that none of the men was moving but all looking down the road towards our front monument. Something was wrong. A string of camels was crossing the road. It was strange because we couldn't see anybody looking after them. I jumped out of my van to ask my surveyor what he thought was going on. At the same time as I made my move the two askaris on my left ran down the road and across to the other side. Just then I heard something hit my van, immediately followed by the report of three or four shots being fired from somewhere down near those camels. Were those bullets meant for me?

The corporal shouted to us to jump in the road drainage ditch and keep our heads down. As soon as he could see that we were doing as we were told, he and his men disappeared into the bush, running down towards the camels but staying under cover of the bush. Only seconds later all hell was let loose down there. Single shots and automatic. I don't know what made me do it, but I looked into the faces of my men to see if I could see any signs of fear. Not a glimmer of concern anywhere! I must say that the thought went through my mind that this must be – it! I was going and I had bloody well asked for it. I looked at one of my chainmen and laughed – he looked back at me and just gave me one of those African grins. God looks after children and bloody fools! Within ten minutes the askaris came back. I said to the corporal, 'What was that all about?'

'Oh, just a bit of trouble but nothing for you to worry about. Now you and your people can get on with your work.'

Honestly!

'Do you want me to come back down there with you?'

'No. You just get on with your work.'

I thought about it for a moment and I didn't like the tone of his voice nor the way he was ordering me around. I concluded that although he was only half my age he was a professional policeman and goodness only knows, 'his work' was very specialised and I supposed he knew what he was doing; so without another word, I did what I was told to do, and told the men to carry on.

I examined my van – there were two more bullet holes. I looked in the back of my van to see if I could find any more important damage but I only found a bullet hole in my tool-box! I have still got this tool-box in my shed at the back of my garden, here in Scotland. Oh well, after all, it was all in a day's work. I dared not think about it too much.

On 26 September Freddie and I drove back to Nairobi, which was 304 miles from Hola, and we got there at half past six in the evening, having suffered two punctures en route. The next day we both called in on our client and made my purely technical report. Fred then went to the garage, where everybody was looking at his bullet holes, to get some spares. I gave him some petty cash and then off to Hola he went. I thought he would have to stop at Garissa because of the curfew and he would have to pick up an escort.

Hoping that the men could bash on without me for a while, I flew down to Mufindi to continue the job with the monuments. I was strangely pleased to see the old hut again; it was always a good sight to see at the end of a hot dusty day on the construction site. It was the same regime for the next fifteen days – twelve hours of work, four hours of drinking, eating, cleansing, picture-going, reading, washing (it was the only way you could make sure that you kept your clothes) and then hopefully eight hours of resting. Friday, 17 October soon arrived and Bob Higgins flew me back to Nairobi.

Life went on; no time to laze around. My diary reads: 22 October '. . . Joe (who had come back to Nairobi from Hola, for a few days off) was at the house a quarter of an hour earlier than arranged. Freddie (who had come back with Joe also) turned up a quarter of an hour late. We got down the road and I had forgotten my bedding. However, we still turned up in Collin Heyes' office (my old Army pal) who worked for my client for the Garsen/Garissa Road, before eight o'clock. Collin was coming down with us to inspect the Garsen/Garissa Job. We left Collin's office by eight fifteen, Joe and Freddie in my Land Rover and Collin and self in the V.W. Camper. We were well on the way to Mombasa when I had to turn back because Collin had forgotten his flight diagram for the air survey (which still hadn't been flown!)! What's the matter with everybody this morning! Because time had now moved on a bit, we now decided to go to Garsen via Garissa and not Mombasa (because of the curfew!). Collin inspected the route thoroughly from Garissa onwards and took many photographs. We stayed the night at the Tana River Camp which was very tropical and exotic, or it would have been if I were staying there with somebody else! Though the monkeys were a thieving bunch of crooks! We only stayed the one night; the rooms were right on top of the crocodiles and the whole place was teaming with game. Comfortable accommodation, excellent food and wine, and expensive!'

The next day, Collin inspected the rest of the route on to our camp at Garsen. Having expressed his satisfaction at the way the job was going Collin left camp at one o'clock for Mombasa and the day after, he would continue his journey to Nairobi. Thank God that was over.

I would like to show you my diary entry 26 October, because it was the last happy day like it for some considerable time. '. . . I'm writing this sitting in the back of the Moonraker, waiting to be given the OK to move the back prism. Feeling very hot with the temperature well into the hundreds; in the shade. It's lovely to have the facility of the Camper's fridge (which now works at last) and to enjoy an occasional glass of milk or cordial. Tried to phone Molly this morning at seven thirty but alas, no operator on duty! Joe is traversing and I'm riding 'shot-gun'. Freddie is frantically planting monuments and Fidelis is levelling like there is no tomorrow. At this moment, I feel life is very wonderful! Moments like these are very nice for as long as they last! Freddie had a puncture and with no bodyguard with him – that wasn't fair – I'm happy that he got away with it. Tried to speak to Molly twice this evening – no reply. We got another eight km of traversing done and Freddie planted twenty monuments. Fidelis is right up behind Joe with the levelling. The new mosquito net is wizard.'

The next day we didn't exactly put the flags out, but the whole crew witnessed my marking the first 'pre-flight marking' on Monument No. 390. This was the first cross of many hundreds placed on monuments over the weeks and weeks ahead. During those weeks we were interrupted by Shifta, lions, buffalo, rain, man, crocodiles, hippo and baboons. However, today, after my demonstration, we got on with our respective jobs. The day after that I had to return to Nairobi and at about midday, when I left base camp, I could see our new pre-flight crosses all along the side of the road and I passed Freddie and his crew making yet another cross on another monument. They all looked very peculiar with their lovely black faces covered in white wash dust! Mike gave me a grin when I passed him and he stuck his two fingers up at me in the Winston Churchill manner; the gaps in his white teeth were even more conspicuous than usual because his face was snow-white! I gave him a Winston Churchill victory sign back and shouted, 'Good-bye Rock Hudson!' (His favourite person.)

About a week later I had a call from Joe to tell me that the traversing was finished (good news) and all the 'tie-ins' to the Survey of Kenya Trig Points. Now they had all joined in on the pre-flight marking. A few days later they ran into more trouble. They had torrential rain, vehicles were being completely bogged down all the way from Malindi up to Garissa; and beyond. Most of the white crosses had been washed away or were even under water. What were they to do? I needed to talk to my client before I pulled my safari out, so I arranged to get Joe to call me again tomorrow; booked the call through the DO to make sure we got in touch. I had been trying to get Collin for yonks and I finally did after having just spoken to Joe again. Collin was in full agreement with me to bring back my safari, while they were still in one piece!

On Sunday the girls and I went over to Ron and Liz for lunch. We had a swim first, then after lunch, at about three o'clock, we drove back to Nairobi to welcome the men back, lock up the vehicles and equipment and then let the chaps get away home.

Freddie and Fidelis arrived home first with a terrible look on their faces. They told me that they had got to Mombasa – no problems – and this morning they all left for Nairobi after spending the night in Mombasa. They got as far as Mtito Ndei when the Land Rover left the road and turned over, putting Joe and the driver into hospital at Voi – and killing Mike. For the next few moments I could not have been more stunned if I had been hit between the eyes with a sledge-hammer. Poor dear Mike. I telephoned the hospital at Voi and they told me that the men had been terribly hurt but they were both talking now. How dreadful. I sent the rest of the men home and then I thought it was better if I went to the Aga Khan Hospital (where Penina worked) and told Penina (Joe's wife) about the accident in person. Molly, bless her, went with me. We arranged to take Penina down to Voi tomorrow. We reported to the Kenya Police. When we got down to the Voi Hospital, quite early in the day, the two fellows had already been transferred to Mombasa Hospital where the facilities for coping were better. Mike was still in the mortuary at Voi.

First reports said that Joe had broken his fibia and had a bad gash on his leg; the driver had broken just about everything. The engine of the Land Rover had landed in Mike's lap. When Molly and I went to the crashed vehicles compound at Voi Police Station to identify the Land Rover, we walked straight past it looking at all the other vehicles to try and identify ours. It was absolutely beyond recognition.

Mike's body was being transferred to Mombasa the next day; apparently, they had better facilities there for preserving it. They kept Mike's body for weeks, waiting for family to claim it for burial, but nobody came forward except myself. At the end, Mombasa City Council had to bury him. I tried hard and so did the Kenya Police to find someone from his family but with no avail. We even put a message on the Kenya Radio. Molly and I went to his native reserve to see who we could find. The village elder tried to help us. He said that Mike's father had died a long time ago and his mother had married another man from a different reserve. And so on. Several people, including some of the police couldn't understand why I was so concerned about Mike. I think that only another surveyor could understand my feelings. Survey camps all over the world and throughout history live a life that is almost unique; I suppose life in the armed forces could be classed as similar but even that is not quite the same. We worked and more or less lived together and shared many serious moments at work and had many damn good laughs together. The job became a major concern to all of us and all of us, no matter what his task, became dependent on each other. It was a bit corny to say we were like brothers because that didn't describe anything but we did become very close. Each other's well-being became a primary concern of all of us. The kind of lives we lived, you couldn't afford to be any different. Nasty rows were not tolerated on safari and unless a man blended with the community he soon found himself out on his ear. When an accident like this hit us, we tended to take it pretty badly. For months the other two were in hospital getting very special treatment and I went down to see them on several occasions. Much water has passed under the bridge since those days, so I don't think there is much point dragging it all up again now. Sufficient to say it wasn't the Land Rover's fault but I think having the night in Mombasa at the end of a safari had a lot to do with it. Most of us, by the Grace of God, got away with it.

Africa has its own unique way of sorting men out from the boys and it's tough. I had to pull myself together quickly, because on 24 November I started my second course for John Mowlems, out at Dandora. These courses were proving popular and my client obviously thought that the cost was worth it. We were talking of offering the course to people outside the company next time. This course went very well and I believe we helped a lot of people. I was already looking forward to the next course.

By the end of the course I had done what we all need to do every now and again: I picked myself up, dusted myself off and started all over again. I was successful in securing a contract at Madogo – about two miles from Garissa! You must think that I'm a bit of a glutton for punishment! The commission was from Pencol Engineering and I was required to do a topographic survey of Madogo Village, both sides of the road, and survey the route for a pipeline down to the river bridge at Garissa. I had made Freddie the party chief for this job and I had come here to give him a hand to get started and to see if there were any problems. James and Fidelis were busy putting all those damn crosses out again for the air survey of the new road. We still had to have our armed escorts, of course, but being so near to Garissa, this wasn't much of a problem.

On 12 December 1980 the Shifta made two attacks very near us and murdered twelve people. The very hot and humid weather, together with these dreadful violent attacks, very nearly made me pack up and go home. Brush myself off indeed! What a year 1980 had turned out to be! I really wanted my head seeing to because every day we were living in hopes of not being shot. On 15 December I entered into my diary how unbearably hot it was and that there was a hell of a lot of military running around with heavy machine gun fire; not very far away but I thought too far away for anyone to be shooting at us. That was the lackadaisical state I was getting in, after months of this. I got a load more surveying done. Christmas was right on top of us.

I'll admit that at times it may sound as if I'm having a bit of a moan. Actually, I'm portraying what daily African safari life is like for the surveyor like myself. It's not as Hollywood portrays it – it's how I saw it, there and then. It's a tough and trying life. So, what made me put up with it?

For a start, I have got to earn my living and meet my commitments. I am pleased to be living in this environment; I feel its magic. I love the sight, sounds and smells of Africa. I feel that I have been granted a gift in having been allowed to walk in and share this beautiful open country with some of His finest creations – animals. I love meeting them face-to-face (but only if I have a fair chance of escape) and then experiencing a mutual inquisitiveness. I have come to terms with the natives of this land and enjoy communicating with them in their language – their colourful Swahili. Africa's trees, plants and red earth are elements in my natural world. I do not live in the past, but I will admit that sometimes I do enjoy sharing moments with the ghosts of one-time fellow travellers. We all have, or had, this unadulterated love for Africa, a raw love which we all shared. I want to stay and share this 'garden of Eden', this bosom of 'Mother Earth', for as long as I am able. I feel sad when I think about how much longer that may be.

During 1981 it seemed that everything in Kenya was trying to eat us. We had an encounter at least once a week! One time I told my client that if I had one more 'upset' over a crocodile I would pull my whole safari out of the Tana Delta Scheme. Mind you, we were doing cross-sections at the widest part of the Tana! It wasn't rare to hear the news that another child (usually a little girl) had been devoured whilst collecting water for her mother down by the river. On one occasion, in search of a missing little girl, the Kenya Police shot what appeared to be a marauding crocodile. They then cut open the stomach and there was the little girl – almost whole.

To do my surveying, I had to travel on the Tana quite a lot in what they call a dug-out. In fact, that was exactly what it was, a carved-out trunk of a tree. These were difficult craft to get in and out of. I often sat in the centre of one of these and although appreciating the cool air as we glided through the still water, I used to be petrified by those pairs of eyes, barely above the level of the water, glaring at us! I felt so fragile. I would wonder, suppose two or three of these characters decided to turn the boat over? This they could easily do, we wouldn't stand a chance. And, what a hell of a way to go!

When we were stranded at Witu because the river had broken its banks, we drove down to it as close as we could, the idea being that Freddie and Fidelis would hire a dug-out with 'crew' and try and get to Garsen (where the dukas are) to get us some food. Before we hired our dug-out we spent an awful lot of time watching three Kenya policemen dragging the river bed in search of weapons lying on the bottom. Earlier that day a dug-out with two policemen on board had overturned. They were fully dressed and even had their overcoats and helmets on. Somebody actually saw the crocs getting them and heard the screams and splashing – but what could they do? It was said that 'nothing at all' of those policemen was found. I still shudder. I can remember when one of my men and myself found a crocodile on the rampage in the flood water, three miles from the normal river course. (Didn't we run!)

The rain had a greater effect on my life than ever before (even in Scotland!) There were times when I thought the rain was never going to end. Tanzania was as effective as Kenya. Strangely enough, one time when I had to move camp because of flooding, we weren't getting any rain at all where we were. It was all falling up in the Mount Kenya region and we were suffering with the consequences, a very full Tana River. I'll give you this, the countryside looked at its best during the rains. All those dead, dried-up looking bushes, thorn bushes for example, burst into bright green leaf and you saw all kinds of bright flowering shrubs and bushes. The zebra look radiant and pot-bellied because there was so much to eat. Snakes – creatures I can never come to terms with – gave me a lot more trouble when the heavens opened up. They were slithering and squirming all over the place, often in my tent. They never seemed to bother my men except for the fact that they loved to go in for a kill.

Most of the areas that I was interested in had got only earth tracks, if any tracks at all, so driving became very difficult. We often had to rely on Shank's mare to get any work done at all. The perpetual driving in and out of deep stony ruts did no end of body and mechanical damage. The high revving played havoc with the engines, not to mention the extra fuel consumption. It all ate terribly into what ever profits I made.

We were kept busy in the Garsen/Garissa area for most of 1981. I lost count of the number of times we had to re-whitewash the 'pre-flight markings' on our traverse points – one every two kilometres, hundreds of miles of them – after they were washed away by rain and then we would have to do them all over yet again. The reason for not flying/photographing was always the same. The anticipated good air survey weather didn't materialise; the unexpected weather conditions did not allow the air photography to be done. I was down in this area a good deal of the time, but I did have to move around a bit to look after other jobs as well.

During the whole year we had to keep falling back on the Kenya Police or the Administration Police for armed escorts while we were working in the Garsen/Garissa areas. Many days we were prevented from doing a day's work because bodyguards were not available; they were out chasing Shifta. This was frustrating to the point where I could pull my hair out. One day, when we were hanging about Garissa, waiting for some bodyguards, I was walking around the ‘boma’ when I looked in on the armoury. There, in the rifle-rack was an old Lee Enfield .303 rifle, the type I used in my army days. Full of excitement over my find, I shot across to the DO’s office and approached the DO himself.

‘Good morning, Sir. Excuse me butting in on you like this, but I noticed that you have a Lee Enfield in your armoury. I used to be a marksman with one of those in my old army days. Why don’t you let me borrow it and then let me get out to work. We will be able to look after ourselves then, if the Shifta should show their faces. After all, I am a trained soldier.’

‘Good Lord, Mr Griffiths, it took generations to get these guns off of you people; I’m damned sure I’m not going to give them back to you!’ he said with boisterous laughter.

In spite of all this trouble we were having in this area, the police were still lobbing out tickets! They gave me one because I had lost the number plate off of my van! This was on the ferry at Garsen. You can’t trust anybody can you?

13

Tana Delta Irrigation Scheme

On 27 February I was successful in securing another contract with Gauff/Dutch Government to do about sixty days' work (ground control) for the Tana Delta irrigation scheme. This was located south of Garsen and at the mouth of the River Tana. So, for a while, the two jobs of the Garsen/Garissa road and Tana Delta irrigation scheme ran consecutively. This new job was quite a big one for us, more in time factor than size. It covered an area of a couple of hundred square miles. I had to cover it with traverses which rather looked like a giant cobweb. Of course, all these traverse stations (one about every half kilometre) had to be levelled too. Oh boy, did this job turn out to be a pain! I love this area for its people and the sheer beauty of its countryside but to try and do a survey here? When I first took the job on there were roads and tracks all over the place and all well-maintained. But, as the job went on, they disappeared, one after the other. Eventually, I had to get around the area some of the time in a dug-out or, by dhow. Very often, only by walking. But the job got done. There were no praises for getting the job done, of course, only the threat of court action if you didn't. We were chased from one end of the site to the other by buffalo, nearly eaten alive by crocodiles and scared out of our wits by snakes. No guns you see, only pangas. It was not like these Hollywood films at all!

We moved to three different camps during the course of this job: Garsen, Witu and Kipini. There were no real problems with the actual surveying; thank God for modern Electronic Distance Measuring Equipment – E.D.M! Well, there was one slight problem: we often had to decrease our traverse leg distances from 500 metres to say, 90 metres because the bush was just too thick to cut with the methods we had (how I wished we had a D8). This way, you had a lot more work in your field book but you didn't have much to show on the drawings for distance covered. There was no doubt about it; my staff, as well as myself, took a hell of a hammering on this venture. Apart from getting thorns in the feet and cuts and scratches from working in virgin bush, there were additional hazards too. One day Fidelis nearly lost his arm whilst going along in a dug-out, when a hippo came up swiftly alongside from behind. It was only his 'sènses' that told him to move his hand inboard quickly. His arm was bruised by the grazing of the hippo's teeth when he missed his bite!

Our food intake was low for weeks too, we just couldn't get any. Africans are very used to this condition. They all get cases of bad breath which they tell me is caused merely by hunger. At one time I was on a diet of bananas, porridge and Bisto – that was my total store content. Then there were long periods when petrol just wasn't getting through to us. It always worked out that you could work tomorrow only because the Agriculture Officer could lend you five gallons and on another day, someone else would help you out!

In the end, we got marooned. Stranded! I didn't know what to expect next whilst working in this area. Initially, we were getting very little rain and yet every day the water level was rising slowly everywhere. Roads were slowly disappearing. This was the first warning that somewhere in the country the rains had started. The next warning that the rains had started was that the vehicles kept breaking down. The next thing was that the supply vehicles (food and petrol) were delayed for days but you couldn't think why. Then the telephones went out for days. Then came more local heavy showers or storms.

To get to the proposed irrigation scheme you had to come over the Garsen Ferry which was owned and operated by the Ministry of Works. The ferry itself consisted of a large pontoon which was attached to a chain which was anchored each side of the river by two holdfasts. The ferry was propelled by about ten men all pulling on the chain between the two anchors. They would grab the chain, walk along the pontoon pulling, run back to the other end again and then repeat. It worked well. There was a concrete slipway each side of the river so that you could drive on and off the pontoon. There was a little bit of tarmac on the ferry approaches each side too. Each side was marked with a high post. For fun, sometimes the passengers would join in the pull. The Dutch engineer with the Ministry of Works said he was closing the ferry as from that day. Help! The water was getting so high the ferry couldn't reach bank to bank – and the velocity of the water was a problem.

I got through to Collin's office at last and they said that Collin had been hospitalised – yesterday. Yes, it was true; there did seem to be periods of nothing but doom and gloom. It was agony to be working your fingers to the bone and yet knowing you were losing money day after day. I was not the only one to have had a tough time working in Kenya. There was a history of us. Occasionally, when things went really wrong for a while, I got to feel terribly lonely; my stomach felt empty and I almost felt sick. Then I said to myself this was all part and parcel of the deal; I had asked for it; now I had to take command of the situation and fight – fight like bloody hell.

Fidelis surged ahead in leaps and bounds on this job. On 13 March, I put him on traversing for the first time and he did very well. He had been studying it for months. He had good agreement in his rounds of horizontal angles and his forward and back Distomat readings always agreed within three mm – which was excellent. He managed to do five kilometres on his first day! I was so pleased with him. In this area we only had very small villages and I wondered if they would ever reach the status of townships. Anyway, keep an eye on them: their names are Kibusu, Ngao, Kau and Kipini. Here are a couple more, Dedi Waredi (isn't that a lovely name?) and Moa.

About a week later, when we were still camped at Witu, I heard the zip of my tent being unzipped. It was one o'clock at night. I grabbed the very sharp panga which is always kept under my mattress and my flash-light. I came awake immediately. I shone my torch straight at the door just as the figure of a woman came into my tent. She had that black cover over her dress, the one that Muslim women always wear but her yashmak was thrown over her head. I could see instantly an extremely pretty face. She had lip-stick on a very full and pretty mouth. I spoke to her in Swahili and said, 'Hello Girl, what on earth do you want? Who are you? Come on, tell me, did someone send you to me? Are you after some money?'

By the time I had finished asking her all these questions she had completely undressed but for a string of beads around her very tiny waist. She was Afro-Arab and undoubtedly had a lovely and full figure. Judging by the firmness of her quite ample breasts, I would think she was about eighteen or nineteen years old. Still holding my panga, I rushed out of my tent and took a quick look around. It was a very bright moonlight night; there was barely a shadow under the trees. I was even more awake now as I took a slower glance around the camp. I walked over to one tree because I couldn't really see under it from where I was standing and I walked over to another one too and another. I was about to shout out for Freddie and Fidelis but I didn't really want to disturb them. Apart from the usual African night sounds, it seemed awfully still and quiet. There really wasn't anyone else around my camp. I felt glad that I hadn't woken up the whole darn place. I was now breathing very heavily, I'm partly ashamed to say. Now, how did I handle this?

I went back into my tent and the first thing that came to my mind was that she was even more beautiful than I at first thought. She was lying on the mattress and completely exposing herself. The next thing I thought, as she was waving me over to her side, was that she was younger than my daughters. The third thing that came to my mind was that if that had been my beautiful Molly lying there, there wouldn't have been any problems! The fourth thing was, I loved my wife so much. The fifth thing was the dreadful matter of disease. And the last thought was that maybe she had been planted here by someone who wanted to make an awful lot of trouble for me. Maybe even tell Molly!

I knelt down beside her on the mattress and took her small hand into mine and with a smile on my face and in a friendly manner, I told her to be a good girl and put her clothes on and I gave her some money and told her to buy herself something nice tomorrow. She quickly sat up and threw her arms around my neck. She was one of the prettiest girls I had ever seen in my life. I stood up sharply, pushing her shoulders away from me and in a very stern voice said, 'Now come on, put your clothes back on and get out of my tent.'

'But I have nowhere to go and I love you. I have seen you for weeks and have loved you since I first set my eyes upon you. Only Allah knows how much I love you.'

'For heaven's sake girl, I'm old enough to be your father and as it is I'm a Christian and I'm happily married to a very beautiful lady.'

'But I have nowhere to go!'

'I'll get the askaris, they are friends of mine, they will soon give you "somewhere' to go," I said, as I walked over to the door of my tent. I suddenly felt very horrible about turning her out at that time of night – but she had got here! She burst out into tears and very quickly dressed and left my tent. It was all over in about ten minutes. I was back into bed like a shot and went straight to sleep. When I was walking through the bush next day, I thought about my visitor and said, out loud – 'I'm mad!'

Before I took this contract on, I knew Wendy would be getting married during the duration of this job. That was no problem, I thought, I'd just leave the men to it and take off for four or five days. Even just a couple of days' break, back in England, would do me the world of good. In any case, I wouldn't miss any of my daughter's weddings for anything. But from the moment I put my first tent peg in on this site, trouble started. As I got nearer and nearer to Wendy's wedding date the problems got worse and worse. Situations were changing several times a day and plans had to be changed just as often. And on top of this, about a week before I would have been due to leave, the ferry closed. I was already losing money so I could not desert my safari in the hope that it would still be there in two weeks when I got back; that would have assured bankruptcy. At the moment, we were keeping the job going, we were producing valuable work, we hadn't stopped and that was important and taking all things into consideration, this kept the clients; the Germans and the Dutch; reasonably happy. I kept our flag flying and that was what they expected of me.

When I saw the difficult situation that I was getting myself into I wrote to my dear Wendy and explained the situation. I also wrote to my son-in-law, Dr Steve Mann, offering the same explanation and asked him to stand in for me and give Wendy away for me. The way I figured it, he was the next in line. What made matters even worse – probably for all of us, was that several times a day, for several days, I phoned Molly but never got through, not to anybody. Honestly, I could have sat down and wept.

When I woke up on the 20 April I finally decided to try and make a run for Nairobi. I thought I must try and get back there before the girls did! Freddie and Fidelis drove me as close to Garsen as they could, which was still a long way from the ferry. We were able to hire a dug-out which took us across the Tana. Strangely, I didn't see any crocodiles that day. But I still treated the dug-out with the greatest of respect; in fact, I told those two not to muck about, not to make a move. That blighter Fidelis decided to have a bit of fun with me and played all sorts of tricks! At Garsen, I caught the Tana River Bus Company bus to Malindi, not being absolutely sure what I was going to do when I got there. I had to go somewhere and that seemed the right direction to travel. Maybe I'd try my luck at getting a flight to Nairobi. What an experience that bus ride turned out to be! I think it found every joint and muscle in my body. The road was in a shocking state, many places still covered in water. At Malindi Airfield, I had to wait several hours but as luck would have it, I got the only available seat on the three fifty p.m. flight to Nairobi. From the Jomo Kenyatta Airport the Kenya Airport bus took me all the way to the Milimani Hotel, which if you remember, was very close to my home. Smokey was very pleased to see me; I could clearly see that he thought we had all deserted him! And guess what? The telephone wasn't working! The trouble with the telephones in Nairobi was caused by the rats eating their way through all the wires' insulating material. They were able to travel for miles underground along the ducts, having the nosh of their lives.

Molly and Fa-Fa came back to Nairobi on 25 April and I was at Jomo Kenyatta Airport in plenty of time to meet them. Needless to say, it was lovely to have part of my family back with me again. I enjoyed hearing all the latest news about the folks and what everyone was getting up to. I must confess I was a little disappointed when they told me that Molly's brother gave Wendy away and not Steve, as I had asked. No explanation was offered!

There came a time when I was running out of work that could be completed without travelling in the flooded areas. There was one piece of work which stood out as a possible; it was high and dry but on the other side of the Tana. The task was to run a traverse and level control from Kipini (but the south side of the Tana) down the shoreline to a place called Adara (a small hill on the shoreline with a Survey of Kenya Trig on the top of it.) The work could be tied-in into a traverse at the south end, which was done before all the flooding got really bad. But to do this I had to get a crew, tenting and equipment across the Tana! I had an idea that there was a way. The men would have to help me and co-operate to the fullest.

My plan was to make up two crews; Freddie in command of one party and Fidelis in command of the second party. They would each have a separate levelling party. I decided to hire, if I could, two dhows to give us the transport and a certain amount of shelter. The plan was for Fidelis to start traversing from Kipini and work south along the shoreline, with another party levelling behind him. Freddie was to sail down south to Adara and start traversing northwards along the shoreline until he met Fidelis. He also would have a second levelling party with him. They would have to carry enough tools and plant and concrete monuments – and water – but no tents! The captain should drop the men off at the appointed place and then meet them about eight kilometres further along the shore each day. The men could either make or find some shelter or sleep in the dhow. They should complete the work in not less than four days or longer than six days. Mosquitos, game and snakes were the unknown factors. I allowed half a day lost through rain every other day. The men listened to my plan, talked about it in many other African languages as well as Swahili and then decided to go for it. None of them were seamen and some of them were even scared to death of the sea, but they gave me the chance to get the job done.

It was important that we should see a mirror being shone between Kipini and Adara because it would give me the chance to tie-in some traverse work in this area. You see, we knew the exact bearing between these two trig points. A Kipini man, Islam Abdullah, owned a scooter and he claimed that he could drive along the beach nearly all the way to Adara. He was appointed as our despatch rider, for as long as his scooter lasted out. I decided to start this 'beach traverse' on 8 April and I started things off the day before by driving to Lamu, to see if I could hire a couple of motorised boats or dhows, but I had no luck. The next day, just on the off chance, I drove down to Kipini and there I was able to charter two dhows and their Arab crews. On the morning of the 10th, we took down our camp at Witu and moved down to Kipini. Freddie and his crew were soon loaded aboard the largest dhow and as soon as I had paid the captain a considerable advance, they were away. Fidelis, who was starting at this end, was away soon after in the smaller dhow and then his dhow returned to collect his levelling crew. The captains and their crews realised that they would have to do all the moving of 'camps' every day to let the men get on with the surveying. As it turned out, the system worked very well.

Whilst they were all over there, I kept myself very busy computing. I'm happy to say that all the traverses computed satisfactorily as did the tie-ins. One circuit of levels after the other were equally successful. This alone lifted my heart no end. When I looked at the pile of completed field-books and comp. sheets that I had accumulated, it all seemed to be worth while. Right, lets see how the battle progressed. The next day was the 11 April 1981 and that was Wendy's Wedding Day – now you should be able to slot everything in!

I liked Kipini very much and now of course it has a special relationship to me. It was a very small village really. It had a couple of *dukas*, a school for small children, a mosque, a 'hotel', a light-house, a customs officer and a policeman. Kipini gave me the impression that throughout the ages everything here had flowed down the Tana and stopped here as soon as the river came face to face with the great Indian Ocean. It grew slowly by a strange series of events; it got here by accident. There was one magnificent building which was regrettably falling to pieces; a relic of past grand colonial days, if not before. There were a couple of rooms in the front that they kept the windows in and were even fitted with doors that locked. The forecourt was slowly being devoured by overgrowth. There was a small weedless area that was commanded by two ancient cannons which pointed menacingly out to the Ocean. I felt they wanted to tell me their story and what a story that would have been, I'm sure. I think this place was known as the DO's office which he occupied when he visited Kipini. They told me that it was always visited by the various Governors of Kenya in the old colonial days. It was built on the highest piece of ground and was only a couple of hundred yards from the village proper. Everywhere, there were chickens and goats and beautiful little children. You couldn't walk far without being in the shade of palm trees. Vasco de Gama must have visited here. Very near the DO's office there was a low-walled Christian cemetery, unfortunately, completely unkept. I was interested in the three graves of missionaries, one of whom came from only a couple of miles away from Inmarsh House! I left a prayer there with him together with a little of my love and affection and I felt happy to break his loneliness and to tidy his resting place for him. One complaint; the place was alive with mosquitos.

To my surprise, Islam Abdullah; our despatch-rider, turned up with a message from Fidelis. He said that he hoped to be back in three days' time. He was now about three kilometres south along the beach and they were getting lots of rain, wind and sand. The survey was finally completed and my dhows got back with all hands. They suffered dreadful weather but they still got the job done. Freddie developed a batch of boils which gave him excruciating pain the whole time. When they got back, I had to take the three surveyors to Wimu for treatment for one thing or another. A sorrowful looking lot they were. All caused by weeks of not getting the right food due to flooding. When Fidelis was coming back in his dhow, his captain decided not to come back along the coast, because of the wind; instead, he cut across the flooded area that he knew well until he met the Tana and then he came back down the river. We set up camp at Witu and the next day I returned to Nairobi with my computations.

On 9 May I spoke to Freddie and he said the river was going down fast. He phoned me again on the 12th and said the ferry should be operating some time that day. Yet another call on the 15th; the river was rising again! On the

24th the river was at its highest. And so on. In fact, the ferry couldn't start again until 24 June.

When I was doing these traverses all over the place, one of the things I could get wrong was a bearing (the direction the traverse is going in). One way I could check whether I was going in the right direction was to compare my carried forward bearing against two trig points whose bearing had been accurately determined previously. If the bearing was a long way out, then I had to scrap it. If it was only a little out then I could correct it to make it agree with the true known bearing. This was the reason for me spending so much time going to trig points to see if I could see other trig points from them. In this area, these trig points were about twenty miles apart so you had to have fairly reasonable weather to assist intervisibility. One of the main problems was that since this triangulation was done, old trees had grown bigger or new trees had come onto the scene, thus blocking the view from one trig to another. I did not have the time or the money to go and find the culprits and trim them down. In actual fact, I found very few trigs that were still intervisable but after a lot of work and patient pursuit, together with a lot of bad language, I found a few to apply checks. Since Independence, I believe there has been little updating in this area.

The job still wasn't done until it was checked. So, the second choice of procedure for checking your bearings was by means of field astronomy. Loads of information was published about the locations of the sun, planets and stars at a given time, so that you were able to compute the position of any heavenly body at a given time. By a further set of observations with a theodolite and chronometer, you could determine the Azimuth (direction) of any star from your position and thus any adjacent line on the Earth's surface. Depending on what equipment was used and the skill of the surveyor, accurate results could be obtained. There was one small problem – isn't there always? – you have got to be able to see this heavenly body at the required time! Still, it can be done and is done often. I was out in the bush nearly every night for weeks, with mosquitos crawling around my eyelids whilst trying to observe. I often found it hard seeing the star I wanted or seeing it long enough because of cloud. One night a buffalo objected to the place I was set up on and on another night a lion expressed the same objection. I always had to keep my eyes open for snakes. I found them difficult to see in the dark, cloud or no cloud. We were able to carry out our final checks at the end of the job when the water cleared away a bit and we were able to get around much more easily.

One evening I was cheered up immensely when Omar Ali, the Agriculture Officer, invited me to his home for dinner. A friend of his had given him a pot full of giant prawns so Ali cooked them in Swahili style. They were absolutely delicious and I was offered all I could eat of them. The conversation was just as rich as the food and extremely interesting. I was still learning about these good folk, their thoughts and way of living.

Tuesday, 10 February was another Red Letter Day. Gay and Steve arrived in Nairobi to spend a holiday with us. Molly, Fa-Fa and myself went to Jomo Kenyatta Airport to meet them and what a great joy it was to see them again. As usual, I wasn't able to spend as much time with them as I wanted, but still, Molly and Fa-Fa had them all the time. A few days after their arrival, I was really naughty and took the day off. We all went to Lake Naivasha and then on to Lake Nakuru and we had a super day. For the next few days after that I had to work on the Madogo drawings for thirteen hours a day. Another price I had to pay for being my own boss! However, Molly was able to give all her attention to our dear visitors. Six days after they arrived I had to fly down to Mufindi again and there was no getting out of it either; at least I was able to catch up on some sleep. While I was away, Gay and Steve made a trip down to the coast anyway, which is what they wanted to do. For years and years Gay has had a bit of a chip on her shoulders about me, which is strange because I love her with all my heart and I always will. I haven't seen her for nearly ten years now. She is my daughter and my first born and it is a pity that something developed as the years rolled on. I could always get her to laugh and I must say she was most thoughtful with presents for me; I'm looking at three of them on my desk now, which she gave to me over twenty years ago. I shall love her and cherish her until I die. She is fit and happy today and that is most important to me. They went shopping the day before they left and that evening they took us to The Carneval for an excellent meal; it was a very happy evening.

One way or another, June 1981 was a very interesting month, full of activity. The day after I consumed my giant prawns was 1 June which is Madaraka Day, a public holiday in Kenya. I lost a lot of sleep that night, not because of the prawns but because there was a perpetual beating of drums throughout the night. I enjoyed watching the dancing that evening. After I had left Ali's house the ladies looked very sensuous as their dark damp bodies writhed to the beat of the drums; one couldn't help but notice their young breasts vibrate to the drums' rhythm. All too terribly exciting for an old chap like me. I lost sleep again on 3 June; a twig had gashed my foot about ten days ago and it now looked as if it had turned septic. Not only was my foot throbbing but I had a terrible pain in my ear! I supposed it was about time that my body reacted to the abuse of bad diet and stress. I called in at the dispensary and asked them to have a look at my ear; they couldn't because they didn't have any batteries for their gadget. On the 6th, even though it was a lot of trouble, I still had to go to Malindi to get some valuable shopping. I suppose the trip wasn't so bad because the MOW now had a dhow at Garsen to ferry foot passengers. The bus still sorted out your ribs, though. (And other parts!)

I left camp at half past nine and arrived at Malindi at two o'clock. I booked in at the hotel where I always stay. It was a good hotel, very comfortable, air-conditioned and with good food: palm trees, swimming pool and pool-side bar, the lot.

One evening I was sitting in the bar of my hotel having a Tusker, when I got chatting to an English couple. They were very intrigued that I should be living in Kenya and that I should be a 'professional safariman' as they liked to designate me. I'm not really quite sure how I got onto the subject, but I mentioned a man I once knew back in 1954 and that I heard that he had retired in this area. I also mentioned that he too was a 'railway man'. That did it!

'Is his name Julian Cobett?' asked the nice chap. 'We met him yesterday!'

I was flabbergasted. I was just about to express my astonishment when into the bar bounced Julian. We were so pleased to see each other, really. It had been nearly thirty years! He still remembered my wife's name and the name of my first-born. The English couple looked so happy for us. Together, we had a jolly good evening. Back in the 'old days' Julian was the section engineer in charge of construction of the lighterage wharf at Mombasa. I could remember him so well with his full moustache, gold rimmed glasses and floppy cricket hat. He used to drive around in a beautiful black car; I think it was a Jaguar. He loved his work and thoroughly enjoyed life to the full. He was tall and of fine physique. I couldn't understand how or why he remained a bachelor. The next afternoon, in the hotel, he amazed me (remember, he was in his mid sixties!) when he came into the hotel for a tusker and a swim. He went to the end of the diving-board, did a hand-stand, held it there for a good minute and then, from that position, he slipped into the water – blooming show-off! People once used to tell me that he was from a 'titled family'. Later that year, when Molly came down to the coast, she too met him again. He took us both around to his house which he had built for his retirement in Malindi; it was baronial, tall, breezy and cool.

When the English couple got back to England, they were going to phone Gay and tell her that they had spent the evening with me. If you lovely people ever read my book, please get in touch with me again.

I had spent most of these two days doing my shopping and for this I had hired a car to do my running around. I must mention that I remembered how painful my ear had been. Anyway, the time had come for me to hand back the car after the driver had driven me to the bus-stop (with my bag of cement, shovel, can of paraffin and groceries!) Fortunately, I only just managed to get on the 'one-a-day-bus' to Garsen. However, all-in-all, I enjoyed my break in Malindi.

I had run out of work that I could do from Witu, so I had to get back to Garsen. The men had already brought one load of stuff from Witu to Garsen and brought it across the Tana on a dhow (still no ferry!). They were able to hire a pick-up from Salim; the guy that owned the duka at Garsen; and he allowed us to leave our stuff temporarily in his compound. We were all able to go back to Witu to spend the last night in what was left of our camp. The next day we packed up what was left and took everything down to Garsen, loaded it into the dhow and took it across the river. It was all getting such a strain; more like performing a military battle. After leaving this load with Salim we then had to drive our vehicles back to Witu, where we left them. They were useless now until the time came when we could get them across the ferry. Fortunately, there was a bus back to the ferry at eleven thirty and we were on it. It only remained to hire Salim's pick-up again and transfer our stuff to our new camp site which was under the big radio tower by the side of Garsen Post Office. We had the camp erected and a cup of tea by three o'clock. We also had a full time escort because the Kenyan police had a guard on the radio tower – just in case the Shifta wanted to blow the thing up I suppose. Well, we were here at last, even though we had no transport.

On the 10th and 11th of this outstanding month, I learnt what it would be like to die in the bush. I was bedded down those two days and Freddie took command of the safari. I had a raging temperature and an awful pain in my septic foot and the boil in my ear. I had hired transport for the teams but I had nothing left in the camp for myself. Therefore, in spite of being delirious I still had to walk the half mile down to the native dispensary and back. The clinical officer seemed efficient and in any case, he was all I could get and he didn't have any eardrops! However, strangely enough, the DO had the same trouble with his ear (apparently, this is caused by dust), so he drove over to the small field hospital at Ngao and collected for both of us. The clinical officer was able to give me a shot to help me out with my problem together with some tablets. I slept the whole of that day and the next. I could remember that I kept waking up feeling so thirsty and thinking how hard my bed felt. Most of the time I had absolutely nothing to drink; I guess I was too poorly to sort that one out. It was so hot in the tent too. This was the time when I would have welcomed a girl coming into my tent in the middle of the night but no such luck! I broke my temperature during the night because I woke up and my bed was saturated and suddenly I felt a little more intelligent. It was about now that I thought I was going to die and I didn't mind one little bit! On the third day I was ready to get back into the fight and take back the command of my own safari. Thank you Freddie.

On 18 June, I had been in Nairobi a couple of days chasing some contracts along and now I had to get the train down to Mombasa, the *matatu* to Malindi and then the bus to Garsen. I arrived at Garsen at half past twelve on the second day. The end of this job was in sight at last; all the traversing and levelling was completed and I only had those seven cross-sections across the Tana to concentrate on. These cross-sections were more or less evenly spaced along the Tana from Garsen to Kipini. I soon had a sounding chain organised, measured and marked up, and our rope uncoiled and cut into manageable lengths of a hundred metres. A boat was organised at Garsen, Ngao and Kipini. I tried everything out at Garsen and found that the chain was too short for soundings in the middle of the river but this was overcome by merely adding a twenty foot sling on the end when required (those half a dozen soundings in the middle of each line). On 21 June I was ready to start my first cross-section. During the whole operation of sounding these cross-sections, only one man fell in the Tana – ME – and within sight of crocodiles – the men moved just as fast as I did to get me back out. I spent the following half hour teaching Abio his left from his right, which was port and which was starboard and which ends were the bow and stern! Never mind, we got the job done and there was always a price to pay. The pull of the water on the ropes was very strong so I had to devise a system whereby the ropes did not touch the water; otherwise, I could see the crocs eventually getting a good feed! We got the second cross-section done – the one at Ngao – on the following day and recorded no real mishap this time. Both ropes were kept out of the water, one rope for holding the boat and the second to give us line and distance off; this worked well. On the way back to camp we bumped into the Dutch MOW Engineer who was terribly excited because he thought the water had subsided a hundred millimetres in one day. He was almost certain that he would open the Ferry tomorrow. At last!

I was thinking, if I were to leave out all the gloomy incidents in my story mine would look a very bright and glamorous sort of life. Unless you have a lot of money, that kind of life would prove very difficult to attain. It would be great to have sufficient money for the purchase of an endless supply of motor car spares! However, my story is to portray to you the 'real life' of a professional safari man, warts and all, not something out of Hollywood or a TV show. There! Read on.

23 June was another Red Letter Day. You had suffered the past weeks with me while my safari was marooned at Witu but today we would break free from our bonds, God willing. My diary for that day reads: '. . . I helped to pull the first lorry across the ferry this morning; this was to satisfy myself that the ferry worked! We went up to Witu on the bus to collect our vehicles. I paid Ali for the two

new tyres he had put on the Datsun and then off we jolly well went. Back at the ferry, I was horrified when the few staff left in charge of the ferry said it would start tomorrow; I just couldn't believe my ears! The canoes that used to ferry people across had gone home because the 'seasonal work' had finished! Hell! After making a lot of noisy protestations and having collected fifteen men together to pull the ruddy ferry (and I had to pay for them!) I got my vans across the Tana by six o'clock. I was too elated to grumble any more.'

We got the cross-sections at Wema and Kibusu done and on the 25th we were instructed to re-mark all the pre-flight marks on the Garsen/Garissa Road – again. Gosh, there were new problems of where do I get the petrol and whitewash from? Anyway, I phoned the client and told them what my charge would be to do all these marks again. They said to go ahead, we would pay, and while I was at it, do all the Tana Delta marks too! (I'd already got through hundreds of bags of whitewash!) As you can imagine, we had plenty of work to keep us busy. By 5 July all marking was well on the way. Unfortunately, we couldn't do the remaining cross-sections yet because the water-level hadn't gone down enough to give us road access. Fidelis was more or less left in charge of pre-flight marking and Freddie and Simeon (assistant surveyor) left Garsen, with me for Nairobi.

I had a new contract with East African Power & Lighting Co Ltd to survey a couple of dams up country in the Kamburu area. I was sure that once I started Freddie off, he would be quite happy to continue alone. Actually, we all went up to Kamburu on Thursday, 9 July. Molly and I were in the Camper and Freddie and Simeon kept the Land Cruiser. We got to Kamburu (the name of the main area) at about eleven thirty and met our contact man from the EAP & L. After the initial discussion we all went along to the first job – Kindaruma Reservoir – and had a good look at it and decided on how to survey it. The EAP & L had already built smart concrete monuments for us, which they wanted co-ordinated and used as our control points. Quite a lot of bush to cut but apparently there would be no trouble getting labour. There was a bench mark on the dam. We decided to level along the north shore monuments and trig height the south shore monuments. Freddie said he must have a boat but otherwise he looked confident and said he wanted to get his camp set up and get down to some work. Molly and I didn't need to sleep in the Camper; in fact, we were back in Nairobi by six o'clock. The time had come to buy some more tents from Lowe & Bonar.

You are not going to believe this! Freddie came back from Kindaruma on 17 July, having traversed and levelled all they could. The clients, in their wisdom, hadn't controlled the reservoir to our advantage and had flooded half the monuments, some of which were now completely under water! We'd go back again later as long as all this mucking about didn't put me out of pocket! I had to keep busy; time was money; so a few days later the three of us went back to Garsen, stopping at Malindi en route. I stayed in The Sinbad and the other two stayed with friends. They were old enough to know what they were doing! I forgot to mention, after leaving Mombasa, we had a look at Kilifi (it comes between Mombasa and Malindi); there was a good possibility I might get another survey to do there. The next day we went straight to Karawa where I was able to employ the services of a guide, to show Freddie and Simeon the route to Adara. At last they were able to get through. It took one and a half hours to get there and one and a half hours to get back. They said the place was alive with elephants and buffalo. I was sorry for one of the chaps because he sure didn't get much sleep the previous night. Karawa was so hot and humid. He was very happy when I told him I was now going to drive to Oda, where we still had another of our Tana cross-sections to do; so he only needed to sit and take it easy. Actually, I found the road was still flooded but 'locals' told me that you could now easily walk there from Colbani. We got to Garsen at about five o'clock, having done a useful day's work. Fidelis was still at Garsen, having done some of the crosses over and over again. Yet he still managed to wear that infectious smile (must be as mad as his boss!)

Entry in diary, 22 July: '. . . I am sitting in the back of the Land Cruiser doing some computing and updating this diary, whilst the men are carrying on with the Tana cross-section here at Wema. (We have got here at last!) We were the first car to get here since the flood! To do the sounding I have hired a boat from the Wema Mission; in fact, right at this moment, one of the Irish Mission fathers is handling the boat for them! He felt that the men couldn't control such a powerful outboard. To get to the river, we have to walk through a shamba of palm trees and bananas. This sort of shamba does all sorts of things to me. I love the shadowed coolness it has to offer and you can always hear the rustle of a banana leaf, if only faintly, when stirred by some zephyr of air. If I ever retired in Kenya (or Tahiti) I would grow a patch of banana trees just to hide my deck-chair during those hot hours in the middle of the day. I would close my eyes and listen to the rustling and then think of all the nice things that had happened in my life and then drop off for a little nap! I can remember doing this once before and saying, 'Dear Lord, if You are going to take me, then do it now!'

Work in the Garsen/Garissa area did seem to go on a bit, partly because of flooding but equally because of additional work. I got everything done, including the crosses (for the umpteenth time) and got the last man away by 5 September. Molly came down and paid the area a visit on 8 August. I think she enjoyed the trip and she certainly looked her old self and quite in place. Because Fa-Fa went away for a week with one of her schoolmates, this freed Molly at a time when it was convenient to fit her in on this small safari! At the end of the first day of travelling, we stayed at the Sinbad and had time to look around the town and get some shopping. I loaded up with an extra couple of jerry cans of petrol, just in case we couldn't get any at

Garsen. This was the evening that Molly was able to meet Julian Cobett after so many years. I was so proud of her that evening for she looked so radiant and beautiful. I could see the sunbeams still dancing in her hair. As I have seen so often before, the bar stewards and dining-room stewards jumped to offer her their attentions. They recognised her superlative quality and wallowed in her African magnetism. We were young and greedy that night! Julian joined us for dinner, during which our very souls were drenched in happy nostalgia. Most of these young waiters weren't born when we were building Mombasa and yet, I could see a respect and even affection passing between us that wasn't so conspicuous between them and the happy tourists.

As we headed up north (not as far as the Shifta) we met Fidelis at Karawa to do the trigonometrical heighting Karawa/Adara. I have a nice photograph of Molly, taken on that day, sitting in her camp-chair under a thorn tree and her feet are by one of our whitewashed crosses! After all these very trying weeks, I couldn't believe that she was sitting here with me. We got to Garsen a little later on and Molly slept in my tent that night – the right woman this time! The next day we had to go down to Kipini to do some jobs, so she was able to go on the Garsen Ferry to see where we had our camp at Witu (where we were stranded) and the old DO's office at Kipini where I had camped on Wendy's wedding day! How about that!

Two days later we packed up our camp and moved back along the coast to Kilifi. I had won the contract to do a site survey for an agricultural college being built by the Japanese Government. After the first day and once I had got Fidelis started, he and Abio were able to carry on by themselves. We were able to go over to the Seahorse quite often for a refreshing swim and some food. The day we arrived it got too dark to set up camp so I put the two chaps in a local hotel and then Molly and I went off to look for somewhere to stay; it wasn't easy; everywhere full at that time of night, we had to go another thirty kilometres towards Mombasa. We eventually stayed in the Sand and Sun at Kikambala. I wonder if any of my readers have been there?

I liked Kilifi. It was a village up a creek but only a short distance from the ocean. Palm trees, heat, breezes in the afternoon, goats, chickens, little children and Afro/Arabs. You also saw a lot of the Kariama tribe, some of their ladies still walking around bare-breasted. However, you saw a lot more covered-up now than you did thirty years ago. Of course, there used to be a ferry at Kilifi but now the village boasted a modern concrete bridge. I remember often crossing the ferry in the old days. I can hear the men stamping their feet on the top of the pontoon which gave off a very thunderous hollow sound as they pulled us across on the chain. They used to chant at the same time, all in complete unison with the foot-beat. Towards the end of the crossing they would sing in Swahili and include words about my car, my wife, my children and me. Then they would add verses about how good I was and that I was going to find it in my heart to give them some 'tea money'! The trip would culminate with loud blasts on seashells – it was magic.

It's amazing how things turn out sometimes. You know I said that Fa-Fa had gone away with her schoolmate; well, they had come down to Watamu which was only a couple of miles from my Kilifi camp. It was a great pleasure to call on Mrs Young and the girls at Watamu. Before we left Kilifi they returned the visit.

On 17 August we were woken before five o'clock by Abio banging two pegs together to shake off the mud. Molly and I packed, had breakfast at the Seahorse and were away by eight thirty, arriving at Nairobi at half past six. Fidelis and Abio had to stay at Kilifi to finish the Topo. That job was completed and the fair drawings handed over on 8 October. In the meantime Freddie had done what he had to do at Garsen and had returned to Kindarama Reservoir to get that job finished. I also went up to Kindarama on 20 August to have another look at the job and then help

Freddie to pack up his camp because I was satisfied that he had done all the field work to that job.

After months of negotiations I was awarded the setting out contract for Mowlems/Canadian Transelec in the west of Kenya. The job was to set out miles and miles of an electric system. It employed some of my surveyors for about nine months. We all left Nairobi on 23 August and arrived at Muhoroni at four o'clock. When we got there we could see the huge sugar refinery from miles away, otherwise, for as far as the eye could see: sugar cane, sugar cane and more sugar cane. I didn't intend to spend too much time on this particular contract myself (my client couldn't afford me!) but it was work my chaps could do well, once I had trained them and they knew what they had to do. It took a few days for the job to collect any momentum but soon a routine was developed and established. I met the clients in the field and we all went and had a look at Lessos, the place where our line began. I have noticed, whether you play sport or not, it doesn't take long to sort out the 'office wallahs' from the 'field men' when a bunch of chaps have to hike across some bumpy Kenyan bush.

I flew down to Mufindi three more times this year, once in September, again in October and then November/December. The paper mill was growing fast; one or two tall buildings already had a roof on. Other ancillary buildings were also popping up all over the place. There were so many more people there now. Makumbako was only a couple of miles away and when I think of Harbhajan Singh and I thumping in two pegs and saying to that lonely old man – the only other person around – this is Makumbako Station! There was nobody for miles and miles and miles in those days. I couldn't see any reason why this place should grow – it was so far from anywhere. That was in 1964 of course. I had loads of work to do, especially setting out works; to name a few, the turbocirculator, the lime burning area, the salt store, coal store, decausterising area, chemical area, roads, rails and machinery anchor bolts in the main mill. I was requested to check a lot of other significant work, done by others: not that I found any mistakes, just better to be safe than sorry. There was quite an informal social life when I was invited to six different homes for dinner and to another couple's home for coffee on Sunday mornings. I was always working on Sundays – when the site was nice and quiet – but I could always 'make up' the hour for coffee; you know Roy! Sharing the company of their lovely wives kept me in touch with civilisation and preserved my sense of humour. I particularly recall the ladies of Bill Bloomfield, Wynn Kenrick, Alen Garner, Ian Blake, Don Corruthers, Don Creighton, Maurice Macracken, Berni Lawrence, Dr David (I haven't forgotten Rebecca, his daughter – 'I am three now!') Gosh, neither could I ever forget Nurse Chui nor the lady schoolteacher.

Apart from meeting all those lovely ladies there were a few other outstanding events on those Tanzanian trips. One was the sight of armed women soldiers on the beach at the coast. Tall, slim, pretty and lovely white teeth, but wearing big boots and sporting heavy automatic rifles. I wondered why this was necessary but I never found the answer.

I shall never forget one of the nights I stayed in the Kunduchi Beach Hotel, down in Dar-es-Salaam. The telephone in my room rang at midnight and again at ten minutes past; when I answered there was nobody on the other end. They came and woke me up at four o'clock in the morning and brought me tea! I looked at my watch and was dumbfounded and I just couldn't open my mouth; I was also frightened they might take my tea away. The same thing happened at five o'clock. 'Just a cottin pickin minute!' I said to the steward this time. The steward appeared not to understand my tone of voice and took off fast in fear of his life. Two minutes later, a receptionist came back and apologised and explained that my room was nearly always occupied by air-crew! That wasn't all. About two weeks later I was booked up in the same hotel again. When I noticed that the receptionist was putting me in the same room as before, I said to him, 'Now look, I don't want the same things happening to me as they did before!'

'Again Sir, we are terribly sorry about that, but let me assure you that it won't happen again.'

'OK, good!'

In December 1981 Collin Hayes decided that he had had enough and went home to England. Strangely, that was a blow and unnerved me. Remember, our friendship went back to our army days in the early fifties. I never saw any sign of affection between us but there was a tremendous respect. I felt that I could never trust him and yet, he did nothing but good deeds to me through all those years. Since I set up my business in Kenya he always made sure that a fair amount of work came my way (without the usual pay-off!). He was such a good surveyor. I think the bond between us was that we were both ex-Royal Engineers. I haven't seen Collin for nearly ten years now and I still miss him.

We weren't happy in our apartment (do you know, I can't for the life of me remember why not!). So, slowly, we did something about that too. We got another apartment only a few hundred yards away, right in State House Avenue (look at the neighbour we had!). It was unfurnished but as it worked out we had two months to get some things together. We surrendered my old flat on the last day of the year and, oh my, what a lovely home we had to move into. Lovely new carpets and handmade curtains and bedcovers; it was truly gracious and very much Molly. But she nearly caught the next plane out of Nairobi when she saw my choice of carpet. So, it was wise to give up my choice poste haste. Half our furniture we had made to order. I must stop this outrageous bragging, but honestly, in spite of my gipsy characteristics, you can see that I am still a very much home-loving man.

I brought all my crews home for Christmas so I didn't have to worry about them. We agreed to spend Christmas over at Karen with Liz and Ron again that year. This was good because that dear woman always did me the world of good and I think Ron enjoyed us cluttering up the place at Christmas. Liz and Fa-Fa were extremely fond of each other – Fa-Fa could tell her things! We had already seen the tree decorated, and the turkey; we felt the spirit of Christmas quite early and we were sure that this was going to be a good one. . . Now came the next blow! Had I been suffering with a premonition? On the 23rd Molly got a phone call from her mother to say that Dad had had a heart attack. I had a lot of time for Sam Vango (my father-in-law) and I was considerably upset about this news. I wished I had a pound for every hour that I had sat down and listened to him playing the piano. He had a magnificent touch. Sam Vango died two days later, on Christmas Day, and Molly left for England on the 27th, the first flight we could get.

Molly leaving me in Nairobi to go back to England was sad enough; the reason for her going back only made my heart heavier. I can't say how Molly felt; she was stunned and I just couldn't get near her. In spite of her deep grief and hurriedly having to pack, she still said that she couldn't leave Smokey like he was without the vet seeing him first. I told her not to worry about Smokey; I promised to take him the next day. Nope, she knew there was something wrong with him and her plane didn't leave until late that night.

'All right then, come on, it's nearly four o'clock, so let's get a move on,' said I.

All the way to the vet's at Westlands Smokey kept looking up to me like a frightened child. The three of us kept talking to him to try and give him some measure of comfort. When we got to Westlands, as usual, we couldn't get parked and the time was running on. We didn't know what time the vet called it a day. I went round the block once more and said to Molly, when we get there, you jump out with Smokey and we'll drive round the block once more and try and find somewhere to park. We eventually got the car parked and Fa-Fa and I charged round to the vet's office. Just as we got there, Molly was coming out. I could hardly see the pupils of Molly's eyes for her tears. She said, 'The lady vet examined him and more or less insisted that the time had come for him to go to sleep!'

I went to run in the vet's office for we were right there but Molly quickly grabbed my arm and I could tell by her lovely face – he was gone. We were heartbroken. We loved him so much. We had all demanded so much of his attention all hours of the day and night and he gave it to us. I could remember the days back at Inmarsh House; sometimes the only place he could get any peace was under the rose-bushes in the garden, especially the peach coloured rose we all knew he loved so much. To this day I have his photograph here in front of me and out in the kitchen; on top of the fridge is his towel he always used to lie on when he suffered the heat of the boiler when he rested back in Inmarsh House!

On 31 December, while Molly was in England, Fa-Fa and I moved into our new home. From that time on 'things' were never the same.

14

Divortium *and Upheaval*

1982 was the most devastating year of my life. I can't hide the facts from you – we have become such good friends – so it's best for me to get it over as quickly as possible.

On the 9 October, Molly and Jennifer boarded the plane at Jomo Kenyatta Airport. They had gone through Customs by half past six and as they went, their faces were full of smiles and neither of them looked back at me to wave. Before Molly left for the departure gate, she said to me, 'Don't worry, we'll see each other again!' That was my Mollykins – my wife. I wished there and then that I could die.

A couple of weeks later, I received a letter from her solicitor saying that they had been instructed to carry out divorce proceedings in two years' time on the grounds that we had lived apart for two years and that she sought the usual settlement.

Our relationship had been strained for quite a long time but I thought that this was due mainly to 'change of life' and I just dismissed it at that. I was obviously wrong. Molly had given a list as long as her arm of what was wrong with me. I could write a book on all my good points at being a good husband and father and I could write another two on my faults. Things weren't always going too well at work and this is when I needed Molly. With Molly I could move mountains. I just couldn't believe all the things on her 'list' but she convinced me that Molly believed it. If even half the list was true then I certainly didn't deserve a wife like Molly. I could write pages on this dreadful subject but that wouldn't be fair to Molly or to you, my dear reader. I will say this, however: that in the eyes of Molly, her mother and our four daughters, I did not come up to their required standard. They felt qualified to make the judgment and they believed they had the right to carry out the execution. Subsequently, while the divorce proceeded on its path of destruction, my daughters broke their bond with me.

That's enough. Now to return to earlier that year.

Fa-Fa had finished her schooling in Nairobi and had been awarded five '0'-Levels, which we were all pleased about. On 3 February she started a secretarial course in a private college in Nairobi and was able to see that through until the end. Molly didn't get back from her dear father's funeral until 27 February. This was Jennifer's birthday which we celebrated with coffee at the railway station (not to be equated with coffee in other railway systems!) in the morning and dinner in the evening at the Norfolk – both places were favourites of all three of us.

On 20th March we decided to have two weeks' holiday down at Mombasa. This was to start on 1 April. When the day came we were all in a very happy mood and we enjoyed the drive down to Mombasa immensely. We hired a holiday apartment out at Bamburi, which turned out very nice indeed. It was right on the beach so that when you lay on your bed at night you were sent to sleep with the sound of the sea breaking and the breezes in the tops of the palm trees. One day we took a drive up to Malindi for the day. We called in to see Julian Cobett and Molly was able to give him a potted parsley which she had promised him. He was most grateful. We had lunch in the Den of Iniquity, you know, the place I have told you about before and my curry was excellent and the girls (mine that is!) enjoyed their prawn salad. The 12th was Easter Monday and our thirtieth wedding anniversary and to celebrate this we walked along the beach to Bamburi Beach Hotel for lunch. Neither of them made any comment about what day it was, they appeared to treat it like any other day. On the 14th we were invited to Julian's house for lunch. After lunch we went and had a look at the large memorial monument on the front, which used to be most conspicuous once upon a time but now you have got a job to find it.

At the beginning of the year I took advantage of the block opposite our apartment. It consisted of a couple of embassies and a judge's house and was surrounded by a minor road, coming off State House Avenue and then finding its way back onto it again. Because I was getting repetitions of not feeling very well (I subsequently was sure that it was the onslaught of diabetic amyotrophy), I thought that I needed to get myself back into some sort of training again, so at six o'clock nearly every morning I used to jog around this block. I would try to do the circuit ten times, trying to beat the time of the day before. I think it was a great help to me because in the peace of dawn I was able to see things more clearly as well as feel a lot better. Of course, every morning of the year was dark at six o'clock. Daylight would appear fast at about six forty five and that was about the time I would finish. A bath or shower as soon as I returned would make me feel marvellous. One strange thing used to happen every morning; each time I went for a jog, I would collect one more dog! In the end, I had nine of these friends. All shapes and sizes. When I first started jogging, I used to be a bit of a menace to all the askaris in the neighbourhood because I would get all the guard dogs barking – anyway, that's what they were all trained for! At first, it used to be just a couple of dogs from adjacent flats or houses that would run with me and they behaved themselves admirably. Slowly, the askaris got to know me as the Mad Surveyor and would open their gates and let their police dogs out; it was much less trouble to do so than to try and keep them quiet! They would just join in the fun and run round and round with me. There were no big fights. Two of the older dogs used to know when the ten laps were up – they just sat down. A couple of times during this regime, there were a couple of dogs that used to stop after about the third lap and make love to each other. They would still be at it while the rest of us did another three or four laps – and then they would join us again! I never knew where they got their energy. Molly said that on some mornings while she was coming out of her sleep, she could hear me and my 'gang' passing the house at about every six minutes! I never found out why these dogs were so friendly to me and to each other. Any other time of the day they were ferocious.

This relationship didn't happen over night; it took weeks to develop to a first name basis. Molly would be a little annoyed sometimes, when she was taking Fa-Fa to college and outside the door she had to step over three or four dogs lying down there and resting! Of course, there would be times when I was away on safari for weeks but after I had been home for a day or two I would go out for a bash. You never heard such a commotion as when those dogs heard my footsteps and they ran out as if they couldn't believe their ears! There would only be four or five with me on the first day but the next, all present and correct, Sir! Really! Wasn't that lovely? There's always love around if you look for it.

I think everybody knew that Mr Roger Whittaker came from Nairobi. It was a very pleasant surprise when Molly and I found ourselves standing by his side when we were all shopping in Westlands. Of course, many of the Africans didn't know him from Adam but Molly and I did. Having said that, all my staff knew him. The last time we saw him was on Saturday, 3 July 1982 at Singh's Grocery Shop. Roger's father also had a shop in Westlands and we had shopped in there many times. Over the years we have seen many famous people in Kenya; Kenya is like that, it draws everybody.

On 1 August all hell was let loose and not by my dog friends. Some members of the Kenya Air Force decided to rebel against the Government of Kenya. And we lived in State House Avenue! I first heard the shooting in the distance at two in the morning but by four the shooting became very heavy and some of it right outside my apartment. At five, I thought that there was a chance that Fa-Fa could be shot in her bed, so I crawled on the floor to her bedroom and made her crawl back along the floor and jump into bed with her mother. I then pushed some furniture around to come between them and the windows. They were very brave because the gunfire was loud and you could hear the bullets hitting walls, etc. At six the whole building seemed to shake with gunfire. Whoever it was, they sure meant business! The shooting continued all day long. They weren't any old renegades; they were trained servicemen (some of them British-trained, I would imagine) and were fighting with some standard of technique and discipline. I had the radio on to try and get an explanation for why people were stopping me from going for my jog; goodness knows what the dogs were thinking! At half past six the rebels made a statement about what was going on and something about 'this corrupt government'. As the day progressed the radio was won back by the Army who were loyal to the President. Nobody knew where the President was for sure but we hoped that he was well and safe. Freddie phoned me and asked about the flight to Tanzania. I told him to stay at home and keep his head down. It appeared to be quiet outside Nairobi; we seemed to be living in the thick of it. The following night all seemed very quiet except for the odd looter being shot – they had been warned! However, at half past seven on the second morning, all hell was let loose again in the downtown area. This time it was all automatic weapons that were being fired. The question did pass through my mind about what I should do if the rebels broke into our apartments. What could I do to protect my girls? I wouldn't think I could do a lot! I couldn't think of a reason why they shouldn't shoot me as soon as they saw me! The electricity went off – another load of shots – a heavy burst right outside the house with return fire hitting the bricks. This was getting too much for Fa-Fa and she got very frightened but her mother was able to cuddle her and comfort her. I spread myself out over the two of them as best I could. Another thought came to my mind and that was, I'm definitely going to get a job with Wilts County Council if I ever get out of this lot!

Westlands had really been ruined; every shop had been torn open and looted. They told me that this wasn't the activity of the Air Force but of civilians. The stories I heard from 'eye witnesses' about looting and rape were horrible. On the third day I took Molly and Fa-Fa for a drive around to try and get some shopping. The town was absolute chaos but there was a massive clean-up operation going on. When the girls saw some of the pools of blood, that was enough; take us back home, Daddy! They had a curfew for a long time afterwards and this quietened the place down. Judging by the hundreds outside the city mortuary, collecting their dead, there must have been a lot of people killed. I wouldn't like to hazard a guess and I would probably get into trouble if I did, so I won't.

I had been turning out a lot of work and my other men were very busy on the power lines. It now looked a good opportunity for us to go down to Mombasa again for a week, commencing 24 September. I always think of Mombasa and Molly as one being complementary to the other; like the other two angles of a right-angled triangle, so I thought a visit might do some good because our lives' happiest memories were of Mombasa. It's all right having these good ideas but I discovered that there was no diesel for the Cruiser available again. Good old Ivan Smith, he was able to help me out, so off we jolly well went.

The girls had more or less 'sent me to Coventry', although I will say this, that when they did speak to me they were polite! I could never stand rudeness. The day before we left for Mombasa, Molly told me that there was no chance for me at all; her love for me was dead. We left Nairobi at nine fifteen and got to Cowrie Shell Apartments, Bamburi long before dark. Even under the circumstances, the journey was very pleasant; Molly doing most of the driving. I got a couple of laughs out of them! The town and hotels were very quiet at this time of year but I thought the weather was magnificent. On the 30th we were strolling along the beach to go and have lunch at the Bamburi Beach Hotel and the two girls were walking in front of me, laughing and chatting away. My chest was hurting; probably the desired effect and I was feeling overcome with sheer horror at what I was just about to say because I knew it had to be said. I called Molly's attention and said, 'Molly, you win, ducks; I don't think it's right for you to treat me like this or for me to keep you here, so I give in. I'll not keep you here any longer. I'm just not getting anywhere. You can go any time that suits you.' Her eyes opened wide and sparkled.

They flew from Kenya on 9 October and that was that.

Jennifer said, 'Thank you Daddy for everything you have done for me.'

15

Steady As She Goes!

When you are self-employed and other people are dependent on your leadership and business attributes; when you have a lot of transport to be paid for as well as a lot of technical electronic equipment, together with rents, insurance premiums and salaries, you can't afford the luxury of going sick or being emotionally upset over family or other disputes. You have to give an awful lot of your power, resources and energy to your clients and your staff. If you do weaken, in any way, you will soon go under and that I would imagine, is a fate worse than death. I had to grin and bear what was happening to me and fight to stay in command. Really.

Work-wise, we started 1982 off well. I couldn't believe it when the Ministry of Works asked me to survey part of Lamu Harbour. Lamu was a small island and you couldn't take your car over there. The passenger ferry is also a very small boat and they had to make several trips to get all our equipment across. Everybody assured me that I would have no trouble getting into the one and only hotel – Petleys Inn. But when I knocked on the door, there was no room at the inn! A government minister, Mr Biwott, and a lot of officials were staying there. However, the manager was able to get me a room in an Arab gentleman's house at the back of the hotel. Whatever happened, I could never sleep in that room again – I must have lost twenty pounds and, the bloomin' mosquitos! I got a room in the inn the next day.

I mustn't give the wrong impression; believe me, Lamu is magic. I love it. Yes, it was hot and there were a lot of mosquitos and it was basically primitive but it was full of Eastern/African Magic. The atmosphere was tropical, mystic, peaceful, paradise-like and sexy! But, you had to take your own partner; I wasn't looking but I didn't notice any spare partners. I had breakfast in the 'Inn' and enjoyed the pleasure of shaking hands with Mr Biwott and having a short but very informative chat.

It didn't take very long for Fidelis and I to check all our equipment, have a good look at the job and hire myself a small motorised dhow to do the hydrographic. Our captain was a real down-to-earth Afro/Arab, even down to wearing a huge dagger! We greeted each other in Arabic and again in Swahili to incorporate Fidelis – that was the Arab good manners. For the last few days I had been suffering from a shocking headache and I didn't know what was causing it; after last night I felt very heavy, unfit and very old. I got loads of sarcasm from Fidelis and very little sympathy. He said to me, 'For only two camels I have bought for you the most beautiful woman on the island and look at you, Bwana, in this state you are going to let me down. You have only got one lovemaking session in you and that's all there is holding you together. She will kill you in only five minutes!'

I was up at half past four and I woke the crew up and then it wasn't more than a few minutes before we were getting everything ready. You see, there was too much wind in the afternoon's high-water so I wanted to catch the morning's high tide. I got all soundings done by ten o'clock; there remained only a couple of hours' hand-soundings to do and these could be done at almost any time and even in a rowing boat. Apart from the flaming headache, I was a happy man. You can't imagine the relief when you get a sounding programme done. To tell you the truth, as soon as I took my last 'fix' on my last 'line', I placed my sextant carefully in its box, climbed over everything to the stern of the boat and with one almighty yell, I jumped into the sea –

sharks or no sharks! It seemed no time at all before half of Lamu jumped in with me. There was laughter, splashing and singing and heaven only knows where everybody came from. I had a little chubby girl in each arm! One of them insisted on pulling my beard and the other was trying to force corn-on-the-cob down my throat with sand, dribble, sea-water and nose-mucus; to give it its own flavour. They were each no more than eighteen months' old. Their pretty Afro/Arab mother saw we were having fun, so she just wanted her babies to join in and thrust them into my arms; I can't turn away from an African child.

The job got done – and done well. The evening before I left there was a very interesting event. I was staying on the top floor of the 'Inn' and below my room was a long narrow passage; real casbah stuff! Well, at about eight p.m. I was working on the 'level book' when I could hear some Arab music and it was coming from far down the passage. I walked over to my window and looked out and there it was. There was a procession coming up the passage and it was headed by several drums and a single trumpet. Following were about fifty women all with their yashmacs on and singing in complete harmony. It all amounted to a very pleasant sound and the acoustics created by the passage added to the lovely effect. They moved along the alley very slowly so I was entertained for about fifteen minutes.

When we got back to Nairobi there was a message on the ansafone from H.P. Gauff: would I please 'whitewash' the marks down at Garsen/Garissa areas again – all of 'em. That pleased Fidelis!

Freddie's party was the first to go back to the West Kenya Transelec Power Grid and this kept him most of the year. The Ministry asked me to go back to Kilifi and carry out a Survey of an extension of the area set aside for the Agricultural College. Extension for goodness sake – it was an area about twice as big as the original! I arrived at the Kilifi Ferry (bridge not completed yet) at six forty but I couldn't get across until seven twenty. I got in at the Seahorse Hotel and it seemed to me I was the only one staying there. In the morning I was able to get my 'nose-bag' on at seven and I had mostly fresh pineapple, fresh paw-paw and fresh mangoes with just a hint of passion fruit. I noticed that the beach looked lovely and clean, having just cleaned off all the seaweed, and the palm trees were doing a lively ballet which meant there must be a breeze, thank goodness! The sky and the sea looked so very blue. There was a beautiful display of highly coloured bougainvillaea all around. Even the birds were greeting such a lovely day. Not far away, I found a cashew nut factory and plantation; it was really extensive. There were dozens of sacks of nuts lying about but I was being watched!

I noticed that I made a note in my diary on 13 May that I thought this was the hottest day I have ever known. After a few weeks the job got done. The morning of the day I left Kilifi two absolutely beautiful French ladies were walking along the beach – topless! I was just enjoying their gorgeous forms when two uniformed policemen walked up to them and obviously asked them to cover themselves. I, for one, wasn't complaining! Of course, this always has been an area under the influence of the Islamic world. Perhaps I'll have better luck the next time I come down!

Another half a dozen commissions came up in or around Nairobi. One of them was in the middle of Nairobi, down by the Nairobi River, which brings an interesting fact to my mind. Did you know, it was a Royal Engineer's sergeant who founded Nairobi? Sergeant Ellis Avenue was one of the last names they changed in Nairobi after Independence (and that was changed to Mama Ngina Avenue, in honour of Mzee Kenyatta's wife.) I'm full of this sort of information!

Although I have headed this chapter 'Steady As She Goes!' I had been finding it almost impossible to carry on as if nothing happened. My life in Kenya had always been with Molly; her spirit was everywhere I went; everywhere I looked I saw Molly. I had found myself at a cross-roads and I honestly didn't know which way to turn at the moment. I knew that I had to go home for a visit, collect a new set of facts, answer some of my questions and then take it from there. It would be a long time before the penny dropped that Molly was no longer a part of me.

I left Fidelis in charge of my office and told him I would phone him at certain appointed times. He drove me down to Nairobi Airport on the morning of 30 October and I arrived at Heathrow that evening. There, I'd done it, I was back in England. I could see Ian Gordon coming towards me and there was no doubt about it, I was very pleased indeed to see him again. It had been a long time and much water had flown under Nairobi Bridge since we last had a jug together. As we walked away from the foyer one of the first things that hit me was, I was not going to catch a train to Mum and Dad in Salisbury, they were gone for ever! God, help me. We got to Inmarsh House at about eleven in the evening. Dear readers, at this stage, I was at rock bottom – if ever you get to this state then give me a call and I will come to you! I was roaming around the house at three a.m. – I thought it was six a.m. and I had to wake up my safari boys! I think a man's mind can only take so much.

Ian and I had loads to talk about and we didn't do much else for the next few days. There was no doubt about it, I had to draw up another one of my job lists: I landed up with 273 jobs that needed to be done in my house, in my garden, in my office, business matters relevant to the Kenya firm, business matters relevant to the UK firm, personal matters and so on. Phew! After a few days, my bank manager took me out for lunch and I enjoyed his company immensely. We discussed my business both home and abroad and I found his comments and suggestions most helpful. By the end of the first week I felt the benefit of all my friends and neighbours and I gathered strength from them, but isn't that what it's all about? I went to Bath and got myself a solicitor to defend myself as best I could and he turned out a damn nice chap too!

I phoned Fidelis in Nairobi and at the same time I thought to myself, wait for it! '*Jambo Mzee*' said Fidelis,

'How are you Mzee? How is UK looking? Is it as cold as you thought it would be?'

I interrupted by saying, 'Jambo Fidelis. *Mimi mzuri sana, Asante*. Yes it is Fidelis, it's bloody cold. How are you and what's new with the business?'

'*Mzuri sana Mzee*. Freddie is still in Tanzania and there is nothing in the mail or on the phone that can't wait until you come back. I'm keeping the men busy on this and that, like you told me to. Mzee, all the girls in Mr Gordon Melvin's office said they miss you very much!'

Blooming insolence. The very sound of his voice cheered me up immensely. So did the voice of Sub Sea Surveys when I spoke to them and they assured me that Ian would be required all next season in the North Sea. I was beginning to enjoy being home but I was still in a bit of a state. I had tremendous difficulty re-orienting my life and coming to terms with the fact that I had no wife, no children and no parents to worry about or care for. I kept myself busy; I had no choice but to do so really; there was so much to be done.

Knightsmead Farm was right next door to me; my only neighbours really, and what lovely neighbours they were too. John and Kitty would often invite Ian and I over for lunch and I had Sunday lunch with them nearly every week-end I was home. They were good Wiltshire farmers. John, from what I could see, did the work of two men, in spite of having had a leg shot off by a sniper in the last war. Kitty was an English rose. There were six children, all grown up and married now. All the boys were very handsome and all the girls very pretty. I've lost count of the grandchildren. Kitty and John would always have a sympathetic ear for me, although they never took sides. I knew that they, like a lot of other people, were very fond of Molly.

I phoned or called in to see clients up and down the country and learnt there was very little, if any, land survey or engineering survey work on the market. The hydrographic survey side had gone mad. In between times I had made several calls to Nairobi and everything there was running smoothly. Fidelis told me that we have been granted a new licence and also that the United States Navy were interested in our services for a big dredging operation in Mombasa. All big stuff and Fidelis was loving it! To add pleasure to all this business, to put back a little colour to my life, to relax, every time my sister visited me I was able to throw a party or two and invite my friends and neighbours; she was good at this and we had a lot of fun. The trips to Bath were always enjoyable too, even though I always visited the solicitor or the dentist! I had to have umpteen fillings, two caps and three route-canals! He too was a nice chap though.

My solicitor and I talked over many aspects of my life and he confirmed that things needed a lot of thinking about and there was little room for wrong decisions. I was also going to need a little mercy from the 'other side' but there didn't appear to be much hope of that! Timing was of paramount importance. I didn't want to part with Inmarsh House for lots of good reasons. Although I travelled a lot to earn my living, I always came back to what was my home. Another reason was, if I decided to work from home; and a lot of people did, Inmarsh House had everything for me: accommodation, parking area for transport not in use and for visitors and it was a prestigious headquarters from which to operate. Another reason, an important one, was that in my current circumstances, without the house I would find that I had completely lost my identity. Well, having made up my mind over that, what next?

To continue working to earn the money to meet my commitments, I had to be able to keep my transport and professional equipment; without either or both, I was stumped. This was where the act of mercy from the other side came in! I also needed a reasonable standard of health, but only God, the doctors and the National Health could help me there. Even when I was walking through the bush in Africa, I often felt there was something wrong with me but I'd always been a bit scared of the consequences if I made a fuss or saw somebody about it. Enough about all this stuff!

I have never stopped loving my country (like most Brits!) and it seems the older one gets, the more one becomes aware that it's HOME. So, that was another big decision made – I decided to come back to England. As soon as I had done this, Ted Taylor Roalfe phoned me and told me to start packing right away because I had better get out of the country within the next few days, before the Inland Revenue man came after me! If it's not one thing then it's another! I mustn't come back to England, on a permanent basis, until after 5 April of the following year, for the same reason as the last. So, it was a bit of a shock to find myself on the plane going back to Nairobi on 3 December, Gay's birthday.

I arrived back in Nairobi at midday and Fidelis was there to meet me. I must say it felt good to be back and I soon got settled in. My return was well celebrated by reversing my car into the Ambassador of Pakistan's car. I had thought I would be spending Christmas in England this year but as it turned out, this wasn't meant to be. Instead, as had become the custom, I spent it out at Karen with Ron and Liz. Now we were going into 1983 and whatever that held in store.

Another three months were going to be spent here and although I was going to be kept pretty busy selling up my home, packing and freighting, I still needed to get a bit more work. I wasn't sure if I was going to be paid in time before I left but that was a chance I would have to take. I would have to make it a condition of any future contract that they paid me on presentation of my invoice (I had a hope!) Freddie got back from Tanzania in plenty of time for Christmas. It was good to see him again.

Ian was kept very busy in 1983 – all hydrographic work – and his services were spread out over several Clients. He did an awful lot of work with these unmanned submersibles, checking oil and gas pipelines. Dennis Hammond, a good friend of mine of DHH, even sent Ian off to Saudi Arabia for quite a long spell. Back here in Kenya we had enough work coming in to pay the bills. In January 1983 I had my first meeting with the Japanese. Their Government were contributing a Medical Research Institute to Kenya (not far from one of the drive-in cinemas!) I think the name of the Japanese consulting engineers was Takenaka Komuten Company and they and Mowlems chose my firm to do the site survey and setting out of works. This was enough work to last me until I left Kenya. And they paid!

I'm sure my publisher will be very angry at me for taking up so much space to talk about 'all' my friends, but I must tell you about this one. He was another grand old gentleman – he could still be alive – and both Molly and myself were very fond of him. His name was (or is) Colonel Conner, an ex-Indian Army officer with an excellent front line record. He was the kind of man one expected to meet in Nairobi years ago. However, they are rapidly dying off now, almost non-existent; more is the pity. Right up until the day I left, we used to meet very often for coffee in the Kenya Coffee Shop. Once he asked the girls and I out to his house for lunch (his *mpishi* used to make the most scrumptious curry – and excellent fruit cake too!). I looked around his abode, manoeuvering my eyeballs very discreetly and noticed all the momentos you would expect to find in such a legend's home, even a tiger skin. There was one particular thing that caught my roaming eye. There, standing on the corner of his desk, was a photograph of him sitting on a garden bench with the late King George VI, both in mufti. After I had returned to England, one of my friends, Stella Brewer (she is always meandering off around the world) went to Kenya for a holiday, just a couple of years ago. She went into the Kenya Coffee Shop (just as you would do now) to see if she could find the Colonel to tell him what I had been getting up to. As she went into the café she could see the Colonel sitting down with quite a few people around him. However, by the time she had got her coffee and was looking for somewhere to sit down, he was free. She went over and sat near him and brought out a photograph of me and put it in front of the confused Colonel. The café was full of the aroma of Kenya coffee and chatting people as he dropped his line of sight down to the photo. He peered at it and then shot up, saying, 'Where is he? Is he here?' Wasn't that lovely? Stella made another precious friend.

Let me tell you another short story about another friend of mine. Again, I was queuing up for my coffee and standing in front of me was a very beautiful lady. She caught me completely off my guard. I had been watching her take a cigarette out of her lovely scented handbag when she turned to me and asked if I had a light. I nearly fainted! I spent far too much time in the bush and this was the price I had to pay.

'I'm awfully sorry, Madame, but I don't smoke!'

That got the conversation going. We sat down together and introduced ourselves, of course. Several days later, because of one thing and another, I went for coffee rather late and, bless me, we met each other again. We sat down together again as if we were old friends and I couldn't help but notice what a beautiful tanned skin she had. After some moments I could feel myself coming round again as I heard her voice saying, 'Roy, you must come home for tea tomorrow and meet my dear husband.' The way she said 'usbond' in her foreign accent was absolutely fascinating.

Gannet Bayone was waiting for me at her door when I came up her driveway and with a beautiful '*Jambo*' she offered me her cheek. Her husband very soon appeared in a white suit. He looked very smart, very handsome and very polished. On the third cup of tea (I had finished all the fruit cake!) I learnt that he was an arms dealer – AN ARMS DEALER – for heaven's sake! He had me gripped by his stories that followed. Once upon a time, when I was in the Army, a sapper woke me up and asked me if I wanted to buy a battleship! That was nothing compared to what this man had genuinely got for sale! I didn't continue that friendship for several reasons; I was scared to!

Early in the morning of 22 February 1983, when I came in from jogging with my neighbours' dogs I had a phone call from my son-in-law in Toronto. Wendy had produced my first granddaughter, Caroline. Both mother and baby were fighting fit. Needless to say, I was over the moon with such news. I had met Simon only three times before, when he was a medical student, which may have been the reason for his tone of voice! He sounded more like a VAT officer announcing that I had overpaid my return by £2.00 and that he was submitting a cheque by return of post! I loved the baby's name; I don't think they knew it, but it was the same as my dear grandmother's.

The day after Caroline was born my mind was still ninety per cent made up that I was going back home. I was trying to be careful, not to burn too many bridges just in case there was a last minute change. You never knew what was going to happen next these days. For example, on 4 March the Mayor of Nairobi was thrown out of office by the police. I had only spoken to him a few days before about the city's future plans! By 22 March, I must have been ninety nine per cent sure of going because I had sold all my office furniture (to my Japanese clients!) and I had sold most of my home. Nearly everything else, including my professional equipment, had been packed. British Airways had guaranteed me a seat to London on 5 April.

Ian Gordon met me at Heathrow on the morning of 6 April 1983 – I was back!

16

Back Home Again

In a way, it was fortunate that Ian wasn't at sea for the next few weeks because he could spend a good bit of time helping me to get sorted out and reorganised. Over these last thirty years or so, I've always kept a job-list going; it didn't mean that the jobs got done but it did help to keep a little organisation in my life! It didn't only consist of 'Replace hot-water tap washer in bathroom' or 'Guild of Surveyors AGM on Friday' but also 'Joy's school on Thursday' and 'Birthday present for Gay's Friend's 13th.' Two days after arriving home, my job-list had listed 319 jobs! (318 of them were marked important!) It took five months to get the list down to a mere twenty jobs.

I had three lawns at the house and over 400 rose-bushes of different species that needed looking after. Upstairs had five bedrooms and a bathroom, all of which needed painting on the inside and out – and the rest of the house before the winter. Upkeeping the books was a never ending task and there was the dreaded VAT return and income tax. The first few months I found it tough to get used to the idea that I no longer had any 'house-staff', not only to look after the shamba but the confounded washing, ironing, house cleaning and cooking. There were a whole string of family and friends coming to stay with me for a couple of nights – and I hated ironing sheets. And yet, it only took a couple of days to feel glad to be back in England and in my home. Having said that, it was only a couple of days later when there was one heck of a white frost – I think my voice went up two octaves that morning!

The day before the frost all my 'stuff', which had come by air-freight, arrived at the house. As we (Ian and I) unpacked I could still smell Africa in my boxes. It brought a lump to my throat! Ian kept an alert eye open for snakes and spiders! I have got to tell you this one, before I go on any further. I had only been home for about two weeks when a threatening letter arrived from the Southern Electricity Board saying they were going to come and cut my power off. Off down to their offices Ian and I charged (I had put my bush-jacket on and carried my panga nice and sharp) only to discover that I had paid my bill, not once but twice; I had sent a cheque and so had Ian. Apparently, that gave their computer something to think about. Ian said that was only an indication of what I had to come (the same as everybody else) as a result of teething trouble with computers.

My beautiful widowed sister would come and stay with us often and her help was never-ending; cooking, making curtains or putting a hand to the garden (bless her). We had many a laugh whilst performing our many 'duties'. However, she used to get on my wires a bit when she looked upon me as not her younger brother but her baby brother! If she caught me using naughty words I would get a real tongue-whipping and I always had to dress like an 'English gentleman', even while working, or I was for it. Being half African, I would often like to wear only my Kikuyu *kikoy* when I got up in the morning to take her a cup of tea in bed. My goodness, I soon had to give up that habit, it just wasn't worth it! She accused me of going native and only the Good Lord knows what tricks her imagination would be playing upon her. Judging by her actions I'm sure she thought I was a lifetime subscriber to the Mau-Mau Brotherhood! It was a vaudeville show.

These were the early days of my return to my new bachelor life back in England. I had only a few ideas in my mind and they were to get my house and garden in order, to get my life into some sort of organised routine and to get my UK firm well and truly re-established and doing well. I also hoped and prayed that some day Molly would come back to me. Fire played a big part in my life these early days too. One day, 24 June to be precise, I had a bonfire going in my garden to try and get rid of some of the cuttings from the garden and a load of rubbish that I had accumulated. There were also a lot of bits and pieces of plastic roofing material (storm damage) I wanted to burn up. A nice breeze blew away from the two houses and I got rid of the lot. That was another important job scratched off my job-list. Several hours later my next door neighbour John, farmer and friend, came storming into my house.

'Here, come with me, come and have a look at this!' he said. He looked so angry, I knew there was something wrong.

I went to the garden fence with him. The fence separated my house from his vast growing vegetable garden. Well, it *was* growing until I lit my bonfire . . . I wished the ground would open up and swallow me, there and then. The toxic smoke (I didn't know the smoke was toxic at the time) from the fire had blown across his vegetable garden and had withered and killed the lot. These were the people that I loved and they had been so kind to me; I wouldn't have wished harm of any kind to come to them and then I did this to them. What could I say or what could I do? As well as offering my deepest apologies to John I offered a substantial deposit on the damage; not that it would put things right but it was some sort of help. I didn't think it helped very much. I lost sleep over that, just through shame. To my surprise, John came across to the house again two days later with a bowl of strawberries from his garden (on the other side of his house) and a jug of cream from his dairy. I love that family and I nearly weep when I think back.

Three months after that 'event', I was working over in my office (which used to be the stables) and David, one of the sons, came running over to me, shouting, 'Mr Griffiths, phone the Fire Brigade quick, the farm house is on fire!'

This I did with the upmost speed.

'Yes Sir, the fire had already been spotted by a member of the public and two engines are already on their way to you. They will be there any second. Has anybody been hurt?' said the lady at the fire station.

I shot over to the farm and saw Kitty running in and out of the house to collect whatever she could retrieve. Not only was that part of the house now becoming full of black smoke but I could just about see gas bottles all over the place. I shouted to David to keep himself and his mother out of there.

The sound of fire engines going round and round the village on the top of the hill was very distinct. I ran out of the farm and across my property to my car park. Fortunately, the key was still in the ignition of the Land Rover so I jumped in and shot up the hill and parked right in the middle of the road. Cars immediately pulled over as if they knew why I had stopped there in such a manner. In no time the fire engines shot around the corner and, following my signals, went down Inmarsh Lane without saying a single word to me as they passed. (It was hardly the time to discuss how England were playing anyway!) The damage was extensive but a lot was saved by the firemen once they got part of the roof off and climbed inside. What magnificent men they are. Myself, I only looked in the back door and got a nasty burn on my forearm. Useless! The family 'took over' my house for a few months until they could get something organised. I enjoyed their company and it was like having a family again. Those days came to pass and the house got partly rebuilt and partly repaired; furniture was replaced and the family were back in, living their day by day lives again.

Another old family friend and one time neighbour (she lived next door to us in Longfield, Kent) used to come and stay with me often. She wasn't that old but she was a page out of German history. Her name was Baroness Gisela. I would enjoy being made a fuss of when she came and stayed or when I went over to her home to stay for the weekend. She was everything you could imagine a German baroness to be. She had also lived some time in Swaziland and Kenya but we never met her in our Kenya days. She was now a 'working class' person, like many of us but she still had that dignity, that noble stance of her past. We were all in Kenya at the same time, those years just prior to Independence. She too didn't hesitate in giving me a hand with the house chores. One way or another, I didn't do badly for myself, did I? Although I haven't seen her for a long time, I can still hear her very German voice saying, 'Griffiths, if these shelves get any dustier, grass will grow on them!' or 'Griffiths, these things are no good, you want to throw them away, yes!'

She was an excellent cook and while staying at Inmarsh she would fill my freezer with pies and goodies that would last for weeks. I don't know exactly where she is now but I do know she is a nursing sister back in Germany. Her father, whom she loved dearly, was shot by the Russians during the war and she had to get out *tout de suite*. If you ever read this, Gisela, why don't you drop me a line?

Towards the end of that first July things were dragging a bit and I could see that one of the main reasons for this was because I didn't yet have a secretary. As luck would have it, there was a lady in the village who wanted to start a new interest in life. Her children had grown up and her husband was a very busy man a great deal of the time (he was a senior armed forces officer). She was like a lot of ladies at her stage of life. She had time (which weighed very heavy) on her hands, she had lots of energy, she was still very attractive and wanted to get back into circulation with the living. I was very lucky. She turned out to be a great asset to the firm. In fact, there were times, when I was abroad, when she would have to take over command – office-wise. Soon after she started, one of the first tasks she had to cope with was getting dozens of personal letters away to potential clients, offering the services of my firm. A lot of the letters were a waste of time, I suppose, but some of them did eventually bring work. The seven years after I came home from Africa we had built up a clientèle of some eighty-six companies and these letters made a fair contribution to that list.

The first job I tackled wasn't until August and that was an overland pipeline at Didcote Power Station. It was nice because I could drive there every day (although, for a couple of days, I took advantage of being able to stay with the Baroness because that was only half the distance.) The second job involved various interim hydrographic surveys at Port Talbot for Nash Dredging and Reclamation. Ian was at sea all the time so now – there was no stopping!

Up until the beginning of 1990 I had ninety-seven survey contracts, some lasting only a week but many of them went on for months and months. A lot of our time was spent on the high seas making charts for one reason or another. A lot of you have noticed on my headed notepaper that at the end of the title of my firm, I have the words 'Home and Abroad', in brackets. Although the title of this chapter is called 'Back Home Again!', it does include the adventures abroad undertaken by my UK office. One job cropped up which comes within this interpretation.

On Friday, 21 October 1983, I was waiting at Heathrow for flight number BA 173 which was due to leave for Khartoum at three thirty five p.m. Baroness Gisela was seeing me off and then afterwards she was taking my VW van back to Inmarsh House. There she would collect her own car and go back home. I had to use my van to transport all my equipment to the airport to get it sent on by air-freight. That was a job that never seemed to get any easier. This time I remembered to get my List of Tools of Trade signed by Customs. It's very difficult to get cleared when you get back if you haven't got this done. Ian wasn't able to help me because he too was working overseas. Anyway, I'd rather be seen off by a lady any day than be seen off by Ian! We had plenty of time left so we sat down and had several cups of coffee and chatted about this and that. I also indulged in one of my favourite pastimes – watching the world go by. When at the airport I can always find something interesting to look at. I asked Gisela to kindly check that I had left my fridge door open and to make sure that I had pulled all of the plugs away from the wall. Oh yes, and please to check that I had locked my office, after having made sure that I had turned the lights off!

'Oh, for goodness sake Griffiths, you are worse than an old woman . . .' followed by a load of German which I couldn't understand, but I had a pretty good idea what it meant. She is good.

An old friend from my Kenya days, Roger Durrant, was at Khartoum at two o'clock in the morning to meet me. I thought this was nice of him and I think it put me in such a good mood I hardly cared about the mass of men and armed soldiers, all pushing, all sweating and all frantically shouting in Arabic. It was terribly hot. Once through Customs and Immigration I was soon driven to a quiet hotel. Sleep was very determined to take a long time to come. Had I packed this? Had I packed that?

The day after next I was up at four thirty a.m. and we were at the airport at six to catch the Chevron Oil Company's plane down to Port Sudan. The plane left at seven and I was nearly cooked to death. Over those last few weeks, since I'd known I was going to the Sudan, I had wondered how I was going to like working abroad again together with all the hassle that went with it. Well, now I know, I was loving it and I'd only been there a day! Dennis Sucre (Chevron Oil) and Peter Holmes (Mowlems) met me at Port Sudan and without any ceremony they drove me down to the site to show me around. There wasn't much to see except a lot of sand dunes and wadis. It was so hot I seemed never to stop drinking bottles of water. There was one outstanding feature – I shall always remember it – a lone palm tree, dead in the middle of the site. You could see it from miles away, if the sand wasn't blowing; it was even shown on the Admiralty Charts as a Conspicuous Tree.

While I was compiling notes for this chapter it was clear that I had enough for a book on its own; some places and jobs just happen to be like that. So, perhaps I can look forward to you joining me in the sequel to this book. But I'm not going to leave you here without giving you a taste of what went on. For instance, I had a lasting introduction to the site. As we arrived near the site and were about to turn off the main road, a passing lorry drove right into three camels and killed the lot. I understand that this is a taboo thing to do in the Sudan and in this case it certainly created a lot of trouble. We weren't involved so we didn't stop there very long watching but those camels were still there, on the side of the road, when I left sixteen weeks later. Every day, we used to stop our cars just before we reached the carcasses and prepared ourselves to drive past them! The Sudanese, in this part of the country, had very unkempt-looking hair and wore their swords more or less under their arms, held in place with a short scabbard strap. We saw several men in argument with the driver and in only seconds they had their hands on their swords. Like I said, we didn't hang around!

Our camp was about three miles from Port Sudan, as the crow flies, and the site was further south about another twenty-four miles. Camp was something else! It consisted of about twenty bungalows, somewhat scattered around, a bar with no beer and a dining-room. It was managed by a French outfit which, by and large, ran it very well. The food was mostly French; however, I could eat most of it. We often had wine with our dinner and I don't know how the caterer pulled off that concession! (The Sudan is a 'dry state'.) Each cabin had hot and cold water and an A/C and these were tremendous assets in a place like Port Sudan, even if we didn't always have water!

The site belonged to the Americans or, to be more specific, Chevron Oil Company. The name of the site was the Marsa-Nimeiri Marine Terminal. It was to be a site with the largest oil tanks in the world, diameters of 88 metres. John Mowlem were to do the civil engineering and I was under sub-contract to Mowlems as site surveyor.

The first task I had to take on was to check the air-survey of the site. I was in the process of performing this check; in fact I was in the eighth day of being on-site, when two pick-ups drove up to me and six men got out. Four of them were armed with swords. The youngest member said to me, 'You! You get off this land!'

Oh dear, I thought to myself, I'm in one of those situations. They all started jabbering in Arabic whilst I, quite frankly, looked on a bit dumbfounded. I must have looked really gormless standing there with my mouth wide open. I was just pulling myself together and making up my mind what to do next, when one of them grabbed my tripod, with the theodolite and distomat still on it and started to yank it away. At sight of this I pulled myself up to my full six-feet-one and then I too grabbed the tripod and in doing so, I said in the strongest possible voice, 'What in the bloody hell do you think you are doing? Let go of this equipment before you break something.'

With that, two of the men drew their swords and the third man shoved me to the ground. Fortunately, the equipment didn't fall over. My five chainmen were looking at me with fear in their faces and were saying something to me in Arabic. The young man held his sword to one side as if he was about to cut my head off. By the look on everyone's faces, I felt there was more in this situation than I knew about.

'You say too many things, Englishman. Now I'm telling you again – GET OFF THIS LAND! You have no right to be here, this is my father's land, not Chevron's.'

I quickly thought to myself, If you don't want to get bumped off, Roy, you had better do what the sod tells you to do. This is not your problem, pack up and go and let Chevron or Mowlems sort it out. Anyway, this gravel is a bit rough on the rump sitting down here!

'All right,' I said, 'let me pack up my equipment and then I'll go away. I haven't got any transport this morning, so we will have to wait at the Dedication Shed.

At least one of the thugs helped me back onto my feet again and even made an effort to brush me off. I went to take the distomat off the tripod and the young one yelled at me (as if he knew he was winning and had got the better of me), 'You go and you leave these things here.'

I've never felt like belting anybody like I felt like bashing this blighter, right now. Our eyes met with raging fire in both of us and I felt that he got his strength through knowing I was outnumbered. Just for a brief moment, my eyes dropped to his sword; it looked awfully sharp and the knuckles of his brown hand were white. I thought, Stop this, Roy, and don't be a fool or in seconds you'll be dead!

Most of my men had run away by now; they went whilst they had the chance. I swallowed my pride, picked up my field book and walked away. The thugs looked at each other with smiles on their faces and I shall never forget that. When I reached the road Dennis Sucre (Chevron) drove up and I told him what had happened. He confessed that he couldn't do much about it on his own and I was inclined to agree.

The next day, Peter Holmes (Mowlems), Bill Jackson (Chevron) and Dennis Sucre (Chevron) went to the terminal and spoke to Sheik Balaab (occupant) and a couple of other gentlemen and presumably got things sorted out. Apparently, the gentleman with whom I had my confrontation the day before was Sheik Balaab's youngest son. I was later taken on the site and in particular the burial ground and was asked to clearly define the perimeter with a fence and to stop messing about and generally get on with the job!

I figured that about 140 control points were going to be required, plus all the computing and setting-out, so I had a heap of work to get on with. Each day when I was traversing, I was recording temperatures of 39°C. I really felt the heat. During the mornings there was no breeze at all; it felt as if there wasn't any air at all to breathe! Several times, as I stood up after putting the distomat back in its box, the whole site appeared to go spinning round and black patches filled my vision as I gasped for air. How dramatic it sounds but how true it was! Most days I would get a hint of a breeze in the afternoons and that just gave me the chance to recover and carry on. The Sudanese didn't seem to sweat at all; they just looked as if they were going to pass out and die.

Most of us would wake up at four thirty and have breakfast at four thirty five. Everybody would leave camp at five twenty ready to start work at six. Work stopped at nine for the famous Sudanese breakfast and this took about half an hour; the Sudanese wouldn't work without this breakfast break. This Sudanese breakfast became an important factor in accomplishing success on the contract! The rest of the day didn't matter very much, as long as workmen got their breakfast. Most chaps had one day a week off but the agent seemed to keep me (a sub-contractor) busy almost seven days a week; but still, I needed to find a lot of money if I wanted to keep Inmarsh House!

Christmas was on me and I hardly realised it was here. I even faintly started to dread it coming – can you imagine that? – and I'm a Christian too. However, all was not lost for when we got back to the mess for dinner on the 23rd; lo and behold, the Christmas decorations were up and what a lovely cheery sight they were! In one sudden shock, I felt the Spirit of Christmas. To my surprise, I had more Christmas cards than I had ever received in my life before. On Christmas Eve we had a grand party; we even had a half dozen ladies who managed to appear from somewhere. We even had some booze but it wasn't enough! But still, as one of my American colleagues said, 'It's lovely to hear the laughter of women, to look at their lipstick and smell their French perfume, to see their full figures and curvaceous hips!'

It wasn't until this party that we were told that we were having Christmas Day off. To my surprise, this was a pleasant day too. We all went to Suakin for the day – now there's a thing. Boxing Day . . . back to work, it was all over.

As the weeks went by Sheik Balaab's youngest son and I got onto talking terms with each other and then we moved on to good friends. The day before I left the Sudanese held a small private farewell party for me with the traditional slaughter of an animal. They presented me with the very sword that I was chased off the site with. I have it hanging in my lounge this very day! I expect Mowlems were glad to see the back of me on 14 February. Chevron laid on a special plane for me (because of all my equipment).

17

Then There Was Maggie

This has been the hardest chapter to write; in fact, this has been my fifth attempt! A lot of painful emotions were introduced into my earlier attempts but I could see that they were not making good reading and they would have bored you to tears. Many of these emotions created sinful feelings which were not worthy of being put down on paper. But there is a much more pleasant aspect to this relationship and that is the one I would like to write about. On my previous attempts I was full of admiration for Maggie and I went overboard with words of praise for her, but, if I was to be honest with myself I could hardly expect you, my dear reader, to believe that anybody could be so perfect!

There are several people in my life that I feel I would rather not have met but Maggie wasn't one of them. Today, I miss her and doubt if I'll ever see her again. I don't even know where she is. I would like to tell you, if I may, how Maggie gradually came into my life. You'll not be bored.

Life was at its best when I was bringing up my children; I loved every minute of it. There was always something to do, there was always something going on in our rich and full lives. They were good children, they had no bad points, only various grades of good ones. I loved each and every one of the four of them for being just what they were. There were times when I felt that I had to lay down the law a bit – of course there were – but the hostile atmosphere would last no longer than ten minutes. But as they grew into their later teens, the job became more difficult. Mainly because their education was better than mine and often they knew more about what we were talking about than I! Those days are over now and I haven't seen or spoken to any of the girls for years; their choice, not mine, and it hurts!

As you know, in 1982 I found that my wife was divorcing me after being my wife, my best friend and my counsellor for thirty-two years! My children, who have now all grown up, didn't want to talk to me. I was living at home alone and naturally feeling very lonely and empty at times; suddenly, no family at all. Even though I had found myself in this sorrowful situation, I realised that I still had to go on living and enjoying the greatest gift of all – LIFE! I wasn't finding an easy way back to happiness; I was sure that there wasn't one. Only time was going to heal those dreadful wounds.

I was gradually formulating a plan for my life but it still needed thinking through. Each time I took a new step in my life it always seemed to be a bloody big one! It was certainly helping me immensely working to get the firm back on its feet again and taking on as much work as I thought I could cope with. I now had a good secretary, I had Ian, lovely friends and neighbours. Things were taking shape as the dust was settling and really, I started to count my blessings, for there were many. I seemed to be coming to terms with my housework but mainly because there were always visiting friends 'doing' for me! However, I could see that unless I did something about it, I was eventually going to get snowed under; I couldn't go on relying on my visiting friends for ever more.

I can't quite remember but I think it was our village postmistress who suggested that I should ask Mrs Margaret W. if she would like to do the job as my housekeeper. This idea I discussed with my secretary who then made arrangements. The next afternoon I was very pleased to meet Mrs Margaret W. when she turned up for an interview. She was rather younger than I expected and looked very smart, which I thought was a good sign. But I thought she spoke rather abruptly; sometimes as if she was interviewing me! It passed through my mind that I wouldn't like to cross swords with her. She had a nice speaking voice and sounded educated; I was surprised that she was looking for this type of work but that wasn't my business. She certainly appeared fit, was married and had two sons. Coffee was not accepted but a contract of employment was.

On 8 May 1984 I had the shock of my life when I weighed myself. I was flabbergasted to find I had lost over two stone, without even trying, but then, I thought no more about it. I did make a note in my diary on the 16 June about how very tired I always felt these days. The previous night I had gone to dinner with Stan and Mary and I actually fell asleep while my host was talking to me! They noticed what was happening which, in turn, made me feel awfully embarrassed and yet, I still couldn't keep awake! I didn't realise that something was developing. Diabetes.

On 16 November 1984 I had another stroke of luck; I was successful in securing a local contract no more than three or four miles away. These local jobs were a luxury for they did give me a period when I could enjoy my lovely home. The job was to survey an old establishment in Melksham. It was an interesting place, very old, and I enjoyed the job very much. It was one of those sites that gave me a chance to produce an attractive and interesting drawing as an end result. Even Ian was able to join me for a week or two. My old friend Stan was able to join our team too and, being a retired builder not only made him an excellent chainman, but he was also a store of knowledge. Inside one of the main buildings there were several manholes and one of these was concealed, over in a dark corner. This one had a loose cover and poor old Stan put his leg down it. He really hurt himself, poor chap; he took all the skin off of his shin.

After Ian was sure that Stan was home and comfortable and in Mary's care, he went off in search of another chainman. We only needed him for a couple of days until Stan was back with us again. Ian had no luck that afternoon. Ever since I'd been in business, I'd always been able to use Molly or one of the girls in such circumstances as these, but I couldn't now. Suddenly, Ian said that he thought 'Maggie' could do this job and it would only be for a couple of days. Anyway, if she couldn't help, she might know somebody else in the village who could. I said OK, let's have a chat to her, on the phone. It's all a bit vague now but I more or less told her, that basically, all she had to do was take the zero end of the tape and hold it wherever she was asked. Fine. First, she would have to have a talk with a friend (presumably a baby-sitter). Maggie was made aware that the rate of pay was more than she earned in my house. She phoned back again while we were having dinner and confirmed that it was all systems go, as she put it. Maggie turned out to be one of the best assistants we ever had. From time to time she was able to come on a lot of jobs with us.

Well, in 1985, the work was coming in fast and furious and so were the cheques. My happiness started to pick up but for the sad news that my dear friend, Liz Marshall, died on Christmas Day in Nairobi. For a couple of days all I could think about was Liz bringing me a cup of coffee out to her swimming pool at Karen and telling me how ugly I was! You must remember me telling you about her earlier in the book? How was Ron going to cope? Terrible. Maggie showed that she could feel my sorrow.

On 26 June 1985 my decree absolute was issued at Bath Family Court and was brought home to me by the resounding comment from my solicitor, 'Your married life is now finished!' Also, that morning I noticed that I had lost three-and-a-half stone without any effort on my part. In fact, I had been eating and drinking very well, especially drinking! This was also the time that I first began to feel a ghastly pain in my left leg. The doctor said it was sciatica!

1986 was another bag of mixed tricks, as they say. One of them was that Maggie had left her husband and that finished in divorce. At the same time Ian took off for Saudi Arabia and was gone for months and months. On the 23 July I spent all day getting upset watching the Royal Wedding, for heavens sake! I could well remember when one of the Sunday newspapers had a photograph of me outside Buckingham Palace, looking up while waiting for the news that the groom had been born! (I was in uniform and I had my hands in my pocket! I think the paper was *The News of The World*!)

It was in September that Jim Fitzpatrick came to see me from Sacramento. The following three weeks are a happy memory. As you can imagine, we had so much to discuss. At that time Maggie was living in Inmarsh House too and I must say that Jim and Maggie got on like a house on fire. We took Jim around to see many of the things that you take your visitors from America to see. He seemed to be impressed most of all with Lord Nelson's ship *H.M.S. Victory* at Portsmouth, St Paul's Cathedral, the Pump Room at Bath and anything to do with the works of Isambard Kingdom Brunel. All the time Maggie and Jim were quite a team and the mirth flowed like water, giving me some darn good hearty laughs – the silly blighters. I've got some snaps that illustrate their antics. Of course, Jim and Molly's friendship went back to our Sacramento days and, naturally, Jim wanted to see her. It was arranged that Jim should go to Virginia Water to take Molly for lunch. It was an all-round exciting meeting because that was the day when Maggie met Molly; Maggie had such high respect for her. These were the two people, different as chalk and cheese, who had become the two most important women of my life (apart from my mother) but I didn't realise it at the time. What pretty ladies they both were, I thought.

Time passed quickly and then we saw Jim off back to California on the 16 September. Jim and I were always a bit tender when we said our farewells and this time we weren't sure when we would see each other again, if we ever would. However, what happened next was unbelievable. As Maggie and I left the departure lounge we noticed about fifty Sikhs all clustered together. As usual, they looked a mass of colour. We were walking along very slowly because Maggie liked to take everything in when she was at the airport. She always enjoyed a good weep watching other people saying their farewells! 'Just a minute . . . Stop!' said I, as my eye picked out one Sikh in particular. I gazed at him until I was certain that I knew who he was. This was my oldest and best friend, Harbhajan Singh! We had lost contact with each other a couple of years previously when he thought I was living somewhere in Kenya. I hadn't contacted Harbhajan since I'd returned because I was too embarrassed about Molly and I being separated. While I was staring at Harbhajan, he was crouched in front of a holy man who was on his way back to India and I believe they may have been saying some sort of prayer. I still stood there, staring. Maggie had a slight smile on her face and her eyes were wide open in a state of consternation. I still stared. Some of the other Sikhs started to look at me very suspiciously. Harbhajan too became suspicious and thought something was going on behind him and then he shot round.

'Roy!' he boomed out!

I have already mentioned this man earlier and I will tell you more about him later.

Maggie was going on 'safari' with us now and had become such a valuable member of the crew. She quickly caught on to many of the day by day chores of the profession and was very conscientious and extremely thorough (which is typical of Wiltshire people!). She took on the responsibility of loading the van every day with stores for work, right down to the correct field book, ball-points and even fuses for the echo-sounder. She could accurately reduce and plot tacheometry, draw tide-graphs, set up instruments and prisms and was a competent 'booker' and leveller. She didn't want to boss all the time but she did have a way of making the team work together and produce our best. She actually kept us on our toes. Yet, even in jeans and a thick pullover and whilst thumping in a survey peg, she looked very feminine and pretty; but not when she got annoyed with anyone! She always gave me warmth in her friendship and a feeling that I could rely on her and trust her. Important in my work. I'm not saying that she didn't bring a little mirth into the team when she was confronted with some heavy object that had to be moved! But generally, other workmen would lend her a hand; in fact, she usually had workmen and fishermen running all over the place for her. I didn't mind, I didn't have to pay them!

1987 was a good year for work also; we were getting plenty. I wonder if any of you saw us? We worked in Edinburgh, New Malden, Brighton, Frome, Lingerabay/Harris, Humberside, Chippenham, Waltham Cross, Castlebay/Barra, Lochboisdale, Largs, Isle of Arren, Port Ellen, Corsham, Mallaig and Westbury.

This will surprise you, but on 10 January 1987 I decided I was going to sell Inmarsh House. I wasn't in a hurry to make the actual sale but nevertheless, I now felt that the house was too full of the wrong memories and it was too big to live in alone. Also, now that I was getting things sorted out I realised I had too much of 'my wealth' wrapped up in the house. I seemed to be working myself to death paying back to the bank some recent loans I had to have. On top of this I found my love for Scotland was growing forever stronger. I had been introduced to and subsequently fallen in love with Scotland very early in my life. Each time I returned, and there were many times, my love grew stronger. Maggie had been up to Scotland on quite a lot of jobs and I really never knew how she felt about it.

As regards to moving to Scotland things were held up a bit because of my health. I saw a surgeon in Bath (eventually!) RUH, and in spite of my lumps and bump he said there was nothing wrong with me! As regards my leg, they said it was sciatica and just gave me stronger pain killers. They confirmed, however, that I did have mild diabetes and said it could be controlled by diet alone. No one seemed concerned about my loss of weight, it seemed; as far as they were concerned my weight was just right. A good night's sleep was becoming unknown to me and then, sleep itself, of any kind. I was still walking awkwardly and felt little demand or desire for amour. Maggie comforted me a lot through this. However, on 4 April, I told the house agent to go ahead and sell the house. The sale was completed by 20 June.

There were only three things left for me to do now, three things that needed my upmost attention. One was to offer Ian a partnership; this in turn would ease the load off of me. Two, was to help Maggie find a job and somewhere for her to live. Three was to find myself a home in Scotland, preferably in that part I loved most of all, the Highlands and Islands. Ian, after careful consideration, turned down the offer, which was a surprise. Maggie found herself a job in Devizes Hospital, doing what she always wanted to do; and they even gave her a room. I made two trips to Scotland, which, in my state, nearly killed me and bought my house at Erbusaig. I was very satisfied with it in many ways. I seemed to have no control of all the things that were going on around me; my world, such as it was, was slipping away from me. I put it all down to this strange illness which no person said I had! Day by day I was losing my strength but, unfortunately, not on Maggie!

On 17 August I said goodbye to Inmarsh House and to my dearest friend Maggie. We understood that she was coming to Scotland when she could to see how I had settled in. I hadn't got three miles from the house when I already missed her. On 24 August Maggie phoned me to tell me that she loved me. Now that made things different! On 7 October Maggie came up to Erbusaig and stayed with me for a few days and that was lovely. If I had been fitter I doubt if I would have ever let her go again.

Molly visited me too on 23 October; I didn't expect such a flood of visitors so soon after moving to Scotland. It was gorgeous sharing Molly's time so privately again. She was so lovely and I was so proud to introduce her around. I would like to have spent a lot more time with her but, alas, loads of work was still coming in and I had to get back to it.

At this time, maybe because of Molly, Maggie gave me up in favour of a few other friends; I could never blame her for this. She had a whole new world of friends, including other nurses that she worked with. Many stayed in the nurses' home too. It appeared to me that Maggie had to have her fling apparently and there wasn't really much I could do about it, except feel thoroughly bloody miserable. I never stopped loving Molly but I knew she could never be mine again but, in spite of the pain, I could never turn my back on her. In my illness, I just couldn't sort things out.

On 13 November Molly came down to Bath to see me and that was another very happy day. I was staying in Bath whilst working for Wessex Water. On the 20th I went up to her home for the weekend and Molly and I felt we were back together again. However, beyond this reunion there were all sorts of complications and because of them, I felt it difficult to relax. If I had been courting a stranger I would have felt relatively more comfortable. I say again, there was nothing wrong with our relationship basically; it was the seepage through of the hostile feelings of others towards me. These hostile feelings had developed more strongly since I had left England in 1979 to live in Kenya. Now I was back on the scene, which was a nightmare for some. And, all the time, I was in such pain.

Molly spent Christmas at Erbusaig with me and it was paradise. We laughed and talked about all the things we liked to talk and laugh about. We played lots of music, the kind we both loved. The Tingle Creek Hotel (next door) provided a lovely Christmas dinner; it was another Hollywood story. To my surprise, Maggie phoned me very early on Christmas Day. If it was designed to damage my relationship with Molly, then it bloody well worked! I thought how nasty people could be. I took Molly back to London for the New Year and stayed with her for quite a long time because the time had come when I just couldn't work any more. Can you believe that the medical world could let me get so ill? For the first time Molly could see the trouble I was in. At night I could only get some rest by laying on the hard floor with my leg up on a chair, thus, finding some temporary relief from pain; you try and sleep on the floor with your leg up on a chair! Boy, behaving in this manner makes it very hard to try and keep a girlfriend!

Anyway, I went to see Molly's doctor, a professor and he frowned and said, 'You need to see a surgeon.' (Another one!) To cut a long story short, I got to see several chaps and it was a neurosurgeon who finally diagnosed my trouble. 'You have a very painful and quite rare condition called diabetic amyotrophy.' A few days in the Royal Surrey Hospital confirmed it. At last, I knew what was wrong with me. The cure was long: by injecting myself twice a day for the next two years and then for the rest of my life – but that is another story!

At this point I really have to leave a lot of hurtful story out; hurtful to all parties. I'll pick up the story again when Maggie returned to Erbusaig for a short holiday in May. Believe it or not, she painted the entire inside of the house, every single room. We were married on 8 June 1988. It was a lovely wedding and we were married in Portree, Isle of Skye, where she wanted us to be married – bagpipes and all.

Fifteen months later we were divorced.

At this time I was feeling terrible and I am sure that many of my dear readers will know what I mean. Those of you who don't are very lucky and may the birds of paradise continue to fly over your heads. A few days after Maggie left Erbusaig I arrived at Harbhajan's home in search of and finding the solace that one looks for from old friends at such times as these. While watching television recently, I heard a doctor mention that the greatest stress that one has to suffer is when the death of a spouse occurs and the second from the top of the list is the business of divorce! Whilst at Harbhajan's I decided to go to Spain, which seemed to be the most immediate thing I could do, to keep me very busy and be occupied. I had to do something before my grief would drive me to despair! Harbhajan and his family did comfort me immensely. I told Harbhajan that when I got back from Spain I wanted to plan a trip to India, where I'd always wanted to go. We had always believed that one day we would go to India together but if I waited for him I would be too old! I may tell you about my trip to Spain in my next book but, let me tell you a little more about my old friend Harbhajan. First, let me get the setting right.

I caught the Sally Ferry on 20 November 1989 and even that was a bit shaky because the French seamen were on strike. But that problem was overcome by having to catch the ferry from Dover instead of Margate as previously planned. The ferry people told me on the telephone to turn up at Ramsgate to collect my ticket, when they would redirect me to another ferry. I was travelling in my camper so I was prepared for almost anything but things were not that bad. I boarded the ferry and we pulled away at eleven p.m. The ferry was practically empty. The thought passed my mind that every time I had caught the ferry from Dover in the past, I had had company. One year I had my father, my stepmother, my wife and four children! The last time I had Maggie. This time I was travelling very much alone – and it was dreadful – it wasn't even summertime. When I drive a long distance, I usually undo my trouser belt and the top button, so, now I was on board, I did the button up, hooked my belt and spritely leapt out of the camper. The parking bays on the ferry were cheerfully lit and there was a fresh draught blowing through the deck. A beautiful stockinged pair of legs jumping down from a high seat of a lorry were noticed as I made my way up top to the restaurant. I felt momentarily excited and I think this was caused by the impending voyage, not by what I had seen jumping down from the lorry! I was soon seated with a jolly fine meal in front of me which I started to devour. Naturally, after I had eaten, I went and collected my Duty Free which then allowed me to enjoy, out on the deck, one of my favourite cigars – a Willem II Señorita. My habit is not to inhale the cigar smoke but to enjoy the aroma and flavour; it's delicious when the end starts to get soggy! The whole act temporarily brought back further memories of a Dutch company I had once worked for.

The twinkling lights of Dover could hardly be seen any more but I could clearly see wisps of fluffy cloud above me, brightly illuminated by the ships lights; one could even see the silhouettes of a seagull or two, who seemed to be enjoying the voyage just as much as I. Lights from other boats – I think they were fishing boats – were bobbing up and down all over the place. Occasionally, I felt a warm zepher of air coming from the ship's funnel, carrying with it a whiff of the hot engine oil which I love so much. To ponder now seemed the order of the moment. I was feeling very sad and yet happy, contented as well as being in a state of torture. My cigar glowed and I felt the warmth of its life; I pulled my collar up. I continued to just ponder, trying to remember exactly what it was that Harbhajan said to me about his business. I wondered whether Bansy was looking any better now, after her operation last year and smiled to myself as I confirmed that I thought she did. My grin broadened as my thoughts went to that cheeky little rascal Raj (one of Harbhajan's grandsons), when yesterday he called me Funny-Face, after I had called him Chicken-Chops! As I continued to enjoy my cigar I chose to continue thinking about Harbhajan and his family. I knew his mother, Ajit Kaur, very well, and his father too, Naranjan Singh. I tried to imagine what it must have been like when these two good people left Ludianna in India, many years ago, probably at about the same time as I was born. I tried to imagine what kind of contract of employment they were given when they left India to work on the Uganda Railways. I wondered what they expected life would be like when they arrived in Kenya.

Meeting Ajit Kaur was one of the highlights of my life. We met in 1954 and hit it off right from the word go. As the years rolled on she became very dear to me – like a mother. They all lived in a very big house in Kilindini

Road which had rooms and passages winding off in all sorts of directions. Mr Nan Singh, another one of Harbhajan's uncles, also lived in the house somewhere! Mr Nan Singh was the head of the Sikh community and became a very good friend of mine. He used to hold magnificent parties in the house, although I can hardly remember ever leaving any of them. Hmmmmm! Mombasa was a good place to live in those days.

It must have been around 1954 when I first set eyes on Harbhajan; he had just been successful in securing a post with East African Railways & Harbours. He was a trainee draughtsman and soon became popular with everybody as well as making his mark on the Railways. When I got back to EAR & H. from Canada, I was posted to the Resident Engineer, Port Reitz Oil Terminal. This was in connection with a big oil refinery which was going to be built at Chamgamwe. It was then that Harbhajan and I met up again; in fact, he worked in my survey section. We worked together in this very busy section for at least two years and never exchanged a cross word. This was the time when we formed our Badminton club, referred to in the beginning of this book. As you know, I then went to America but I had the good fortune to meet Harbhajan again in 1964, when I once again went back to EAR & H. If you remember, he stopped me from losing my mind in Makambako! Actually, we were put in the same independent survey party on safari in Tanzania. We had to work very hard on that job but we still found time to have a good laugh and cook a meal together.

I moved to the other side of the funnel; there might be less draught there; I was feeling a little chilly. I wondered what Maggie might be doing right now; one o'clock in the morning! It was no good letting my thoughts drift in the wrong direction. Where was I? Whenever I think of Harbhajan, there are always a few memories that never fail to come flooding back to me. One of them is that when we were on safari, I would always know he was approaching my tent by the loud and rapid stomping of his feet, the accompanying swishing of the elephant grass and the clucking of chickens as he shooed them off to the left and right. When he approached my house in Mombasa, he would announce his arrival in a different way – all my children would stop whatever they were doing and suddenly shoot out to the garden when they heard the screeching of his car tyres and the blaring of his car radio as he rounded the corner. One day, he gave us all a surprise when he approached the house at the usual top speed and then leapt out of the car almost before it skidded to a halt! There he was, fully dressed in a Kenya Police sub-inspector's uniform – I didn't even know until then that he was in the Special Police! As well as the usual white shorts and tunic he wore a navy-blue turban and it all looked so very smart.

He was a bit rough (but not spiteful) with my daughters but he had a way with them that made them adore him – bit of a good-looking blighter too (but that was then!) I can always remember the time we worked in Mombasa. Much of the time we worked on the water (hydrographic surveys) or along the shoreline (land survey/setting out works) but there would always be periods when we would be in the office. This would be the time when we would hard-boil a couple of eggs in the RE's Secretary's kettle! After we put these through our egg-slicing machine and peppered them with black pepper, they would go down well with our coffee. A small act but it would bring joy to our lives. How I remember us having a break from work and sitting under the shade of some palm trees and looking out across the blue sea of Port Reitz from its white sandy beaches. It was magic! Even more so when out came the flask of coffee and the hard-boiled eggs.

I had dozed off for a minute or two and was woken by the ship's siren which announced that something was happening. Looking over the side, I could see that we were close to berthing and that people were sleepily walking around the quayside. I just had time for another quick cup of coffee for I had got a little cold and damp; then I had to go down and get my car.

All right! That's all I'm going to write about that particular part of my life. Now let's move on to the end of my trip through Spain, to the point in time where I was sitting back in Harbhajan's home, having a lovely cup of Indian tea. Harbhajan had always been a good listener and he wasn't any different on this occasion. Bansy spent a lot of time by my side too, listening to all my mutterings and looking at my latest collection of snaps. I could smell the curry cooking; it smelt heavenly.

'Have you finished?' asked Harbhajan.

'Yes,' said I, 'Why? Have you got something you want to say?'

'Yes. Are you ready? We're going to India together!'

I just sat there with my jaw dropped and gazed at him. I had seen him in these moods before. I waited to hear what he had to say next. Bansy looked at me with a smile on her face, indicating that her man was about to say something very important. Honestly, she was like an older sister to me, except that I was a good bit older than she was! Raj, who was sitting on my lap and just looking on, insisted that I took the wrapper off another one of his toffees for him.

'What do you mean by that? We are going to India.'

'While you were in Spain, I've talked it over with the family. I haven't had a decent holiday for the last twenty years and the family think that now is the time to have one. This fact, together with your trouble with Maggie, convinces me that I too think the time is right for both of us to go to India together.'

'I see!' was about all I could come up with at that moment. I wanted to believe what he said but I wasn't sure if I heard right! I soon started to get charged with a feeling of intense excitement when he said that we had to go to Poona first, to collect some tree saplings to take to his farm in the Punjab. I've known this dear man for nearly forty years, but I never knew until now that he had a farm in the Punjab!

'We are going at the end of February.'

I looked at Bansy and gave Raj a squeeze and Raj wanted another toffee. 'Right Harbhajan, you're on.'

It was pretty well decided that I was going to spend Christmas with my Sikh family, so I didn't have to drive all the way back to Erbusaig immediately. This was good because I wanted to go and see Stella Brewer and Ted and Judy Taylor-Roalfe while I was down in this neck of the woods anyway, as well as see a lot more of Harbhajan and his family. There was a perpetual flow of people in and out of Harbhajan's home, many being members of his family I had known since the year dot and a lot of others were folk from East Africa; many of whom I'd known since railway days.

Having found out where Maggie lived, I went down to Wiltshire to see if I could see her and tell her about a possible plan for living in Spain. She was furious; wanted to know how I got her phone number! Wasn't a bit interested in the house in Spain. By the tone in her voice I could feel that there was somebody else in the room. Even though my phone-box was right outside her house, she didn't want to see me, not even for a minute or two. Her attitude was so foreign to me; coarse and uncivilised. Why on Earth did I even bother! Merry Christmas, Roy!

In spite of the huge cavity, I had a lovely Christmas with a very happy family. They were very westernised (dare I use such a term!) when it comes to celebrating such events; they certainly understood about Jesus Christ. We had loads to eat, loads to drink, loads of fun with the kids and lots of laughter. It was a happy holiday and I wondered what would I have done without that family.

18

My Return to Kenya

Visitors were still perpetually coming in and going out to wish Harbhajan a bon voyage. This man was so loved and respected by everyone, his family, his friends and those that work for him. He was a short man but very heavily built and as strong as a horse. He had an unforgettable baritone voice and the face of a fierce warrior and yet he came across as a gentle person. Yet, woe betide those who crossed swords with him! He used to cast a spell over Africans; they would work so hard for him and yet he would have them rolling around in hysterical laughter. He was born in Nairobi but was more or less brought up in Mombasa. We both considered Mombasa as our 'home town'. Oh, these stories could go on for almost ever, but the time has come for us two old chaps to catch our flight to Nairobi.

There were a multitude of people at the terminal to see us off. It was a jolly time and for just a moment I felt very important. Isn't that silly? I didn't kid myself for long, realising that if I had been going alone there wouldn't be a single person there, except maybe a VAT officer and an Inland Revenue officer; they will see me off at my graveside! The ladies looked so colourful and pretty. The kids were hanging on to their grandfather's legs, indicating that they didn't want him to go. 'Come on Harbhajan, we're going to Kenya – we're going home.'

Monday, 5 February, 1990. Almost a whole night without sleep and suddenly three o'clock in the morning became six o'clock in the morning! Must put our watches right! Life was stirring all over the aircraft. I went to the toilet and had my injection and on the way back to my seat I looked out of the window and saw the most magnificent dawn; the sun was just sticking its head above the horizon. We had to wait our turn to land and I recognised the Machakos Hills as we flew around them. There was Nairobi and then it disappeared just as quickly as we turned towards her to make our landing. After about the third bump, I thought the pilot was having difficulty in making up his mind which runway we were supposed to be making our landing on. However, we landed quite near the airfield! This was eight fifteen local time.

We had just joined the flock at Customs and Immigration when Harbhajan said to me how great it was to be back in Kenya. Two men came rushing through the crowd towards us; they were both Sikhs. One was dressed in a very smart suit and that was Harbhajan's nephew. The other was dressed in a major's uniform of the Kenya Air Force and he was a distant relative. After rapid introductions we were given the VIP treatment but Customs still went through our cases with a fine toothcomb. Just outside the airport entrance and standing all on its own, a big car was waiting for us. We drove off to the Air Force base where we dropped the major off to work. Harbinder, the other gentleman, Harbhajan's nephew, gave us the latest local news whilst he drove us through Nairobi to his house, where we would be staying. Nairobi looked magnificent and brought a lump to my throat. It was a beautiful sunny morning and yet the air felt cool and fresh. I had the same feelings in my stomach as I had when I first came to Nairobi, thirty-seven years ago. I tried to fend off attacks from the ghosts of Molly and the girls. No matter which way I turned my head, no matter how much news was being fed to us by Harbinder, no matter how many irrelevant questions I asked, the ghosts came charging back at me. I could hear Gay, Joy, Wendy and Jennifer all calling 'Daddy!' Molly was standing on every corner with her arms outstretched towards me. At the end, I just engulfed them in my arms and let them enjoy this homecoming with me. There were a few changes but not enough to destroy Nairobi's identity. This was still very much Nairobi and Harbhajan shared that opinion.

We were soon at Harbinder's house and his askari opened the gate to let us in. Mota Singh came out to meet us. He was Harbinder's father and Bansy's brother. He remembered me well from our Iringa days; he used to live in Iringa in those days but now he lived in Nairobi. He and his sons were the proprietors of a big construction company, the Ruaha Concrete Company.

We then went back down town to Harbhajan's large old house where members of the Naranjan Singh brothers had always lived. There I met two more of Bansy's pretty sisters and quite an old and majestic aunt. We had a gorgeous lunch, after which we went back to Harbinder's house and there was another lunch waiting for us! It was another beautiful meal prepared by a lovely young lady, Pam, Harbinder's dear wife. We saw a lot of Pam over the next few weeks and we always found her such refreshing company, with a complete command of English. The rest of that day was a very happy one and we were magnificently entertained. I didn't wake up until eight the next day and that was when I was being bathed in gorgeous sunshine. I didn't waste much time in getting up and while the servants were preparing my breakfast I took a stroll around the shamba and enjoyed watching the beautiful jacarandas dancing against a backdrop of deep blue sky. This must be God's own country. We spent a lot of time down at Harbhajan's old house that day; well, they were his direct family and they had an awful lot to talk over. Anyway, I could sit for hours and look at pretty ladies and as it turned out, their husbands, when they came in, were good company too. These chaps had known me for thirty years. You don't just gatecrash into these sort of families; it takes an awful long time to become one of them.

Harbinder came to the old house at the appointed time to collect us and we went straight to the International Hotel and had dinner with a very amicable friend of the family, Mr DB Kimutai. He was a director of the hotel, I believe, and he was a very learned young man with one of those precious qualities, a strong sense of humour. There were just the four of us at the table and I hadn't had so many damn good laughs for ages; what I needed. He had spent a lot of time in the UK and had been to Harbhajan's house several times for a meal, so Harbhajan and I were really at ease with him. We learnt that he was in a high government office as well but he seemed to soon join our relaxed holiday mood and be at ease with us two old timers. I hope the day will come when I shall meet him again. The hotel was magnificent as was the service and food. The floor show was very cordial as they sang a song, in Swahili, with Harbhajan's and my name in it! I think Harbhajan has got a recording of it somewhere. Our host had a lot to say about Scotland and liked the country very much. While we were eating dinner he asked me had I ever thought of coming back. I replied that I would love to some day, that was if 'the boys' down at Customs and Immigration didn't give me a bad time! Nonsense he said, when you get here you just tell them that my name is Uncle Roy and I have arrived! You shouldn't have any problems! If only that were true and I could do that!

The next day we took it easy. Harbhajan and Pam went down to Nairobi shopping and I wrote about 35,000 post-cards. I was also developing a friendship with another young lady. Her name was Hardeep (she wrote it in the back of my diary on top of my VAT return figures!) and she was the daughter of Harbinder and Pam. I guess she must have been about seven years old and had an absolute command of English, as did her parents. Basically, I think I'm not too fond of kids but they never seem to be aware of this fact. I awoke one morning, only because I could sense someone was looking at me. I opened my eyes and there she was sitting on the floor by my side.

'Hello darling,' I said.

'Now you keep awake because I want to show you my colouring-book. Look, what do you think of this picture? And, what about that one?'

This went on for quite a while. At one time she told me quite bluntly that she thought I was colour-blind! Getting a bit restless, I said to her that I thought it was time I got up.

'OK!' she said.

'But I have to get dressed now but I can't because you're pens and pencils are now all over the floor,' I said, indicating that I thought she should make a move and pick them all up – and perhaps get out.

'No!' she said. 'You can go to my bedroom and dress and don't forget to close the door while you are in there!' she added, pointing her finger at me, as much as to say that I had better do as I was told.

It looked like I had got another boss!

In the late afternoon of that day, Harbinder, Harbhajan and myself, took off on safari. We eventually wanted to get to Lodwar but for today we would settle for getting as far as Eldoret. The drive was excellent and loaded with nostalgia for both of us. The escarpment still looked breathtaking in the evening sunset; so did Naivasha. You now drove on a beautiful tarmac road but what I saw I couldn't believe; you had to stop and pay a toll! This was truly out of character with the Kenya I knew. I could well remember the old road; it too used to be tarmaced for part of the way. Where the road crossed the railway line, near the bottom of the escarpment, you stood a good chance of meeting lions. Today, it all looked so civilised and upkept.

We stopped at the house next door to the State House, Naivasha, for that was the home of Pam's parents. I found them a pleasant couple. Her father was a retired headmaster and they say that with education comes personality; this is certainly proved in this case. Of course, being a Sikh also, a lot of Punjabi was spoken but when he reverted to English, I found his conversation friendly, refreshing and entertaining. He and the President were fellow teachers when they were younger men, so I understood and they had still remained good friends.

The rest of the drive to Eldoret was in the dark. Harbinder owned a cottage there which we were able to use that night. But first, we went and had some grub in the marvellous Eldoret Club; it was still in an excellent condition, clean and with a well-polished look. I noticed one of the State Houses was right next door to the Club! Although it was gone midnight before we all turned in, we still got up at half past six and had a good breakfast in the Club. We then returned to the cottage where the Mayor of Eldoret was waiting for us to bid us welcome and to talk over some municipal business with Harbinder. I found the mayor (Coun. Hussein K Kitur) a charming and dedicated man, dedicated to his town, his job and the President. Whilst walking in the garden with him he was able to name for me some of the local flowers which I'd always wanted to know but never did. Harbinder started to look a bit impatient and indicated it was about time we shoved off.

Further along the road we had to stop at Kitali to have a look at one of Harbinder's building sites. While Harbinder was conversing with his agent, I couldn't help but think back to one of my closest friends, Doug Valpy. I mentioned him very early in this book, do you remember him? He was the young engineer I 'hated' back on my first tour in Kenya in 1953! I thought of his dear mother too and if I remember correctly, she too was a school teacher. I called in on one of the bigger *dukas* there and asked them if they could remember the Valpy family who had a tobacco farm at Kitali? I might as well have been enquiring after Tom Mix! Then it dawned on me that the shop proprietor had probably not been born when Doug lived there!

On we bashed to Lodwar. Now, I had been to Lodwar before, in the old days. All I could remember about the place was that it consisted of a few tin huts, a few government quarters, a few cattle pens (which were never used) and some government tents; one of them my own. It was one of the hottest places I'd have ever known – and still was. It used to take three days to get my safari there from Nairobi in those days and that was flogging it. Now, with all the new modern drained roads, you could do it in one. You could still see the ruins of old washed-away bridges and the old tracks making their way through the bush and river crossings. Get caught there when the rains came and you were in big trouble! The flash-floods were unbelievably frightening. The drive was enjoyable even though it was very hot; I think the car's air-conditioner contributed towards our comfort, but we did have a shower of rain. As we got near Lodwar a high wind whipped up the sand and dust a bit. The hills looked very impressive and I found the sight of the camels amusing. The sight of the beautiful and bare-breasted girls kept us all quiet for a bit. In the hotels you were warned that it was an offence to stop and photograph these beauties. I couldn't agree more with that ordinance.

Lodwar was now a growing township. In spite of the heat and wind, we enjoyed a late lunch of lake fish in a Lodwar bar; there was so much of this tasty fish (talapia) that I was able to make a pig of myself. We spent the rest of the afternoon in the Ruaha Concrete Company's yard before we made the last stage of our trip to the fishing lodge on Lake Turkana. Terrific! After Lodwar, you left the tarmac to make your way to the lodge. There were many tracks that you could follow but no signs to signify which one to take. Some of them strayed to absolute disaster and yet other people had followed them; time and time again it appeared! However, good old (young) Harbinder got us there with no mishap.

The lodge consisted of a number of two-man bungalows with a central dining room, lounge and bar and all quite open for comfort's sake. A welcome shower and another tusker prepared us fully to attack the excellent dinner. I mean to say, this place was in the back of beyond and yet, they still managed to put on a tasty well-presented five course dinner which would be a credit to many first class hotels in Europe. I take my hat off to them. You were warned about crocs around the bungalows but I didn't see any. Although the footpaths were well lit until quite late when the generator was turned off. From then on, it was every man and crocodile for himself! They did leave a torch by your bed, just in case it was 'needed'. I would have liked my room fan left on for a few hours after I'd gone to bed, but of course, they went off when the generator closed down. Having said that, in the evening we were blessed with a romantic breeze blowing off the Lake, which was particularly appreciated when we were eating our dinner. Unfortunately, this breeze died down at about midnight which was when we all turned in, rolling about and laughing our heads off. At that stage, we were ready to laugh at anything and we had certainly forgotten to look out for crocs.

I was woken by a camel trying to pull the roof off of my bungalow. This didn't matter very much because it was time to get up anyway. I was the first to have showered and had his breakfast which was quite understandable because I didn't have to 'set my beard' and put my turban on! We left the lodge at about nine, after taking some more photographs, just like typical tourists! Harbinder still had some business to see to in Lodwar so this gave me a chance to get some more postcards written up and posted. I had no idea how often the mail was collected from Lodwar.

We didn't leave until nearly six in the evening and stopped at the Club at Kitali for a drink and a bite to eat. There we had the pleasure of meeting the Member of Parliament for the Turkana District. I was enlightened by listening to the informed conversation and after a while, I too was able to exchange some points of view with the member. It was nearly midnight again before we reached the cottage at Eldoret. The cook had a lovely curry waiting for us but at that time of night and with my damned diabetes, there was no way I was able to get stuck in to my favourite meal. In spite of the late hour, the two boys were getting pretty happy and were phoning all over the world, including Bansy in London! They even phoned Molly but they didn't get a reply. Pity! It's funny how the family out here accepted Molly but politely did not accept Maggie. Harbinder thought he could remember 'Aunt Molly' from when he was a small boy home from school, when he lived in Tanzania. Made me feel very old.

Harbinder had also spoken to Cabinet Minister Biwott and we were to meet him tomorrow lunchtime in the Eldoret Club. When I thought about this, I wondered whatever next? I could remember meeting Mr Biwott at Lamu when I was doing the survey there; time certainly marches on. I left those two and went to bed, listening to them singing their heads off – in Punjabi!

We met Mr Biwott at the Club. At first, he was dealing with several of his constituents who had been waiting at the side of the entrance road for him. This was a thing that was done in Kenya. After a while, the minister's secretary indicated to Harbinder that he was to have his turn. The minister left with us soon after he had a few words with Harbinder. We left in our car as soon as Harbinder had introduced Harbhajan and I as his two uncles. The minister shook hands with both of us without showing any signs on his face that I must have looked 'a bit odd'. We drove through the Kerio Valley and I was absolutely awestruck by such grand scenery. The conversation flowed fairly freely as we talked about this and that until we arrived at Mr Biwott's house which Harbinder was building. After a while, we bashed on a bit further along the worst roads I have ever travelled on, then up a long hill where we eventually arrived at a new school which Harbinder was also building. All this was in glorious countryside all dappled in brilliant sunshine.

Evening was falling fast so we decided to head back to Eldoret where we said goodbye to our distinguished and good friend. Before he left us he let me know that the road from Garsen to Garissa was now nearly finished and my irrigation scheme at Kipini was almost completed as well. It was nice to learn what happened to projects that I had worked so hard on. The boys and I had a drink at the Club with the past Mayor of Eldoret and then a much wanted dinner. We slept at the cottage again.

The next day the three of us drove back to Nairobi, enjoying the views of Mau Summit and Molo (where Kenya's good mutton comes from). We went to Lake Nakuru (famous for its flamingos!) and passed the Escarpment from a different aspect. It was only just before we arrived in Nairobi that Harbinder sprang another surprise on us. We were not going straight home but to a garden party first. It was one of Harbinder's friend's wedding anniversary. There must have been well over a hundred people at this huge barbecue. The wine flowed like water and for blotting-paper we had such goodies as giant prawns in a delicious barbecue sauce. All the guests were Sikhs; I was the only non-Sikh person there; what an honour. Even so, I did feel a little out of it because mostly only Punjabi was spoken – no other reason. There was another surprise too: Harbinder's brother, Manjit, had arrived back from England. I had met Manjit several times in the past at Harbhajan's home in London. That party got really noisy but very happy.

There were always things that had to be done and one afternoon we went out to Karen to see Ron Marshall. It was horrible going to that house and Liz not being there to greet me. Ron had changed and looked a lot older. His brother from New Zealand was staying with him at that time. He asked me some questions about Molly as if she were still with me. Otherwise, we didn't have an awful lot to say to each other. I promised that I would go back but I never did. I also bumped into Ivan Smith that afternoon and that was a happy and pleasant surprise. He had changed too; he wasn't so youthful. Ivan, who used to look after my transport situation when I had the firm in Nairobi, had left the transport business and was now drilling all over Kenya for water and site investigations. I was pleased that he immediately recognised me and he certainly remembered Molly and Fa-Fa. I was beginning to feel as if I had never left the place.

Harbhajan's cousin drove us down to see Digger Hemsworth whose office was right opposite the New Stanley Hotel. Fortunately Digger was in his office and the first thing he said was he thought it was about time I showed up again. By Jove, he had aged and not without reason. He told me of the accident down at the Tsao Park when his son and two dogs were killed. His lovely wife was badly injured in the accident too, but she was coming out of it all right. One of his daughters was still home in Nairobi and the other, Sue, Wendy's friend, was still in Australia. Digger knew more about my daughters today than I did. Wasn't that awful? The other two people I saw that day were my old askari and Molly's maid. To my surprise, she threw her arms around me as soon as she saw me and she was normally such a shy little thing. They wanted to know all about Molly and the girls, so I had to cook-up a few tales because they would never have believed the truth!

During the next few days, we spent a lot of time just mooching around Nairobi and taking it all in. We had some more of Harbhajan's family and friends to visit too. One such person was Balbir S. Bhachu. He was a man I took to immediately. He was another Sikh and owned a big timber factory. He probably made the parquet floor in your lounge! I met him first at a garden party at his own house; a fine barbecue it was too. We met again at many subsequent parties that followed over the next few weeks. Harbhajan had laid a couple of floors in London made of East African woods and they looked very warm, colourful and beautiful.

One day Harbhajan and I had a conducted tour of Balbir's factory, which turned out extremely interesting. After the tour there was the usual Sikh hospitality – one beer after another – then we all went down to the Nairobi Royal Golf Club. That's where we stayed and drank and ate and laughed till gone midnight. Balbir took me around to one of the other bars and showed me the pride of the Club. It was a letter signed by the old Prince of Wales, Edward, saying that he would be pleased to be patron to the Club.

On the way home we called in one of the night clubs in downtown Nairobi (I had never been in one yet!) Some very pretty girls joined our party and the prettiest one took to me! I enjoyed her lively personality and appreciated her well-dressed and shapely form. I asked her what her age was and she replied – sixteen! I felt dreadful as I realised that all my daughters were older than she was. If she had been about twenty four, I could have got accustomed to the situation, but sixteen! I told Harbhajan, who was quietly sitting and watching and not talking to anybody. He knew me so well because within minutes we left for home. It was fun for a while and an experience; we haven't got anything like that in Erbusaig!

At one time we had to keep ourselves amused because Harbinder had to leave us and go to Nakuru State House to attend a meeting with the President. A day or two later, on Friday 16 February actually, Harbinder had to see the President again. This time the three of us drove to Nakuru together where Harbinder left us with his in-laws while he went next door to see the President. It was hoped that Harbinder could arrange for us to meet the President if the President was willing; after all, it was Friday afternoon! Unfortunately, although Harbinder stood with all those to see the President, he could not see them because he was very involved with another sudden matter. One of his cabinet ministers had been missing for days and his body had just been discovered, murdered and brutally mutilated. This was a minister who was popular with everybody.

I had seen President Danial Arap Moi many times, mainly because I had lived in State House Avenue, Nairobi and I used to see him being driven up and down past my house. At several public functions I came face to face with him and he looked me in the eye, but never did I have the chance to actually meet him. I guess he recognised me as the bloke who lived up near his place, if nothing else! I respect Danial Arap Moi and have followed his career for many years. Hanging in my hall is a picture of him with Mzee Kenyatta.

17 February was a great day because that was when we went to Mombasa. We were supposed to be going first thing in the morning but while I was having my coffee everybody else was still in bed, even Hardeep! They must have been partying somewhere last night long after I had gone to bed.

Anyway, it wasn't much longer before that glorious sunshine stirred the rest of the house and then one after the other appeared. Harbinder had to go into the office first and deal with some business, so Harbhajan and I went down to Westlands, filled up with petrol and went and had a cup of gorgeous Kenyan coffee. Harbinder was free by lunchtime when Pam joined us to go down to the Aga Khan Hospital to visit Mota Singh, who had decided to admit himself into hospital with a painful hip. When we all decided that Mota was going to live through this coming weekend, Harbinder, Harbhajan and self said our farewells and took off for Mombasa. We were on our way, I couldn't believe it. Harbhajan and myself were acting like two excited little kids and Harbinder had a job to control us and he had to tell us to quieten down and behave ourselves.

The drive down was absolute magic. Unfortunately, Kilimanjaro wasn't visible that day but we did get a glimpse of Mount Kenya. The road had tarmac now, all the way down. It seemed only yesterday that we had to slow down every now and then because of 'drifts' and bad corrugation; often you would have to slow down to let a 'grader' do his job, to stop the track disintegrating into 'tank-traps'. I noticed there was a lot more habitation along the length of the road and that people were much better dressed. Houses looked humble but very clean and organised and it left no doubt in my mind that the people of Kenya had come a long way since 1953.

We stopped to go in and pray at the Sikh temple at Makindu which was a pleasant experience and seemed to put everything back into perspective again. I can't remember if in 1953 there was a temple there. I do know, though, that a lot of Sikhs, as well as others, were eaten alive by lions when in the process of building the railway. In fact, things got so bad that the Uganda Railways had to employ a professional hunter whose name was Hunter! His job was to whittle down the number of man-eating lions in the construction area and to offer some sort of protection to the staff. There was much of this activity in the Makindu district. I would have hated being the surveyor in those days! Not very far from Makindu there was a place called Hunter's Lodge, named after that hunter. His house was still existing. Hunter had been dead for quite a long time now but his mother had died much more recently.

There was also some sort of eating place-cum-hotel there now – nothing much else. I saw busloads of tourists stopping there for refreshments; many of them had no idea of the history of that place and I do think that's a pity, don't you? When old Mr Thompson, Molly and I stopped there for a tusker in the old days, we had to find the place first! I think Mr Hunter was alive and living there in those days.

In a way, all us surveyors were hunters, if we wanted to survive, except that our roles were somewhat reversed. We hunted for the game, found it and then tried to keep the heck away from it, while we did our job! It even sounds a bit romantic now, but as I've said before, I used to get a bit fed up with it, when everything was trying to eat me up before I even put my first peg of the day into the ground. It was Hunter who closed his book by writing, 'Africa is like a sleeping giant and is best left to sleep!'

It didn't seem all that long after leaving Makindu when we started to notice the sand alongside the road and then the palm trees. That meant we were getting near! Along came Maji Chumvi, then we were on top of Chamgamwe and then Kwa Jomvu. Any minute now – there it was – M O M B A S A ! We even passed the evening train on its way up to Nairobi and we laughed and waved back at the smiling passengers. It must have been about eight o'clock in the evening when we drove over Makupa Causeway. Without hesitation, Harbinder drove straight to the lighthouse (or where the lighthouse used to be) along the Front, to capture the Spirit of Mombasa and to purchase that old favourite of one and all, casava, the tuberous roots of a tree toasted on charcoal, which is delicious. After indulging in this treat in this carnival atmosphere, we drove over the Nyali Bridge and booked in at our five-star hotel, the Mombasa Inter Continental. It was palatial, it was heaven. I think my room was about £153 per night and Harbinder refused to let me contribute one single penny. I had a mini-bar in my room so I laid back in a warm bath with two or three ice-cold Tuskers. That moment in time was the only moment that I didn't think of anybody else; I just enjoyed breathing in the air of Mombasa again. Mombasa owns my very soul and I love her with all my heart.

The three of us were absolutely beaming when we met in the foyer to get back on the road and head towards Mombasa for dinner. We landed up in the Tamarind, a luxurious restaurant, born since my days and situated on a creek over-looking Nyali and Mombasa Island. It was on top of what you could almost call a cliff, overlooking the creek. As the palm trees swayed in the evening breeze we could see another floating restaurant drifting around below. This was a dhow which had been converted and you could see people on the top deck eating by candlelight. The piano music blended in with the whole tropical scene. By the time we were having a brandy with our coffee it was already midnight; time to go to the Bora-Bora Nightclub, or so Harbinder thought. I stood up straight, placed my napkin on the table, shook my head while I pulled my shoulders back and thought, 'Oh well, here goes!'

It was a bit disappointing because there was no floor-show that night, but what the heck, we went in anyway. The inside décor was excellent and the lights were very low except on the dance-floor. The music was pounding away and the dance-floor was crowded. I'd never seen so many real live, colourful, attractive and fitter looking men and women at one time in all my life. And, were they dancing! I wished I was young again! Never mind, I still got up and had a go and thoroughly enjoyed the dance. I felt a little embarrassed at first but it didn't take me long to notice that not a single soul was looking at me, nor did anyone give a toot; there were a lot nicer 'things' for them to look at. My partner was a young and very pretty Masai girl. Whilst laughing and enjoying myself, the thought went through my head that there was a time when I could never have imagined dancing with a girl of this tribe! I wondered if they had always been around! The music finally stopped and I thanked her; not really being sure if you did that these days. She just gave me a rich deep smile, showing her dimples and perfect white teeth. The music started again and before I had completed my turn to go, she grabbed my hand and said, 'Have another dance with me Mzee.' Really! At the end of that dance, I was saturated with perspiration; I remembered all of a sudden that I was in Mombasa! I asked the young lady if I could buy her a drink but she declined the offer. She said she had one at her mother and father's table! Now was the time to excuse myself and I went and sat with the boys again – before I had a heart-attack. I liked this!

It was now one thirty in the morning and Harbinder looked as if he was getting restless again and wanted more action. He thought it was time we took off for the International Casino. We went together and when we got in I had a good look around the place and to a certain extent, I was impressed. I watched Harbinder playing; not that I had a clue what he was playing at. After a quarter of an hour, I felt myself yawn; I couldn't hold it back. This really wasn't my scene and I was getting quite overcome with tiredness. I begged my buddies to be excused but permission wasn't granted! I had another glass of whatever it was and decided not to check my blood-sugar level for at least another couple of days. There was nothing I could do but just stand there and grin and watch. After another quarter of an hour I could see my chance to slip off to bed and I was sure it would be a long time before I was missed. The bedroom was extremely comfortable; needless to say and as I walked across the room to put the kettle on, I studied the pictures on the wall. There was a tray put out with lots of packets of tea, coffee and chocolate drink; you know the sort of thing; and I found my favourite brand of coffee. While my coffee was cooling off and filling the room with its delicious aroma, I looked out of the window and could see the white foam along the edge of the gently breaking sea. The palm trees around the garden and swimming pool were highlighted by the hotel's flood-lights. Over in the corner a couple of folks were engaged in amorous activity, and they weren't all that young either. Jealousy would get me nowhere! They say you are only as old as you feel and these two seemed to be proving a point. Being in Mombasa automatically makes you ten years younger, anyway. They looked suntanned and fit too. God! I'd got to do something about myself, starting tomorrow; where were the biscuits! The lovely bed in the cool a/c bedroom felt welcoming and just for a little while I thought of only one woman and then sleep.

Although it was very late before I went to bed, I was still up and walking the beach just after dawn. I said *Jambo* to the guys who were tidying up the beach and passed the time of day. A vendor was already putting out his wood carvings and mini-drums together with a good display of batiks in matching colours and artistic designs. I'd never seen locals making these last mentioned things and I wondered who made them and where did they do it. The air was warm yet fresh and there was a large background boom coming from the outer reef. Judging by the patterns on the sand there must have been an early morning shower. An elderly couple walked hand in hand up the slope of the beach, after having had an early morning dip. Even so, I could still smell the woman's lovely perfume. I was now ready for a cup of Kenyan coffee and a good breakfast; loads of fresh and tasty pineapple, mangos, paw-paw and passion-fruit. The men turned up when I was eating my Machakos marmalade and drinking my third cup of coffee.

It was not very far from Bamburi to Mombasa so we were soon there. I got excited when I noticed that my concrete 'water' markers were still sticking up out of the ground along the side of the road, marking the water-main that I put in years ago. Memories! Downtown Mombasa had changed considerably and was in the process of changing even more; there were huge buildings going up all over the place. I reckoned it wouldn't be long before it looked like Florida! Every now and again we came across little patches that we recognised and which had survived the onslaught to date. In fact, the Old Town, the Arab sector, had changed very little.

We spent the rest of the morning visiting some of Harbhajan's old friends and it was a treat to watch him enjoy himself so much. Not very far from the railway station we called in on Mr Kuldip Singh; it was the first time that I had met him and I enjoyed his noble company immensely. He offered to put me up in his hotel down at Bamburi should I decide to stay in Mombasa a little longer than the other two. Actually, I decided to take Kuldip Singh up on that offer because Harbinder had to see the President the day after the next in Nairobi. The two guys knew how much I loved Mombasa and it was their suggestion that I stayed down here until Friday. They sure meant what they said because after we left Kuldip Singh we went straight down to the station and booked a ticket back to Nairobi on Friday night's train! So, I even got a railway trip on this safari!

While we were down at the station we took some photographs of the old corrugated iron offices right next door and adjacent to the main station. These were the offices of the District Traffic Superintendent. For many years Molly had worked in there as his secretary. Outside, there was a huge mango tree and I understand it was growing there before the British built the station. Hundreds of times I'd parked under the shade of that mango tree, waiting for Molly to come out. I can still see her tall slim body jumping out of the side-door, dressed in her 'shift' and Indian sandals, showing her sun-tanned legs to an advantage. She would always give me a broad smile, revealing her lovely white teeth against her suntanned face. Sometimes a breeze would flick her black short-cut hair and just flutter and lift the hem of her dress. Why did those moments have to go for ever?

We lived at Tudor Creek then and when we travelled home in the car, my body was always hot where it had been burnt-up on the construction and I would enjoy the coolness of her soft fragrant body through the thinness of her dress. What memories!

Let me come back to earth. In the afternoon the three of us took a glass-bottomed boat out to have a look at the coral growth and the inshore marine life. It was marvellous. To me, it was the height of luxury to be sitting under the shade of the canopy of one of these boats, just bobbing up and down and feeling the tropical breeze wrap itself around me. This time I even had an ice-cold Tusker on board – good old Harbinder, he thought of everything. I looked at these two while we were flopping around in the boat; they looked so happy and relaxed in their swimsuits and no turbans on, their hair tied up in a bun on the top of their heads.

Harbhajan was Harbinder's favourite uncle and I felt so aware of the honour to be drawn so close to these powerful men. Harbhajan was taken ill that night and we had to have the doctor into him, who then gave him a shot. Apparently, it was caused by some sort of allergy and the doctor expected Harbhajan to be quite recovered in the morning. He was. We were going to a night-club that evening but naturally, we had to cancel it – thank goodness!

The day when these two chaps had to return to Nairobi had arrived. While Harbinder paid the bill it took us just a couple of minutes to collect our things and shove them in the car. Harbinder had to see a very important man the next day. The first thing we did was to get me in the Indiana Holiday Apartments which were owned by Kuldip Singh and where I would be spending the next four days. I had a lovely self-contained apartment which was a/c and had everything you could possibly need; except that! There were two beautiful swimming pools and my next door neighbour was the Bamburi Beach Hotel where Molly and I stayed when we did our market research back in 1979. I spent many pleasant hours over the next few days in this hotel. The guests in the hotel seemed to be mostly German, although I did hear an ocassional English accent. I had about half my meals there and the other half in the Indiana.

After the chaps and I had a gorgeous curry lunch at an Indian restaurant, they took me back to the Indiana Apartments and then off to Nairobi they went. I missed them almost immediately. They phoned me every day just to make sure that I wasn't getting up to any mischief. I'm not saying that I wasn't still enjoying myself; it was just that Bamburi and Mombasa were full of old memories and once I was on my own they tried to play havoc with me. I snapped out of it, counted my blessings and blooming well enjoyed myself. That afternoon I noticed how suddenly my perspiration started to flow quite freely (forgive me!) and then over came a very big black cloud. It didn't rain at Bamburi; it just got very dark and oppressive. I always think the whole scene turns very dramatic! Then, just as suddenly, out came the sun again.

For the first time in my life I used the Kenya Bus Service to go down to Mombasa. The bus wasn't all that clean but the passengers were noticeably clean and smartly dressed compared with those days I once knew. I really don't think that I'm mean but I noted in my diary that the bus fare was only K.Shs. 4.50 as opposed to the taxi fare which was K.Shs. 220.00; that was if you were lucky! There were at least another half dozen white people on the bus – a sure sign of the times. I walked just about the length and breadth of Mombasa Island and thoroughly enjoyed it. I was amazed at how many roads and lanes I remembered, not to mention buildings and even telegraph poles! The two navigation leading lights out on English Point were still in use; I positioned these years ago; can't understand why any ships have never gone aground!

I had a lovely shower, a rest and then went round the corner to the Bamburi Beach Hotel for a meal. This hotel was a dream in the evenings. At the same hotel but down by the beach they had a Chinese restaurant which produced an excellent meal and at a very reasonable price, as far as Chinese restaurants went! Every evening, after dinner, the African dancers laid on by the hotel would put on a display of their lovely art and culture. I was proud of them as they 'showed-off' to the visitors. They were lovely to watch and then, as the evening wore on, they would try and get the guests to participate in the traditional dances. I got talking to all sorts of people and they couldn't hide their interest when they heard me talking to the stewards in Swahili, which was completely unnecessary because the stewards spoke English, German, French and Italian. The stewards would enjoy the act as much as I and would join in the 'game'; it gave some local colour which was what some of the guests were looking for, no doubt. Little did they know that I used to come to these beaches when there were only a few grass huts for hotels – even then there were only two or three of them. Not including our pride and joy, the Nyali Beach Hotel.

Friday, the day that I had to get my train back to Nairobi, soon came around. Mind you, the family in Nairobi wondered whether it was a good thing that I should return. I had better explain this! As I told you, last week a Cabinet Minister was murdered and as a result bad feelings in Nairobi were running very high and there had been some nasty demonstrations in the town. However, it was finally decided that I should return. I didn't mind one way or the other! Most of Friday morning I spent in my room just being quiet and thoughtful. Anyway, I had a bad night the night before because I'd bruised my big toe; all to do with my poor legs and the after-effects of my wretched illness. It wasn't because I was drunk! After coffee I looked at the dancing trees, the lovely sunbathers and listened to the birdsong and then decided to have another shower before going down to see what was happening in this lovely world. I strolled along the Bamburi Beach enjoying the cool breeze, had a few beers and then a good lunch at the hotel. I just didn't want to leave all this.

The hotel taxi took me to the station where I arrived at five in the evening. That meant I had two hours to kill which I found very easy to do. There was the usual activity on the station which there always was a couple of hours before the train left. Half the way up the platform there was a refreshment bar, on a raised platform about six metres square; I remembered when they modified it in 1954. They would bring you a good cup of tea, or coffee, for only a few shillings. From that vantage point (you have to get there early to make sure of a seat) you could see everything that was going on. There were always nuns, army officers, pairs of girls with their rucksacks from other parts of the world, pairs of boys and their rucksacks from other parts of the world, families and batches of tourists. Sometimes it was like looking at colonies of ants when they were all excited and rushing up and down. This was not the same as, say, a train leaving Paddington; this was a memorial event – one that anybody would swear had never happened before!

The bell rang. All the bedding had been loaded into the various compartments and only a few doors were left to be slammed. Voices were raised and the train's siren sounded off. Then that huge diesel engine started to roar. We jolted and then we were off. Dead on time. On the train I thought my compartment wasn't as good as such compartments used to be, but still quite comfortable. I had the bottom bunk and shared the compartment with another Englishman, who had the top bunk. I thought the corridors were much narrower than they used to be, or had I put some weight on! I had to walk back through ten of these coaches, along those narrow corridors, to get to the dining-car and I could not recall ever having to have done that before! Dinner was announced by the sound of a travelling gong and the meal was well worth walking all that way back for. Later, I turned into bed with those familiar sounds as the train sped towards Nairobi and heaved up to 5,450 feet.

I awoke at half past six when the steward knocked on the door and entered with a tray of tea. Looking out of the window I could see that the Bush was covered with a layer of early morning mist. It was noticeably much cooler. We were going round such a sharp curve that I could see the huge diesel engine in great detail. He was tugging, heaving and roaring just like his warlord predecessors used to. He was doing all that was within his power to maintain that tradition. I had my injection of insulin and then walked back to Mombasa for my breakfast. Harbhajan and Harbinder were at the station to meet me; they reminded me of the terrible twins as they came marching towards me with big grins on their faces. We jumped into the BMW and drove to the office, looking at all the damage done to downtown property by the demonstrators over the recent murder. Such a shame. It was lovely going into the office knowing that I didn't have to do any work! We spent the next few days still visiting friends locally and as far as Athi River. There was also a big party in honour of Harbhajan and myself and that turned out to be a laugh a minute, even though an awful lot of it was in Punjabi! That went on until half past two. Never a dull moment.

We didn't catch the flight to India that day as my partner in crime told me we would. Instead, we finished up in an observation car on our way to the Masai Mara. Apparently this is a must for all visitors and yet, Harbhajan and I both confessed that we had never heard of the place in all the years we had lived in Kenya. It was beautiful bush country and teaming with game. I had driven across the country over the years but never thought of it as any place special; I just looked upon it as another part of Kenya although I certainly considered it as Masai country; I may have called it Narok when I come to think of it. In those days it was a place where I personally would not have liked to get a puncture! But, it was all different now.

The three of us were up at half past six and down at the office by eight, where our observation car was waiting for us. Harbinder couldn't come with us because he had to make another million so that he could pay the bills for his two uncles! The two of us were soon settled down and off we went.

It was a lovely crisp and sunny morning and everywhere I could smell wood fires, which is always pleasing to my nostrils. It took five hours to drive to Mara River Camp which was run by a private concern. It was about a hundred kilometres past Narok Township. The road was diabolical. You had to use the old escarpment road for part of the way and that had been abandoned for years. It almost disappeared in places and was now densely inhabited by monkeys. There was tent-type accommodation in the camp with a shower and toilet built on the back of each tent. The tent was very comfortable and was placed right alongside the Mara River, where you could see the hippo in great detail. We had an acceptable lunch at about two and then a short rest. Well, it wasn't quite a rest because we decided to step into immediate action by taking a walk along the river bank to see if we could get a closer look at the hippo. We could already see them from our tents but we thought they were a bit far off. There was nothing to be afraid of for we had been confronted with hippo dozens of times, when we were younger men. So, along the bank we crawled. We weren't exactly holding hands but we were nervous enough to be almost doing so. There was no doubt about it, we were a lot closer. Suddenly, a pair of hippo let out a thunderous snort; they were on our side of the river and just below us out of sight. You never saw in your life before two grown up men move so fast! We raced against each other up the bank and towards the camp, laughing and screeching like two little school boys! I forgot all about my leg, I can tell you! It took us an hour and a pot of tea to get over that. You wouldn't have believed we were two old professional safari men by the way we behaved, honestly.

That was not all. At about five o'clock, the driver took us to where he thought we might find some rhino. The track was in a terrible state because of some recent rain. In fact, we came to a halt; we couldn't get any further. The air was very still and the clouds looked very dark and menacing.

'But look,' said Harbhajan, 'over there. What a beautiful herd of elephants!'

I looked and estimated that they must be about 400 metres away and said so.

'Yes, that's true, but they are heading towards us. If we get out and walk down the track, between the puddles, for about fifty metres, we will be able to get a real good picture of them,' said Harbhajan.

I agreed whole-heartedly, as we jumped out of the vehicle and started to walk down the track. The driver silently shook his head in opposition to our action. The elephants were moving exceptionally slowly so we stood our time. They were definitely coming towards us and two of them started to get a bit of a move on. Out of the corner of my eye I could see the driver walking quite fast and yet cautiously down towards us. For a second it appeared to me as though he didn't know whether to speak to us in English or Swahili. He eventually came out with it.

'Whilst you two gentlemen have been watching those elephants, have you been also noticing those two lions crawling up on you from behind over there!'

I, for one, didn't bother to look; I made a dash for the car. Both Harbhajan and myself were back in the car before the driver and he was half our age! That released a storm of half nervous and half embarrassed laughter. We did see a host of game and many birds but we had to get back to camp by six o'clock or they would come out and look for us – and now we knew why! A nice warm shower, a clean shirt and a couple of Tuskers were followed by a very good dinner. Two American guests nearly died of laughter listening to our stories. I didn't know quite what to think of that! We turned into our tents by nine and I went to sleep listening to the chatter of monkeys and the snorting of hippo. There was a very heavy thunderstorm and it poured with rain, but not a drop got into my tent. This was my beloved KENYA.

Next morning I was woken up with a tray of tea. I was soon showered and shaved and had my breakfast and was ready to go. All very well but, there was heavy evidence that we had a lot of rain last night and we realised that this might hinder our proposed movements. Even from the camp we could see that some of the tracks were awash. We were supposed to tour the game reserve today; however, looking at the tracks and that big dark sky in the north, I developed my doubts. Well, we had come all this way and the driver was willing, so we decided to at least make an effort. We went a little way on the recommended route and we did see quite a lot of game but we had to turn back because the state of the road just wouldn't allow us any further access. That was when we got stuck!

We spent the next day saying our farewells to all our friends because at midnight we left Nairobi for Bombay. On my part, I would never be able to thank anybody enough for their hospitality and help in making this, my holiday of a lifetime – especially my nephew, Harbinder. I look forward to the time when they will come to Erbusaig. I was amazed at the number of friends who were able to make it to the airport at that late hour to see us off. There must have been at least sixty. My dear friend and I knew we were coming back again. Those of my dear readers who have been to Kenya know what I am talking about. I agree with Mr Roger Whitticker when he sings that song from his heart – 'My Land is Kenya.'

19

Why My Book?

'Why on Earth are you writing a huge book like that? You are not a celebrity; who wants to read about you?' said a very old friend of mine. I love this friend with all my heart but she has never been an inspiration to me. But still, I must confess, the same thought had passed my mind several times! The first literary agent I had contacted said the very same thing; however, the book is written now; it's done! I felt I had a story to tell and so great was my compulsion, I had to tell it. That's the first reason for my book.

There have always been lots of other reasons why I shouldn't write on this day, or the next, or why I should write at all! Nevertheless, I'm a little pleased with the fact that I bashed on. It hasn't been easy for me, not one little bit, especially when I've had to do all my own typing, for which I've had absolutely no training at all! That makes me a glutton for punishment, you might say.

From way back in my school days I can still remember the face of my English teacher, although I have long forgotten her name. She used to make me enjoy writing compositions and I always managed to get an eight or nine out of ten! She claimed I was always dreaming and if I wasn't dreaming then my imagination was running berserk. Miss had retired once but had come back to teaching as part of her personal War Effort.

Whilst on the subject of dreaming, as a youngster I was very impressed by what was turned out by Hollywood; so impressed was I that I used to try and emulate the life of some of my favourite film stars. As I arrived at my later teens, the Army had its way of diluting the aforementioned impressions. The Lord Jesus, Nelson, Winston Churchill, Field-Marshal Montgomery, Joshua Slocum, President Kennedy, old-time Greyhound Bus drivers and my late brother-in-law have all left indelible marks on my mind.

So many times over these last twenty or so years, when I have been 'chewing the fat' with one friend or another, they have said in unison to me, 'Gosh Roy, honestly, why don't you write a book?' Mind you, sometimes I was a bit dubious about interpreting the meaning of their comment! Nevertheless, I mostly valued these suggestions and they were stored in the back of my mind and they eventually helped to compose my third reason for my book.

The following conglomerates of events also had a tremendous driving force for writing. In 1973 I started up in private practice; in fact, this was the time when I made my first attempt at this book. I did this to help take my mind off all the facts, figures and drawings I got professionally involved with and to help with the lonely feelings I suffered when working so many miles away from my family. Then, in 1979 I started a second consultancy business in Nairobi, Kenya; now here was another story that I felt I just had to tell. Much has already been written about the places I mentioned; even movies have been made about them; but, the presentations and points of view were often different from the way I saw things. Frequently mine was a different aspect, maybe because these were events as witnessed by a working 'ordinary man'; a surveyor.

As I have mentioned, in 1982, whilst living and working in Kenya, my wife divorced me, something I found hard to bear after thirty two years of marriage. But I have tried to restrict my thoughts, my feelings and the story of my family life to points that would be of interest to all my readers and not only my immediate friends and family. For the same reasons, I have kept the technical dialogue to a minimum; there are technical volumes written by far more qualified persons than myself. While all this was going on, I started suffering excruciating pains, day and night, in my stomach first and then my legs. This went on for over a year before diagnosis of diabetic amyotrophy was made. Anyway, the two divorces and my illness were interesting, in a morbid sort of way, and they needed to be mentioned to make my story balanced and complete. My physique and feelings took quite a hammering and subsequently, I found it an ever-increasing challenge to handle all the sudden and continuous changes in my basic living. I knew that I wasn't the only person who had to suffer these miserable events, but I had to write about them in an attempt to sort myself out. All the time I thought writing about it might help others if they wished to compare notes. It has been therapeutic to me.

In the two years following 1985, pain wouldn't allow me to concentrate and the growing fear of what was wrong with me was hardly conducive to an incentive to create and write. Because of the damage done to my legs through my illness, it just wasn't safe to return to my professional life. Each time I tried, I added further damage as a result of falling when my legs gave way. Yet, one has to carry on. That was when the idea came through again; why don't I get on with this book? However, it was almost impossible to start again. I had piles of old notes and unfinished typed pages!

There was no doubt about it, I was dragging my anchor! This was my reason for my new trips to Spain, Kenya and India, in quick succession. I could gradually see that it was becoming a matter of pulling myself together, taking a look at my situation and then plotting a new course with all the energies that I can muster. What happened in 1990, by shear coincidence, is what started this book off again. I was in India with my dear friend Harbhajan Singh. We were invited to a cocktail party which was held in a penthouse suite overlooking Bandra, near Bombay. We had met our host on our arrival but now we were enjoying the company of two lovely young ladies. However, it wasn't very long before our host, who incidently was a film producer, joined us for a chat. He was very interested in Harbhajan and myself, he said, two men being of totally different cultures, one a Sikh and the other a Christian. Yet, they were such close friends; you could say almost brothers. It was at this point that another guest said, if our host was so interested in these two, then he should read Roy's book! Oh dear! 'What book is this? Who is your publisher? I would like to see this book, there just might be a film in it!' said our producer friend. 'Just a minute there! Not only has the book not been published yet, it hasn't even been finished!' I felt I really missed a golden opportunity here!

I then told him about some of the opinions that I had received about my potential book which, on the whole, had discouraged me from pursuing my objective. 'Look,' he said, 'you must complete your book as soon as you can. Then, try and get the right people to have a look at it. You can then see what can be done with it. Perhaps very few people know you now, but they soon might, if for example, a film comes out of it! There's different ways of becoming famous. In your case, first the book, then the film and then the fame!'

God bless him for saying that. How jolly kind of him. Most flattering. Very stirring and stimulating. Honestly though, I couldn't share such enthusiasm and confidence as our film producer friend, but I'm grateful for such encouragement. I needed very little more encouragement than that which Harbhajan gave me – to finish this book as soon as I returned to Erbusaig. Another reason for publishing.

As the following weeks went by, I had my first awareness of the loneliness of serious writing. It gradually dawned on me that the book wasn't really only about me, it was about a lot of other dear people as well. Other people and a lot of other places. In the process of refreshing my memory, I used so much energy and concentration I almost incarnated the people I knew. In a rather peculiar way, I also developed a rapport with my imaginary readers; you! This is another strong reason why I have got to get my book to you. You can't imagine the number of typed sheets that have landed up in the waste paper bin, after having put my thoughts and feelings on said paper and then saying to myself, 'People don't want to read about this stuff . . . I'd bore you to death!.'

You agreed, so I tore it up and tossed it into the bin! At one time, I said to myself, 'if my reader wouldn't want to read this, or that, particular sentence, then why on Earth do I clutter up my mind with such rubbish!'

It seemed to me that any thought that was worth the paper it was written on was possibly the only thought worth retaining, if you understand my drift.

When was I going to know enough to write a book? I'm now in my mid-sixties and I've been trying to increase my knowledge all my life, but there is still so much more to learn. If I don't write my book now, I will never be able to do it. It won't be long before it's my turn to die. Now, there's a thought! It drives me into a state of panic to think that I could die without leaving a record of the enchanted safari of life that had been granted to me; or a record of my humble achievements whilst I was here on this good Earth. Perhaps nobody will find the time or desire to read this book, but it is here if they want to. If one person finds some joy in reading what I have written, then I feel my time has been well spent.

I believe that we are made up of a lot of people whom we have met in our lives and who have impressed us for one reason or another. We have formed a habit of emulating those features about them that had impressed us so. Parts of these features fade over time but some particles remain with us for ever. A lot of our character is developed within us and is unique. I have told you about many of the people who have influenced my personality and my life. Maybe some of my stories have reminded you of someone you knew and had influenced your life.

As I have said, in other places, I had to reduce this book from 600 pages to 300 pages and that was a very hard job indeed. Some lovely people and some colourful stories had to be slashed. I feel the only thing I can do now is to write some sequels. I would love to bring those characters back in and perhaps amplify some of the actions. If my tales have stimulated some of you to do things that you've always wanted to do, then I'm pleased about that. Another message I hope I have got across, especially to the young, and that is, you don't have to be rich or famous to search for and find a life-style of Enchanted Safaris.